IDEAS OF THE GREAT ECONOMISTS

IDEAS OF
THE GREAT
ECONOMISTS

SECOND EDITION

JOHN W. MCCONNELL

BARNES & NOBLE BOOKS
A DIVISION OF HARPER & ROW, PUBLISHERS
New York, Cambridge, Hagerstown, Philadelphia,
San Francisco, London, Mexico City, São Paulo, Sydney

This work was originally published under the title *The Basic Teachings of the Great Economists*.

First BARNES & NOBLE BOOKS edition 1980.

Designer: Robin Malkin

ISBN: 0-06-463511-2

80 81 82 83 84 10 9 8 7 6 5 4 3 2 1

CONTENTS

PREFACE

Ideas of the Great Economists is an updated and revised presentation of *Basic Teachings of the Great Economists*. Like my earlier work, it is an introductory text for the general reader or beginning student. A chapter is devoted to each of eleven major categories of economic study and together they cover all the main areas of the subject.

Each chapter acquaints the reader with the views of the great economists, from early times to the present, on the topics under discussion. Leading economists of course appear in many chapters. Thus we arrive at rounded knowledge of the views of such major figures as Adam Smith, Thomas Malthus, David Ricardo, W. S. Jevons, Von Böhm-Bawerk, Karl Marx, John Bates Clark, Alfred Marshall, Henry George, Thorstein Veblen, and many others.

In updating the survey, I have introduced discussions of the important work of more recent economists, including John Maynard Keynes, Paul Samuelson, Joseph A. Schumpeter, John Kenneth Galbraith, Milton Friedman, and Walter Heller, which appear in the chapters covering the topics to which they have given special attention.

It is my hope that this book will give readers a very real acquaintance with economics as part of their general background, and will prove an open door to one of the most challenging aspects of modern society.

JOHN W. MCCONNELL

IDEAS OF THE GREAT ECONOMISTS

1. The Nature of Wealth and Value

PLATO · ARISTOTLE · AQUINAS · MUN · QUESNAY · TURGOT ·
CANTILLON · ADAM SMITH · LAUDERDALE · RAE · LIST · SAY ·
RICARDO · SENIOR · JEVONS · KARL MARX · WALRAS · VON
BÖHM–BAWERK · MARSHALL · GALBRAITH

*Economics is sometimes called the science of wealth; but
what is wealth? What gives things value? Are things valuable
because they are useful? Because they are scarce? Because
they require labor to produce them? Because someone is
willing to pay money for them? What conceptions of wealth
exist under a system of intense nationalism? Do religious or
ethical principles influence our ideas of wealth and the
methods by which it is obtained? Is public wealth the sum
of private wealth?*

As far back as research into the life and habits of mankind can
take us, there is ample evidence that every society has spent much
of its time and not a little of its thought upon securing those material
things which support life and increase its satisfactions. To describe
this activity and to define the general principles underlying and
controlling it is the subject matter of economics.

To be sure, the lines of separation between what is economic
behavior and what is not are often blurred and indistinct. In one
direction economics fades off into the field of philosophy and psychology. What do people really want in life? What are the basic
needs which they feel compelled to satisfy? How do they arrive at
evaluations of the objects surrounding them?

1

In another direction we find economics influencing and being influenced by social institutions. The activities of the family, the state, the church, the systems of law, all are inextricably interwoven with the processes of production, exchange, and consumption of material goods. Any attempt, therefore, to describe economic matters as though they were confined to a separate and distinct area of life results in an exceedingly artificial discussion.

Economic problems are paramount in our age. But this has not always been the case; in the past, concern with the material was frequently subordinated to more important and more respectable pursuits. At the utmost, economic activity was considered as a means to an end. It remained for our modern industrial civilization to turn things around so that those actions which directly or indirectly result in economic gain are considered as the most worth while.

THE BEGINNINGS OF ECONOMIC THOUGHT

Of all the ancients the early Greek thinkers contributed most to economic theory. Confined as their ideas were to a largely superficial treatment of domestic management, the revenue of the city-state, and the regulation of occupations, they nevertheless dealt with the basic concepts of modern economic knowledge. Plato (427–347 B.C.) made his chief contributions in his discussions of the division of labor. He noted the variety of men's needs and the variation in men's abilities and came to the logical conclusion that if everyone did the thing most natural to him greater production would result with a smaller expenditure of effort. Furthermore, specialization presupposed merchants to carry on exchange and a system of currency to facilitate the process.

Plato's ideal state as described in the *Republic* is a strange mixture of the real and the imaginary, of current practices interwoven with what ought to be. It would be difficult to look upon these general outlines of the ideal state as basic economic concepts, though such proposals as the subordination of the individual to the state, the specialization of labor, the rule of the wise, communism in wives and property, rules for the family, inheritance, and limitation of population all certainly presuppose an acquaintance with economic matters. The *Laws*, written some years later, is a more realistic appraisal of the practical methods necessary to hold a city-state together.

Aristotle (384–322 B.C.) probed deeper into the character of economic activity and expressed himself more directly on these matters. Wealth, he believed, was of two kinds: true or genuine wealth, which was limited in supply; and wealth gained through unnatural acquisition, which was unlimited. The former was derived from specialized productive activity, such as agriculture and mining, in which labor was applied to raw materials. The latter was acquired through the exchange of things having different values. This emphasis upon natural wealth forecasts the view of the school of French economists known as the Physiocrats.

Aristotle could not conceive of money having a productive use, and thus thought that usury appropriated unjustly the natural wealth earned by another. Money was merely an arbitrary, not a natural, form of wealth. Its value was determined by man for his own convenience. The need for money was great, however, since it was the means whereby values were made comparable in the process of exchange. Money also performed a certain service; it enabled persons to defer the consumption of goods for a time, since its value tended to remain constant. In determining values, Aristotle emphasized the usefulness of the article as fundamental. His acknowledgment of the distinction between value in exchange and value in use places him today in the company of any number of modern economic thinkers.

Centuries passed before another figure of Aristotle's stature paid serious attention to economic ideas. Thomas Aquinas (1225–1274), an Italian cleric, was the next to do so. Like Plato and Aristotle, Aquinas regarded economic matters as incidental to the conduct of the state and the development of certain ideas. The society in which he lived was largely dominated by the Church and Christian philosophy on the one hand, and the philosophical ideas of Aristotle on the other. Economic activity of course went on. Since Aquinas was a native of southern Italy, he certainly knew the importance of trade to Italian cities. His economic contribution was in making the Christian teachings practical for his time, and in finding a common ground upon which ethical and moral principles might exist side by side with buying and selling.

Though early Christian doctrine had looked askance at wealth, Aquinas took the attitude that wealth and private property were not in themselves either good or bad; it was the use to which they were put that determined their moral status. Property was a trust placed in private hands to be used for social good. Aquinas believed that wealth was as likely to serve the development of an individual's greater virtue as it was to accomplish his moral degradation.

In addition, Aquinas concerned himself with the economic issues of just price and the prohibition of usury. Both were practical applications of the principle of justice, which was considered the abiding rule of human relations in medieval Christian communities.

To harmonize both religious and secular knowledge with the practices of the time and with each other was no small task. The completeness of his accomplishment has given Aquinas a permanent place among the great intellects in history.

WEALTH

Wealth in one form or another has held a more or less prominent place in the history of every civilization. It has brought ease of life, prestige among one's fellows, and power. Naturally it has been much sought after, and being such an important factor in social life, has received great attention from philosophers, religious leaders, and rulers. However, our concern is primarily with the views of the economists.

The systematic treatment of wealth as an economic matter begins in the great age of discovery and exploration, roughly during the fifteenth century, a period marked by voyages of discovery to the new world of the west by men whose chief interest was the search for silver and gold. Thus was started a chain of events which led to the formation of an economic theory called Mercantilism.

During the Middle Ages, Europe was a loose conglomeration of cities and feudal estates with vague lines of authority binding together the dukes, barons, freemen, and serfs of the same language or the same area. Whatever unifying force existed was exercised by the Church. As commerce and trade increased in scope, political units expanded in size and the heads of states acquired more power, usually at the expense of lesser nobles and the Church. This process was not a simple one, for it was accompanied by such complex movements in history as the Reformation, the Commercial Revolution, and the birth of new political philosophies. The end result, however, was the rise of the great states with absolute monarchs whose courts were the most extravagant in the Christian era. The demands of the latter played no little part in stimulating the study of economic life made by the Mercantilists. They were concerned with the ways and means by which nations could become wealthy.

THE MERCANTILIST DOCTRINE   The Mercantilists thought of wealth primarily as gold and silver, or—to use a term common at that time—treasure. Most followers of this doctrine acknowledged, perhaps indirectly, that consumable goods were ultimately more important than money; yet since most people wanted money it was always possible to buy what was needed, whether it be goods for domestic consumption or materials of war—including mercenary soldiers. Consequently an abundance of money was more desirable than an abundance of goods. In the absence of a natural supply of silver and gold a favorable balance of exports over imports was the broad way to wealth.

Thomas Mun (1571–1641) gave the clearest exposition of the Mercantile theory. Mun was an Englishman with an active interest in trade. As a merchant he had amassed a large fortune and he subsequently became a member of the Committee of the East India Company and of the parliamentary standing commission on trade. The statement of Mercantilist principles is found in his book bearing the enlightening title *England's Treasure by Foreign Trade*. His main contention was that to increase the wealth of the nation, England must sell to other countries more than she bought from them. He advised his people to cultivate unused lands; reduce the consumption of foreign wares and avoid frivolous changes in fashion; be clever in selling to foreign nations, holding prices high on necessities and cutting prices on goods having strong competitors; carry English goods to foreign nations in English bottoms, thus getting the price of the goods and the fees of the transporter; be frugal in the use of natural resources, saving them as much as possible for export; develop industries at home to supply necessities; make England a center for exchange between other nations, thus increasing the trade in and out of England; trade as close to the primary producer as possible, thus eliminating or acquiring for England the fees of the trader; place no embargo on the export of money because it is necessary to foster trade between other nations from which England can earn a profit by acting as middleman; place no taxes on articles made primarily for export. These tenets imply close cooperation of the government and business interests.

Italy was the home of the earliest and most positive exponent of the Mercantilist doctrine. Antonio Serra admitted no quibbling over what constituted wealth—it was gold and silver. In his pamphlet, *A Brief Treatise on the Causes Which Can Make Gold and Silver Abound in Kingdoms Where There Are No Mines*, he set forth certain rules for the production of an abundant supply of the precious metals aside from a natural supply. He advised emphasis upon manufactures; an abundant population; an extensive foreign trade with a favorable balance; and positive government regulations fostering and protecting such trade.

A more nationalistic twist was given to Mercantilism by Antoine de Montchrétien (1576–1621). In his *Traicté de l'Œconomie Politique*, published in 1615, this French theorist berated his country not only for the importation of goods which by a little effort the people could produce for themselves, but also for throwing their country open to foreign traders who drained off its natural wealth and for importing foreign books which undermined the strength and vitality of French culture. Montchrétien deviated from mainstream Mercantilist thought in his emphasis upon domestic trade to the exclusion of foreign trade. His point was simply that France could, if all would labor industriously, be self-sufficient and maintain a high level of material existence. He also acknowledged that wealth was constituted not of money alone but of commodities maintaining life. To make sure that sufficient quantities of such commodities were available for all was the chief business of the state. It was this theory which led to his coining the term by which economics was long known, *political economy*.

The last of the Mercantilists was Sir James Steuart (1712–1780). His *Inquiry into the Principles of Political Economy*, published in 1767, was the most systematic and comprehensive survey of the Mercantile theory up to that time. Steuart's viewpoint was a strange mixture. He believed that a favorable balance of foreign trade was necessary to keep up the wealth of the nation in terms of money; yet he realized that an excess of currency might be detrimental. His discourse on such topics as population, value, agriculture, interest, credit, and taxation was sound and in line with the best thinking of his time; but throughout the work there is an emphasis upon the responsibility of the state to regulate, control, and direct economic activity in the interest of national advantage. It was this aspect of his treatise which prevented his rightful recognition in England, yet made him respected above Adam Smith in Germany.

In the works of Philipp W. von Hornick, Johann Joachim Becker, and J. H. Justi (Austrian and German economists of the eighteenth and nineteenth centuries) a particular brand of Mercantilism was expounded. Their ideas on wealth were similar to those of the true Mercantilists except that while in their theory money was important to the wealth and power of the state, economic self-sufficiency was likewise important. Hence all kinds of produce, agricultural and industrial, was wealth as long as it was produced at home. The same articles produced abroad and imported actually represented a loss of wealth. These writers were predecessors of the more modern economic nationalists.

THE PHYSIOCRATS   The reaction to the ideas of wealth held by the Mercantilists came first in France where the theories of the Physiocrats became prominent. The name *Physiocrats* was first applied by one of this school's early members, Dupont de Nemours, and was later changed by the members to *Economistes*. When the latter term became a general designation for persons of all shades of thought who dealt with the subject of political economy, scholars again referred to this early school as the Physiocrats. The father of the school and the best exponent of its doctrines was François Quesnay (1694–1774), a physician who delved into economics as an avocation toward the end of his life. Wealth, he said, does not consist in the quantity of money a nation can store up but in the quantity of raw materials available for the purposes of man. Thus, the increase in wealth of a community consists in the surplus of agricultural and mineral products over their cost of production. This excess is called the *produit net* and upon it depends the well-being of the nation. Manufacturing gives new form to raw materials, but their increase in value is only found in the quantity of other materials used and consumed in the elaboration. Commerce merely transfers wealth from person to person. What the traders gain is acquired at the cost of the nation and should be as small as possible. The professions are useful but "sterile," that is, they draw income not from what they create but from the surplus created by the producers of raw materials.

The Physiocratic ideas on political economy did not develop from an appraisal of that phase of life alone, but rather as an integral part of the school's view of the world. Dupont de Nemours defined Physiocracy as the science of the natural order. The system of thought assumed that there were natural laws which governed man and the universe. To attain true satisfaction in life it was but necessary to discover these laws and conform to them. Since the basis of satisfactory human existence was believed to be in nature, the Physiocrats made the logical deduction that nature was the only true source of wealth; manufacturing and trade were *sterile* or at best creators of artificial wealth.

Quesnay's belief in the existence of a natural order of things which would serve man's purpose better than the existing order led to certain other ideas of a very modern hue. He believed that every individual should seek the greatest amount of pleasure for the least effort, as this would insure rather than endanger the natural order. Physiocracy gave birth to the famous doctrine of *laissez-faire*, *laissez-passer* (that is, let things proceed without interference). The work of the legislator was to aid in the discovery of natural laws, and not to interfere with their operation by artificial control. Everyone should have the right to enjoy the fruits of his own labor— hence private property became to the Physiocrats a cornerstone of the natural state. As Quesnay took great pains to show, the arguments for a favorable balance of trade were logically and practically unsound. But although all trade was essentially unproductive, it was necessary to keep it free so that the natural forces of competition might exert themselves and control the economic activity of the nations. Another leading Physiocrat was A. R. J. Turgot, who will be discussed later.

ORIGINS OF THE CLASSICAL SCHOOL: ADAM SMITH   The question of what constituted wealth and how nations might acquire it continued to be the most important economic problem of the time during which Adam Smith (1725–1790) lived and wrote in England and Scotland. One needs no further proof of this than the title of his world-famous book, *An Inquiry into the Nature and the Causes of the Wealth of Nations*, published in 1776. Smith realized that goods had both value in use and value in exchange, but he was convinced that the only objective and measurable value, and hence the only reasonable basis for a systematic analysis of economic principles, was exchange value. With this in mind, wealth could have one meaning only for Smith; it was the sum total of all exchange values which an individual or a nation possessed. The central theme running through *The Wealth of Nations* is the importance of the division of labor as a means of adding to the store of wealth. This does not mean, as some maintain, that Smith was the formulator of the theory of industrialism. It does mean, however, that many of Smith's economic theories were rooted in his contention that the division of labor was the chief means of increasing wealth. It is labor of all types which produces wealth; not nature or the labor of agriculturalists only, as the Physiocrats contended. From this premise Adam Smith derived his labor theory of value, which states that the value of an object is equal to the quantity of labor it can demand in exchange for itself. From it also arose his emphasis upon exchange as the focus of economic activity, for obviously if there is division of labor, exchange becomes the only way whereby everyone can acquire what he needs to sustain life.

There has been lively controversy as to the sources of Smith's ideas. The passing of time has shown that he must be considered as the founder of economics as a social discipline in its own right; but there were important forerunners to Smith who contributed to his thinking. Francis Hutcheson (1694–1746), Smith's teacher and his predecessor as Professor of Moral Philosophy at the University of Glasgow, intimated the importance of the division of labor, and the possible use of labor as a basis of value. Moreover, the general outline of *The Wealth of Nations* seems to have been drawn from Hutcheson's *System of Moral Philosophy*, published after his death. Although better known as a philosopher than as an economist, David Hume also contributed much to Smith. His essays on economic subjects laid the basis for Smith's appraisal of Mercantilism and the opposing justification of free trade. Lastly, while Smith takes some pains to dispute many of the theories of the Physiocrats, he unquestionably owes much to his acquaintance with Quesnay and Turgot, especially in the development of his ideas on the distribution of income. Smith's treatment of the ideas of the French school, however, surpass even their best presentations in clarity and practicality.

CRITICS OF THE CLASSICAL SCHOOL   The first and most important of Smith's critics was a Scottish peer, James Maitland, Earl of Lauderdale (1759–1839). In his book *Inquiry into the Nature and Origin of Public Wealth and into the Nature and Causes of Its Increase,* published in 1804, Lauderdale reasoned that since exchange value is a basic consideration in estimating wealth, and since exchange value may be determined in part by the scarcity of the object, one is led to a conclusion at which common sense revolts, that wealth can be increased by making things scarce. When the riches of an individual are increased by the augmentation in the value of his possessions, he argued, the wealth of the community must have been decreased, and a conflict in public and private interest is therefore inevitable. Lauderdale further criticized Smith's theory that the nation's store of capital might—like an individual's—be increased by saving. He apparently was fearful of a condition of an oversupply of capital goods and underconsumption of consumers' goods. In this he anticipated modern economists by well over 125 years.

John Rae (1786–1873) was another critic of Adam Smith, taking much the same line of attack as Lauderdale. In his chief work, *A Statement of Some New Principles on the Subject of Political Economy*, published in 1834, he said that while individuals grow rich by securing a larger proportion of the wealth already in existence, nations grow wealthy by the creation of new wealth. For this reason he assigned to invention a place of primary importance. Rae wrote on other economic topics with an insight far beyond his time. His arguments for protection of infant industries were used by John Stuart Mill; his objection to the lavish consumption of wealth, purely for the sake of show or to excite envy in one's fellows, was later elaborated by Veblen. Rae's keen psychological analysis of time as an explanation of interest and the accumulation of wealth are exceptional not only for his time but for ours.

As one goes from the English-speaking economists of the early nineteenth century to those of central Europe, the criticisms of Smith and his views upon wealth become more comprehensive. Whereas Smith assumed that economic life could be treated systematically without reference to other phases of life, and its operation controlled by natural laws inherent within itself, the early German and Austrian economists began with the opposite assumption. Economic life, they believed, was bound up with all the rest of life, and since the welfare of the state was so dependent upon it, economic activity had to be subordinated to and guided by the government. Adam Müller (1779–1829) was one of the first to follow this reasoning. In *Die Elemente der Staatskunst*, published in 1810, he pointed out that the question of what is wealth must be discussed in the light of what produces wealth and what conserves and maintains it, by which he meant the state. Like Lauderdale, he believed that, contrary to Smith, consumption, not abstinence, was the way to increase wealth. Müller's career as administrative officer and finally as councillor in the state chancellery of Austria gave a practicality to his works in spite of the vague world philosophy which underlies his main principles.

Friedrich List (1789–1846), who was Professor of Economics at Tübingen, administrative official, member of his state legislature, and political reformer, wrote in much the same vein as Müller. He believed Smith was wrong in confining his work to an analysis of wealth defined in terms of exchange value to the neglect' of the productive forces which underlie these values. The well-being of a nation is assured by the development of productive powers rather than by the accumulation of wealth, he argued. In one respect List went far beyond Müller. He conceived of productive forces as the entire institutional life of the state—its science, law, government, religion, and arts. Teachers, physicians, judges, and administrators do not produce wealth directly, but they develop what is more important, the productive powers of the nation. Something of the Mercantilist outlook clings to List. He believed in national self-sufficiency and in national wealth as distinct from individual wealth; he advocated protection as against free trade; and he emphasized manufacturing. List's major work, *Das Nationale System der Politischen Œkonomie*, published in 1841, was a popular exposition of his theories. It was repetitious and poorly organized but its popular style got it wide circulation and consideration.

Two other aspects of the nature of wealth as described by Adam Smith were criticized by scholars who in most things were his close followers. The great French teacher and popularizer of the theories of Smith, Jean Baptiste Say (1767–1832), objected strenuously to the restriction of wealth to material things capable of being preserved. In Say's opinion "immaterial products," such as physicians' and musicians' services, were wealth even though the value of their actions was consumed in the moment of production. He could see no reason, for example, why the work of a painter should be wealth (that is, bearing a value capable of being preserved) and the work of a musician not be. The argument has been carried even further: Why should not talent itself be considered as wealth?

John Stuart Mill (1806–1873), prominent in many fields of thought in England, did little toward originating new ideas of wealth. His chief contribution was the systematization in English of the views held by Smith's classical school with such reasonable modification as he saw fit to make. In this respect he and Say followed similar lines. Mill said that wealth consisted of all useful or agreeable things which possessed value in exchange; they must be material and susceptible to accumulation. Like Say, he included talents and skills.

There is a final criticism of wealth when defined as the sum total of all material objects having value in exchange. It is a criticism from a purely ethical point of view. Implicit in the writings of both Müller and List, it was first advanced directly by the essayist John Ruskin and later by Stuart Chase in his *Tragedy of Waste* (1925). Things which possess value in exchange may include a great deal that is personally and socially undesirable. Narcotics have value in exchange. In the field of medicine they make an important contribution to social well-being; but used as a habit they are distinctly bad. As Chase saw it, our society is burdened by the production of useless and harmful objects, frequently pushed onto the public by high-pressure advertising. Ruskin met the problem by coining the word *illth* to be applied to such objects.

At most points, the early socialists were critical of ideas advanced by the followers of Adam Smith, but on a definition of wealth they seemed to agree. As a matter of fact, the socialists were not as much concerned over what constituted wealth as they were over how it was distributed and who owned it. Karl Marx (1818–1883) held that material possessions were not the only things of value, though they were prerequisites for achieving nonmaterial values. Hence it was necessary to provide everyone with the material means of existence in order that all might enjoy the nonmaterial advantages of society.

VALUE

As economic theory bordered on maturity, economists began to realize that definitions of wealth implied preliminary conceptions of utility and value. Early economists assumed an understanding of these terms or ignored them; those coming later felt that they needed to be more precise. Utility is defined as the power to satisfy a want or serve a purpose. If, as some claim, wealth includes all things which have utility, fresh air and sunshine are wealth. Yet that seems too broad an interpretation. To restrict the all-inclusive nature of this definition, the idea of scarcity was introduced. That had its fallacies too, for—as has been pointed out previously—it is not common sense to hold that if items have become less plentiful, wealth has increased. And it is just as absurd to hold that if the quantity of goods in the country has increased—which may result in a decline in the value of each unit—the nation is thereby impoverished. A third way of analyzing wealth was to consider only those things which can be procured with difficulty. Thus the pain involved in the production was the essential factor in differentiating between things which were wealth and those which were not. Problems here are obvious. Is all labor of the same importance, the same quality, the same speed? If not, who is to determine the relationship between some labor and other labor? How could various kinds of wealth be evaluated for purposes of exchange? Thus, around the focal points of utility, scarcity, and labor, the theory of value has been evolved over the last two hundred years.

If one were to look at the definition of value as a philosophical problem, it would resolve itself into the age-old conflict of the ideal versus the material. Value in the former sense is a subjective matter; it is an estimate of the power of an object to give satisfaction. In the latter sense there is a striving for objectivity: it is the quantity of an object which another object can command in exchange for itself. Attempts have been made to set a quantitative measure upon the utility possessed by an article in order to make the subjective aspect of value as concrete and exact as the objective. To most economists this is artificial. It is doubtful whether the gap between these two estimates of value can ever be bridged satisfactorily.

VALUE THEORY: EXPERIMENTS IN A NEW IDEA   The volume of literature written on value, even before economics took form as a definite discipline, was considerable. Naturally the ideas were somewhat vague, but many of them hint at later ideas of great consequence. With the decline of the self-sufficient feudal manor and the rise of the town and the appearance of commerce, the religious control over estimates of value dwindled. As Aquinas pointed out, the utility of an object might vary considerably depending upon the need which an individual felt; but this had little bearing upon the objective estimate of value (except in unusual circumstances), because the idea of the just price tied value inseparably to the value of the labor of the craftsman as judged by the standards of custom and status. What Aquinas was saying was reiterated centuries later. The value of an article, in the long run, is determined by the quantity of labor necessary to produce it.

Sir William Petty (1623–1687), a British writer on economic statistics, added land as a value-producing factor, maintaining that "while labor is the father and active principle of wealth, earth is the mother." He believed that land as well as labor should be considered in any evaluation system. At another point in his works he said that the cost of a day's food for an average man is a better measure of his value than the day's labor.

John Locke (1632–1704) disagreed with Petty. He held that labor determined value. Land as such was valueless; it was only by the application of labor that it yielded any value at all. Capital was labor stored up in tools and equipment. This theory reappeared in Ricardo and in socialist thought nearly two hundred years later. Locke was quite aware of the short-term effects of supply and demand upon price, or market value. Over short periods, and in a superficial sense, supply and demand affect value, he said, but in the long run labor alone (which is the principal cost of production) determines value. It is interesting too that he understood the principle of elastic and inelastic demand: "Things absolutely necessary for life must be had at any rate; but things convenient will be had only as they stand in preference with other conveniences . . ." The idea of competition of substitutes was also known to Locke.

Though Adam Smith usually gets the credit, it was John Law (1671–1729) who first used the diamond-water example to illustrate his exchange theory of value. Water which is useful is plentiful and has no value in exchange, while diamonds which are useless command high prices. In his *Money and Trade Considered*, he said:

> Goods have a value from the uses they are applied to; and their value is greater or lesser, not so much from their more or less valuable or necessary uses, as from the greater or lesser quantity of them in proportion to the demand for them.

A return to emphasis on utility as a criterion of value is noted in the writings of the French economist Turgot (1727–1781). In fact the systematic formulation of this concept is sometimes credited to him. He was aware that value was created by several factors, but held that the most important was the need of the individual, or, in other words, the utility which an object possessed to the individual. There was, of course, great variation in utility from individual to individual, from time to time, and from place to place. Future need and difficulty of attainment also influenced evaluation. As far as market price was concerned, Turgot understood the importance of supply and demand, and believed that midway between the various offers and demands a price would be set.

Richard Cantillon (1680–1734) was a French banker who laid the foundation for the classical theory of value in his *Essay upon the Nature of Commerce in General*, published in 1755. (Adam Smith acknowledged his debt to the work of Cantillon.) The intrinsic value of a commodity is the measure of the quantity and quality of land and labor entering into its production. Market prices are set by supply and demand and do not always reflect intrinsic value, although for commodities that are in constant demand and general use the market price is stable and remains close to the intrinsic worth. Other prices vary greatly, in general being determined by supply and demand, but also fluctuating according to the whims and fancies of bargainers and the aggressiveness of sellers.

Twenty years after Cantillon's *Essay* came Smith's *Wealth of Nations*. At the outset Smith distinguished between the two types of value—value in use, and value in exchange. These two values are seldom equal, for things which have value in use may be plentiful and have no value in exchange, and vice versa. At this point he uses the diamond-water illustration employed earlier by John Law.

Although not a thoroughgoing advocate of the labor theory of value, Smith believed that value in exchange was rooted in the labor necessary to acquire it. In fact labor was the original purchase price paid for all things. While gold and silver vary in the amount of labor they may purchase, the quantity of labor necessary to produce a commodity varies but little from time to time. The labor value is the real price; the money value is the nominal price.

But it was only in the simplest societies that commodities were really exchanged on, or in consideration of, their labor value. When land became scarce, and capital important, their owners could exact a fee for their use which had to be met out of the market price of the commodity; consequently labor costs no longer were the only costs which established real price. It is not clear whether Smith believed that rent and interest came out of value created by labor or whether additional value was added from a different source to provide for their share.

Smith recognized the difficulties inherent in the labor theory of value. Since he had already intimated that it could apply only in relatively simple communities, he did not worry about such problems as how various degrees of skill and speed were to be equated, or how persons in entirely different occupations would balance their effort. Nevertheless, he indicated that labor never could be evaluated on a purely quantitative basis, for esteem and prestige modified the evaluation of different kinds of work.

Market values fluctuated above and below the normal values set by the cost of production (costs of labor, land, and capital). Prices could not continue long at variance with normal value, for a kind of magnetism made up of forces in the economic order itself tended to draw them together. However, monopolies and "natural causes" might temporarily or permanently sustain market values above the normal value level.

FORMALIZED THEORIES OF VALUE: RICARDO, SENIOR, MILL, MARSHALL   For more than twenty-five years no serious criticism was raised against Adam Smith's analysis of value. Then a great economist arose, who, although associated with the classical tradition, in some respects took issue with and overshadowed the founder of the school. David Ricardo (1772–1823), the son of a London stockbroker, made a fortune in the stock exchange at an early age and then retired to study and write in the field of economics. In analyzing the process of evaluation Ricardo assumed that competitive conditions existed. He ruled out the short-term market value as non-essential, and dealt exclusively with the long-term or normal value. Both scarcity and the quantity of labor required to produce articles influenced their value. Certain objects which could not be reproduced at all had their value set by scarcity alone. There were really so few of these that they need not be considered in the development of value theory. The economic life of the nation was carried on with commodities which could be produced in infinite quantity if sufficient labor were expended. For these, labor costs set the basis of value. Since rent was paid on land only in terms of its superiority over the poorest land under cultivation, and capital was merely stored-up labor, logic indicated that only labor contributed to value. Qualitative differences in labor, as, for example, between skilled and unskilled, between the professional and the common laborer, were of no moment since the market had long ago adjusted the differences and these were subject to little variation because of the power of custom.

In spite of the tenacity with which Ricardo held to the pure labor theory of value, changes of titles to chapters in successive editions of his *Principles of Political Economy and Taxation*, first published in 1817, forecast a clear modification of the power of labor alone to determine value. His efforts to discount the influence of profits and rents on value appear to most economists either as outright failures or as an arbitrary definition of terms to reinforce his theory of value.

The next great economist in the classical tradition was Nassau Senior (1790–1864), a man trained in the legal profession but who spent the greater part of his life as a teacher of economics. Senior built upon the foundations laid by Smith and Ricardo, but he was closer to the former in his conception of value. He disapproved of Ricardo's labor theory of value and tried to show that a misplaced emphasis led people to confuse the fact that labor was necessary with a limited supply and thus with value. It was Senior's belief that scarcity was a fundamental aspect of value whether the scarcity arose because of the difficulty in applying labor or because of natural causes. But he added that the costs of production, which include expenses of capital as well as labor cost, also influence value. Of the expenses of capital, he said that these were but the necessary payments for the sacrifice of present enjoyment which made possible the accumulation of capital.

It remained for Alfred Marshall (1842–1924) to rework the old classical theory of value into something which would stand the test of modern industrialism and large-scale business enterprise. Marshall was Professor of Economics at Cambridge University, England, from 1885 to 1908. Schooled in the classics and trained in mathematics, he was well fitted to do the work of synthesizing and revitalizing economic theory. He made value problems the center of his system of economics. His chief contribution lay in bringing together and harmonizing the utility and the cost of production theories of value. Not so much in England, but on the Continent and in America, theorists had revolted against the cost of production theory in favor of utility. To these writers it was essentially the power of a good to satisfy human wants which gave it value, not what was spent in producing it. A homely illustration provided Marshall with his insight into value theory. A pair of scissors did not cut with either the upper blade or the lower blade alone, but with both together. However, value theory is not quite so simple, he commented; and proceeded to show why. Value is almost entirely influenced by demand when a short-run point of view is taken, for once goods are on the market the consumers' willingness to purchase determines the price. In the long run, said Marshall, supply is important— the price of a commodity cannot vary greatly from the expenses incurred in producing it.

This exposition of Marshall's brought to the classical theory of value new life and a sense of reasonableness. Yet some economists strongly advocated a revision of classical theories. The principal criticism was that in attempting to be objective and scientific, the theories dealt only with the external aspects of economic phenomena. Specifically, in emphasizing exchange values, utility or use value was neglected, when actually utility was more important in understanding value than any of the more obvious characteristics of exchange.

Another deviation from the classical doctrine is found in the work of Karl Marx and other socialists. The socialists extended the labor theory of value to further limits, using it as a tool both in an economic and an ethical sense to prove their contention that rent, interest, and profits were unjustifiable charges upon the true values created by labor alone.

THE MARGINAL UTILITY SCHOOL   Hermann Heinrich Gossen (1810–1858) anticipated the work of W. S. Jevons in England and the later Austrian school of thought. Gossen claimed that the value of things is proportional to the ability to provide enjoyments, but as the quantity available increases, the satisfaction of each succeeding unit decreases. The satisfaction that each unit gives is modified by the cost of production of that unit; hence value is represented by an equation of two unknowns—satisfaction in consumption and the cost of production—and value is established at that point where marginal utility and marginal disutility balance one another. The methods used by Gossen were statistical and graphic. He hoped that through quantitative methods economics might be lifted to the plane of an exact science.

The English-speaking world is better acquainted with the theories of value, very similar to Gossen's, presented in the works of William Stanley Jevons (1835–1882). He had a varied career as assayer of the mint in Sydney, Australia, and later as lecturer and professor at Owens College and at University College, London. The unique contribution of Jevons to economic theory lies in his insistence upon the need for understanding consumption. (Gossen's earlier works set forth most of the theories developed by Jevons; but Jevons stated that he had no knowledge of Gossen's work until years after his own *Theory of Political Economy* was published in 1871.)

Jevons emphasized both the infinite variety of human wants and the idea of marginal utility which ultimately determined exchange value. As he explained it, the exchange value of two commodities could be determined by comparing the degree of utility possessed by the relative quantities available after exchange had been completed. For example: A has ten units of an article, while B has three units of another; A might be willing to give five units of his article for one of B's; but if he wished a second unit of B's article it is hardly likely he would part with five more units of his article, because that would leave him with none. Although B might be willing to make the second exchange at the ratio of 5 to 1, he would be less willing to do so at 3 to 1. Nevertheless a compromise might be reached where exchange could take place at some other ratio, say 4 to 1. This and other manifestations of the value theory and utility, Jevons presented in the form of graphs, using artificial incidents and quantities to illustrate the application of his theory. Indeed, it is on this score that the most telling criticism of the whole marginal utility school of thought can be levelled. The school seeks mathematical certainty for its theories but has no adequate measure for utility, which in the last analysis is largely an individual matter. The appearance of exactitude is misleading. To Jevons's credit it must be said that he recognized the difficulty of finding quantitative expression for his utilities, but he claimed that he overcame this by dealing with people in the mass, and with the relationship of many utilities rather than with the utility of one commodity alone. In a detailed analysis of utility, Jevons noted several different types. For example, the sum of the utility of all the available units of supply is total utility; that of the last unit consumed is final or marginal utility.

The work of the Marginal Utility School was carried on in Switzerland by Léon Walras (1834–1910), a Frenchman who spent much of his life as professor at the University of Lausanne. In 1874 he published his *Eléments d'Economie politique pure*. Value, he said, is the total utility of a given commodity, but its value in exchange is not judged merely on its own relation to supply but rather in a relationship to all other desirable things. The value of one object in terms of another will be judged by a comparison of the marginal utility of each. This, of course, is similar to Jevons's analysis. To some extent Walras tried to harmonize cost of production and utility theories of value, for he considered supply as well as utility, but formal connection is never made and his treatment rests essentially, as does Jevons's, upon subjective matters given quantitative expression.

THE PHILOSOPHICAL APPROACH TO VALUE: THE AUSTRIAN SCHOOL
While Jevons was working on his utility theory of value in England a similar line of thought was developed by Carl Menger (1840–1921) in Austria. Menger is looked upon as the father of the Austrian School, which presses the subjective analysis of economic causation to the extreme and carries forward the original German criticism of the exchange theory of value. To Menger, value is really the utility which goods possess; exchange and disposal is merely the external evidence of what is inherent in the mind and in the nature of the good. Obviously such value can be nothing more than a subjective phenomenon, so Menger completely ignored objective evaluations.

Friedrich von Wieser (1851–1926), one of the best known of Menger's followers, made all of economic theory the problem of value. He even went so far as to suggest that the purpose of economic investigation and the function of the state is the maximizing of values. Value, he believed, arose only from utility. Far from dismissing the cost of production as a factor in the value of any commodity, he acknowledged its importance while demonstrating—to his satisfaction, at least—that costs of production were in reality matters of utility. Cost of production was more than the payment necessary to attract productive forces into operation on a certain article; it was the payment necessary to make this use of available productive forces more desirable than some alternative use. This did not mean that cost value superseded use value. The latter was still primary and it alone set the limits to cost value—and in so doing limited the supply of a commodity which would be produced. The proposition might be stated this way: Assuming that use value of article A equals a sum of money X for Y units, it is first necessary to assure the producers of A a return better than they would receive by producing another article B; but under no circumstances can they be assured a return greater than X, which is the sum of money representing the value of Y units.

The best-known member of the Austrian School, at least among English-speaking peoples, is Eugen von Böhm-Bawerk (1851–1914), a university teacher and three times minister of finance of the Austro-Hungarian Empire. It was not alone in the field of value theory that Böhm-Bawerk made great contributions to economics. He subscribed to the marginal utility theory of value: that is, value is determined by the power of the least important want satisfied by the supply of goods available. He recognized and subscribed to the theory that the power of one good to satisfy wants influences its power to acquire other goods in exchange for itself. In a sense this was a substitution of a subjective exchange value for the older subjective use value, and it drew closer to the value theory of the neo-classical thought of Alfred Marshall.

THE SOCIALISTS   Another branch that grew from the original classical root was the socialist theory of value. The early socialists, William Thompson (1783–1833), John Gray (1799–1850), and J. F. Bray (1809–1895), were ardent supporters of the labor theory as applied to value. In their doctrine, the term *property* is frequently substituted for *material goods*. Making this allowance, we find their writings filled with declarative statements that labor is the source of all value (a theory first advanced by Ricardo), and that if people secure property (material goods) without labor they are defrauding the worker of what is rightfully his. Thompson believed that machinery was stored-up labor in the first instance, and that management was a form of labor; hence both had the right to a return. Bray said that labor created all value, and in exchange equal value should be exchanged for equal value; any deviation from this practice was unjust. Gray said: "It is labor alone which bestows value." The work of these men is not so much an economic analysis of values as an ethical evaluation.

→ Karl Marx (1818–1883) had prepared to be a university teacher, but he became absorbed in the social reforms of his time and took up the writing of political pamphlets and tracts instead. Exiled from Germany, he spent the remainder of his life in England except for short excursions to the Continent. His interest in reform never flagged, and while his work was chiefly academic it was designed to establish the scientific validity and the historical necessity of his reformist views. Marx conceived of value in the Ricardian sense as the labor necessary to produce an article under average conditions "with average degree of skill and intensity prevalent at the time." Such a modification thus accounted for the variation in market value from the time of production until sale. While differences in quality of skill may produce variations in value, the variations in skill are themselves accounted for by the variations in the cost of the worker's training. These differences are established by custom much after the fashion described by Ricardo.

Marx's theory of surplus value was presaged but never stated clearly or explained in Ricardo's writings. It may be briefly stated in this way: Labor is paid on the basis of its physical reproduction and maintenance costs; but the laborer is required to work hours over and above the hours necessary to meet these costs. Thus every additional hour that he works above the point necessary to produce sufficient articles to supply his reproduction and maintenance costs (wages), he is producing value which is appropriated by the employer. This value above his reproduction and maintenance cost is *surplus value*. Marx accepted the thesis of Locke and Ricardo that capital was stored-up labor. The value of raw materials was the labor necessary to produce them. Thus costs of capital and raw materials were justifiably incorporated in the final sale price which approximated the cost of production at all times. It was not in the sale price of each unit that the employer received surplus value but only on additional units produced in the extra hours of labor exacted by him.

Attempts to put the labor theory of value into practice on numerous occasions, especially in the Utopian communities founded through the inspiration of Robert Owen, proved the theory's impracticability. No one was able to solve the problem of how to equate the labor time expended by one man on one article against that expended by a second man on a second article.

CONTEMPORARY ISSUES

Looking back across the several hundred years of economic thought on the subject of wealth and value, several issues seem to stand out clearly, not alone for the questions they raised in times past but for their pertinence to the contemporary scene. The very nature of the economic world in which we live makes money of great importance. A nation or a person accumulates money because of its intrinsic qualities—durability, ease in exchange, and relative stability in value. This was the opinion presented by the advocates of Mercantilism. It was not in the quality of their reasoning that the Mercantilists were unsound; it was that they failed to take the long-run effect of their policies into account. Mercantilism as a working principle never died. Until World War II it was followed assiduously, concerning itself with a short-sighted policy of amassing a store of money while neglecting the inevitable consequences of such a general thesis of selling more than one buys.

A new emphasis was given to the concepts of wealth and economic growth by John Kenneth Galbraith (1908–   ), a Harvard professor and a maverick among economists, in *The Affluent Society* (1958). Galbraith's main point is that economic thought and analysis has heretofore assumed a scarcity of economic goods. Wealth was created and/or acquired through work and exchange, and value existed because goods were scarce. Today, he says, despite the existence of poverty among certain groups of the population, there is widespread affluence. Generally higher incomes lead to undesirably high rates of saving or to wasteful expenditures making no contribution to the improvement of society. In Galbraith's prescription for a healthy society, a greater share of private income should be utilized to create public wealth in the form of facilities and services which no individual can provide for himself, such as higher-quality public education, mass transportation systems, recreation facilities, and a fostering of the arts. Thus, while classical economics describes the production and distribution of wealth as private enterprise, Galbraith takes the position that the improvement of living standards in general depends upon the development of public wealth.

2. Land, Private Property, and Rent

MORE · GROTIUS · PETTY · TURGOT · ROUSSEAU · BENTHAM · SMITH · SAY · MALTHUS · RICARDO · MILL · PROUDHON · MARX · ENGELS · SAINT-SIMON · GEORGE · VON THÜNEN · CAREY · BASTIAT

How did land become the property of individuals? Is land most useful and productive when individuals own it or when it is owned by the community as a whole? Why and how do forms of land ownership change? What is rent? What determines how much rent should be paid for a given piece of property? Does land become more valuable or less valuable, more productive or less productive as civilization advances? Should land be taxed more heavily than other forms of property? Does the fact that no one created land make rent an unjust source of income? Are minerals and energy sources proper objects of private ownership?

LAND HAS EVER BEEN a center of man's interest and a constant basis for his disputes. For thousands of years man lived under the Biblical saying of God to Adam:

> Cursed is the ground for thy sake, in sorrow shalt thou eat of it all the days of thy life. Thorns also and thistles shall it bring forth to thee . . . In the sweat of thy face shalt thou eat bread, till thou return unto the ground.

And this condition still exists for many people in the world today.

LAND AND PRIVATE PROPERTY

Among primitive tribes, when hunting, fishing, and the gathering of vegetation was the means of existence, the ownership of land was not a concern. The temporary use of it was all that was desired among these nomadic peoples. The introduction of agriculture as the principal source of food brought a radical change in the idea of land tenure. Interest now centered on a particular plot of land for the planting and growing season. From here on, the evolution of private property of land is a rapidly developing story in which ownership by tribal chiefs, family holdings, and serfdom and vassalage are intermediary stages.

Under feudal law, no one held land absolutely in his own right; each person held it by grace of a superior, with the king being the only true landowner. The decline in feudal holdings came as a result of the increase in trade, the rise of towns, the extension of the use of money, and the emergence of new social groups such as merchant-employers and wage workers.

Why private title to land should become a characteristic of some societies is difficult to explain. The most plausible explanation is that it is the result of demand by individuals; once they have cleared the land, improved it, and continued to care for it over a long period of time, they should be guaranteed possession.

Despite vast stretches of underpopulated farm land in North and South America and Australia, and despite phenomenal technological advances in agricultural science, the scarcity of land in relation to total population in most of the world and the persistence in some areas of primitive methods of land use leave hunger as the world's most baffling problem.

But man's concern with land as a source of food has been forced to share the spotlight with his concern with land as the source of other materials essential to the rapid growth of industrial economies. A variety of minerals, iron, coal, and water power have for two centuries supported industrial growth only to give way to oil and other limited resources as the object of man's most aggressive search.

While the term *geopolitics* is seldom used anymore, efforts to discover and control natural resources form a dominant theme in national aspirations throughout the world.

THE VIEWS OF PLATO AND ARISTOTLE The first writers on economics of whom we have record were concerned with land. They assumed the importance of land as a factor in production, and devoted their attention principally to the question of ownership. In the *Republic,* Plato called for communism in land among the rulers of the State as a means of removing sources of discontent. But later, in the *Laws,* he advocated private property in land and houses because the people were not capable of managing their affairs in common. Private ownership was in a sense a trusteeship held from the city, and enlargement of land holdings was distinctly forbidden. Aristotle did not favor communism. To him private ownership, through which an individual was assured the result of his labor, seemed more likely to elicit the best efforts and the most conscientious attention to obligations. He did advocate restrictions on the accumulation of property, mainly through limitations on inheritance.

AQUINAS Writings of the early Christians give no clear picture of what the Church held as a policy on private property in land. Some favored the communal ownership of property; others upheld communal ownership as an ideal but recognized the inability of the members generally to follow such a practice. Aquinas, the spokesman for the religious viewpoint of the Middle Ages, presented able arguments in favor of private property. It was advantageous because of the greater care an individual owner would take, because of the greater industry that would be exercised, and because it reduced friction among members of the community. But he held that individual owners should consider their property a trust from God and be ever willing to share with others in need.

PROTESTS AGAINST MEDIEVAL LAND TENURE With the breakup of Feudalism, two conflicting strains of thought emerged. Out of the misery of the common people and the extravagance of the courts

a matter of contract when societies were formed. Private property, however, should exist only where there is enough left in common for others, and where the owners could adequately put such property to use.

Strong support of Locke's theories came from the Physiocrats, the French school of economists headed by Quesnay. They viewed property and authority as the very foundation of the natural order—property especially, because it stimulated the production and accumulation of wealth. Quesnay thought of private property as the real basis of the economic order of society, and other Physiocrats looked upon it as the root out of which grew all other social institutions. In a violent reaction to the Mercantilists, Quesnay and Turgot claimed that all value was derived from land. Labor on land produced a surplus *(produit net);* labor applied in other areas created nothing, but shared in the surplus derived from land. This emphasis upon land, coupled with a firm conviction of the sanctity of private property and the rejection of royal interference in economics, fostered profound changes in the economic and political life of France, culminating in the French Revolution.

Jean-Jacques Rousseau (1712–1778) looked upon property as a violation of natural rights to which most of the ills of mankind could be traced. By acquiring property, certain individuals were able to increase their wealth and gain control over their fellows. To Rousseau, the established order of society was an evil which perpetuated unnatural, man-made injustices and inequalities.

THEORIES OF LAND AND PROPERTY REFORM Although Rousseau died before the French Revolution, many of the theories concerning property which he set forth in his *Sur l'Origine de l'Inégalité Parmi les Hommes*, published in 1755, were elaborated by the anarchists and socialists of the century and a half which followed. Among the first was William Godwin (1756–1836) in England. Godwin was the son of an austere and conservative dissenting minister. Although trained for the ministry he found his beliefs shaken by the writings of the French philosophers. In his *An Inquiry Concerning Political Justice and Its Influence on General Virtue and Happiness,* published in 1793, he analyzed the problem of private property. In his opinion, property not only distorted judgments and values but was intimately tied up with the system of coercion and punishment which marked the modern state. He saw that private property in land prevented the access of some persons to sources of food, clothing, and shelter to which all had a right, since the good things of the world were a common stock. The rights of private property, he held, are of three types: first, those granted to an individual because they are more useful to this person than to any other; second, those representing objects which have resulted from the person's own labor; and third, those created by law and passed on through inheritance. The second and the third are obviously in conflict with the first, which was the most natural and fundamental right. Consequently, the second and third types of property should be abolished and a state of equality should be introduced where natural rights would be secure against usurpation.

It was the second of Godwin's types of property which received the greatest support both from theoretical economists and social reformers; human labor became the source of value as well as the justification of private property. However, there was one who took up Godwin's viewpoint. Pierre-Joseph Proudhon (1809–1865) was the brilliant son of working-class parents. His education was achieved at great parental sacrifice. In later years he obtained a higher education while earning his living as a printer. The winning of several prizes for essays on contemporary subjects fostered his literary career, but marked him as one of radical and revolutionary opinions. He believed that every man had a right to the materials necessary to produce his means of existence; but since population never remained constant, continuous redistribution of property would be necessary. Hence it could never become a private possession. Furthermore, property must be used in conformity with general utility, but this also undermined the very foundation of private property, which was the unrestricted right to its disposal. He held that, for the reasons cited, society itself could be the only property holder.

The popular economic arguments that private property could be justified because of the labor expended to produce it, seemed to

Proudhon disproved by the social conditions existing at that time. Men labored on lands and in factories but received no title to the goods they produced. Value in land was not finally created by the single act of clearing and improving; it was re-created and increased each year by the careful attention of the tenant. Yet the tenant received no property right in the land. Even if labor were rewarded with the totality of what it produced, injustice would still continue. Here Proudhon used the Ricardian theories of wages and value to prove his point. Wages are the cost of maintaining and reproducing labor. Since talents are natural endowments and society supplies the materials and training for the skilled workman, why should one man receive more than another as a result of his labor? Absolute equality was the only just principle to apply. Since labor was responsible for value, anything taken by the owners of property was theft.

The most objectionable feature of property to Proudhon was not the simple fact of ownership, but that ownership gave the proprietor a right to any increase in value which the property might acquire. Since owners were few and laborers many, the drain of interest, land and house rent, and profit was enormous, and was responsible, in Proudhon's opinion, for economic crises.

The most numerous critics of private property were the Socialists. For the most part their criticism rested upon two assumptions: first, that all value was created by labor; and second, that the labor necessary to produce a thing was the only justification for private property. Adam Smith and Ricardo had already accepted the first of these tenets but never bothered to explain the justification for rent, interest, and profit. It remained for the Anarchists and Socialists to point out the ethical implications of this theory.

John Gray gave a clear statement of this point of view in his *A Lecture on Human Happiness* (1825). He said that labor is the foundation of all property. But land cannot be created, and those who claim rights to property through conquest, merely taking possession, or inheritance do not have adequate basis to hold title to property. That ownership might arise from clearing and draining land Gray readily admitted, but he confined ownership to as much land as the amount of labor in obtaining it might justify. He claimed that if the possession of land itself was unjust the charges made for its use by another were also unjust. Consequently owners accepted the result of another's labor and gave no equivalent in return for it.

J. F. Bray followed much the same line of reasoning in his *Labour's Wrongs and Labour's Remedy*, except that perhaps he was more absolute in his denial of the right of anyone to own private property in land, since this would interfere with the right of another to use the land for productive purposes.

The theories of the French economist Comte de Saint-Simon (1760–1825), who was himself a possessor of great wealth (gained, it is believed, through speculation), were not nearly so absolute as those of the early English Socialists. His main criticism was not directly of private property but of the system of inheritance which made it impossible for members of new generations to begin life with equality of opportunity. He believed there was some justification not only for private property but also for paying the owners of capital a return. Rewards, however, were not to be apportioned in society on the basis of ownership but rather on the basis of ability and social contribution.

The socialist analysis and criticism of the institution of private property was most completely propounded in the comprehensive works of Karl Marx and Friedrich Engels. As long as production was a matter of an individual's labor with his own tools upon raw materials which he owned, no dissatisfaction arose when the individual owner appropriated the product. In modern civilization, however, the owner continued to appropriate the product, paying the laborer a wage equivalent to mere subsistence. This, according to Marx and Engels, was unjust, for it was the appropriation of values created by the labor of others. In planning to do away with private property they contended that nine-tenths of the people no longer owned property anyway. The essential means of production would not be destroyed; in fact, they would be employed for social interests rather than for individual interests. Only the power to derive earnings from ownership would be eliminated.

It is difficult to discuss the question of land and private property without confronting philosophical literature. One might dwell at length with profit upon the writings of Bentham, Kant, Hegel, and Fichte, who defended private property as an expression of individuality, as the rightful return for one's labor, as the natural result of inequalities, and as the spur necessary to secure production. Only in a mild manner did these writers restrict the use of property so as to conform with the best interests of the state.

Jeremy Bentham (1748–1832) evolved a formula of "the greatest good for the greatest number" that did much to serve as a justification for the institution of private property. Bentham agreed that ideally greater happiness would result if a measure of equality existed in the distribution of property, but this he claimed could not be. Equality could not last. Furthermore, if people could not keep all that their labor produced they would not work. He did advocate the regulation of inheritances to prevent too great an accumulation in the hands of a few.

The discussion of private property in the work of John Stuart Mill shows clearly its dependence upon Bentham's theories. Mill argued that production followed certain fundamental laws that were as unchanging as laws of the physical world. This was not true of the distribution of wealth. Mankind established its own principles in this matter, and they could be changed "if mankind so chose." He maintained that while the present results of the system of private property were intolerable, a better organization of the laws of property might be worked out to retain the institution of private property which he believed to be, on the whole, desirable. He condemned that aspect of private property which guaranteed to some persons the fruits of labor and denied it to others. He defended payments made to the organizers of business activity, for he believed the provision of machinery and raw materials was accomplished only by labor and abstinence and that these had a reasonable claim upon the final product. On the question of inheritance he had strong views. Within the limits of reason and practice, inheritance should be curtailed; but he cautioned all to understand that, while those who did not inherit suffered a disadvantage, it was not nearly as great as the disadvantage which would have been felt had no saving and inheritance been possible. Only by saving is capital acquired and only with capital does man's labor improve its productivity. Mill objected to land rent more than to any other aspect of the property relationship. The most uneconomic feature of it was its tendency to increase as population increased without any effort on the part of the owner. To remedy this he advocated taxation of the surplus.

HENRY GEORGE AND THE SINGLE TAX   One of the most important figures in the conflict of ideas on the subject of private land holding was Henry George (1839–1897). The son of a publisher of religious books in Philadelphia, he gained wide experience through travel. A brief adventure in politics brought home to him the power of vested interests. This experience, along with his observation of land booms following early railroad construction in California, plus the obvious poverty surrounding him, and his own firsthand acquaintance with it as a young man, produced the ingredients for his famous work *Progress and Poverty*, published in 1879. The last part of George's life was spent as a lecturer and journalist popularizing his ideas. It was George's theory that poverty tended to increase and wages were forced down even though productive capacity and wealth increased, "because land, which is the source of all wealth and the field of all labor, is monopolized." Private property is justified only by the labor expended to produce it; hence labor provides the only right to property. What a man makes is his own; the process of exchange does not change this fact. To George this had the aspect of a natural law. He drew from this proposition the obvious conclusion that no one had a right to anything which he did not produce. Nevertheless, men exact rent for the use of land which they did not create, and reap the increase in value for which society alone is responsible. It is this toll exacted by the land owner that fosters poverty and stifles progress.

To remedy this condition George offered one solution. It was not necessary to confiscate property; "it was only necessary to confiscate rent." This would be done by abolishing all other taxes and introducing a *single tax* on land. In theory the scheme appears sound:

Merely tax the surplus or unearned increment above necessary expenses of land use. But practical difficulties arose and the proposal has remained theory save for a small number of modified local experiments.

PRACTICAL MEASURES OF LAND REFORM   Land reforms of a more practical and less theoretical and radical nature have been devised from time to time throughout human history as necessity demanded them. Such programs have seldom been the work of scholarly economists, but usually that of professional politicians and statesmen. There were the reforms of the Gracchi in ancient Rome whose purpose it was to preserve the small farmer from extermination at the hands of the great land owners. Then there was the program of land reclamation by the Cistercian order of monks which helped to re-establish individual freedom by opening up new lands to free tenants. Later the Inclosure Acts of eighteenth- and nineteenth-century England broke up the village commons in order to provide additional areas for tillage. More modern programs, such as the U.S. government's free land policy of the last half of the nineteenth century, and its more recent attempts to safeguard the farmer through mortgage and crop loans, aid in soil erosion, and crop reduction payments, have sought to adjust land use and land ownership, not only to economic, but also to social needs.

In communist countries, government ownership of land is accompanied by collective farms and communes as devices to secure the efficiency of machine technology and the effective organization of farm labor. Even so, arrangements in these countries provide for limited amounts of individually cultivated land and private sale of produce as production incentives to the more energetic sectors of the population.

RENT

THEORIES BEFORE RICARDO   The injustice of private property in land has long been a point for philosophical speculation. Accepting the realities of private ownership as they exist in the non-communist world, the fact of practical importance is that some payment is necessary to bring privately owned land into productive use. The professional economists have concerned themselves with questions emerging from this condition of our economic life. What is *rent?* From what conditions in the nature of society and the economic process does it arise? Where do the surpluses out of which rent is paid come from? Why are some lands more valuable and capable of exacting more rent than others? A great deal of idle speculation and fine theorizing has accompanied the efforts to answer these questions, and not a few modern economists have dropped discussion of rent as a separate subject from their works, merging it with treatments of capital and interest. However, the theory of land value and rent is of significance not only for its influence upon economic theory generally, but also because of its relationship to historical movements.

The earliest known modern discussions of rent came from Sir William Petty, a seventeenth-century English economist. In his treatment, rent is the surplus over and above the maintenance cost of the workmen and the production costs of the crop. The value of land is really determined by the number of persons for whom it can provide a livelihood. Petty was exceedingly farsighted in some matters. He saw that values of land and amounts of rent tended to increase directly with the population; and he was aware that an increase in production could be secured either by cultivating more land farther from the center of population or by adding labor or fertilizer to the present land. In both cases an increase in price of the foodstuff was warranted by the additional costs either of transportation or cultivation.

The origin of rent as visualized by the Physiocrats, especially Turgot, is the same as that of any value. It arises from the land itself. After taking from the produce of the land the subsistence cost of labor and materials needed for cultivation, and taking out a new supply of seeds, the remainder *(produit net)* apparently is the equivalent of rent, for it goes to the landowner. In a competitive society the rental on land is determined by consideration of the probable produce, the price at which it will sell, and the prices offered by others desiring to use the land. If competition is keen, rent will be the total amount of the surplus; if not so keen, the renter may be able to retain some of the surplus.

The work of Adam Smith does not contain any conclusive statement on the nature or origin of rent. Actually, it is possible to draw three different conclusions as to what Smith thought rent to be. In the first place, he shared the Physiocratic doctrine that land produces a surplus over and above the expenses of the labor and capital applied to it. This might be considered rent. Second, rent may be a fee paid to entice the owner to use his land, and the investment it represents, for productive purposes rather than withdrawing it for some other use. And third, from the renter's viewpoint, it is the result of monopoly in land and an unjust exaction from the value created by labor. That is, under natural conditions when land was plentiful, the man who applied himself to the land received the total produce as his own. But when all land is occupied, the owner can exact a portion of the produce of the soil merely because of a legal relationship he holds to the soil, and not because of any value-creating labor he has performed.

J. B. Say, who in most cases was the great exponent of Smith's theories, discussed rent from a different perspective entirely. Rent, he claimed, was in the first place produced by the supply and demand for the products of the land which set a price providing a surplus over and above all costs of production; and, in the second place, it was an interest payment on improvements necessary to ready the land for cultivation. These theories were not elaborated by Say, but they were taken up and given prominence by other economists. It should be noted, however, that Say, engaged in heated controversy with Ricardo over the latter's analysis of rent, always insisted—as later economists have insisted—that where the demand is greater than the supply, a price will be paid which will give a surplus over costs of production. This is the real basis of rent.

THE PESSIMISTS: MALTHUS AND RICARDO   The problem of rent came full force upon England in the early nineteenth century when the increase in population caused such concern over the food supply that the Corn Laws, which set duties on the importation of grain, were abolished. Popular debates on the subject were numerous. It is probably due to this historical circumstance that the theory of rent figures so largely in the writings of English economists. Thomas R. Malthus (1766–1834) and David Ricardo (1772–1823) were the principal contributors to the literature on the subject during this period. (Although many of the ideas met in theories of Malthus and Ricardo had been set forth fifty years earlier by James Anderson, apparently his writings never came to the attention of Ricardo or of any of the prominent economists of the time.)

Malthus came from a large family. He was educated as a clergyman, but his theological training broadened his field of interests and continued study centered his attention on economics and population. Later in life, he was appointed Professor of History and Political Economy at the East India Company's training college. His writing upon the subject of rent began with two pamphlets written during the Corn Law disturbances in 1814–15. The second, *An Inquiry into the Nature and Progress of Rent* (1815), is the most important. Malthus agreed with the Physiocrats that land produced ample sustenance to maintain those who tilled it. He added his observation that population tended to increase faster than the food supply, resulting in an ever increasing demand for agricultural products. Land differed in fertility, and the labor and capital applied to different areas yielded different results. The difference in productivity of the best land over the poorer constituted a surplus which went to the landlord as rent.

Ricardo's statement is not greatly different from that of Malthus. "Rent," he says, "is that portion of the produce of the earth which is paid to the landlord for the use of the original and indestructible powers of the soil." There is no rent when land of nearly equal fertility is present in sufficient abundance to supply human needs. When an increase in population causes land of inferior quality and less advantageous situation to be called into cultivation, rent is paid. Assuming the presence of land of three degrees of quality, let us suppose an increase in population creates a demand for food, making it necessary to call into cultivation the land of the second quality. The greater costs of production, either in labor or transportation, will cause the price to rise. Obviously the smaller costs of production on the first quality land in relation to the price paid for each unit of the product will yield a surplus to the first land over the second. This, says Ricardo, is rent. If further increase in population brings land of the third quality into production, rent on both first and second quality lands will rise. The price of natural products will be determined by the higher labor costs necessary to produce the additional quantities needed under the least favorable circumstances. As Ricardo put it, "Corn is not high because rent is paid, but a rent is paid because corn is high." The laws of supply and demand and the cost of production on the least favorable land fix the price of corn.

An alternative analysis of rent is frequently presented, calling into discussion the law of diminishing returns as applied to agriculture. Instead of seeking the less fertile lands, additional expenditure for labor and fertilizer may be used. But beyond a certain point, application of additional capital and labor to the land produces proportionately less return. This principle had been carefully described by Sir Edward West (1783–1828) in his *An Essay on the Application of Capital to Land*, published in 1815. Therefore one might analyze rent from the point of view of the diminishing returns, either as less fertile soil is brought into cultivation to meet increased demands, or as additional applications of capital and labor are made to the land originally under cultivation.

VON THÜNEN   A theory of rent similar to that of Ricardo was developed about the same time in Germany by an agricultural economist, J. H. von Thünen (1783–1850). The son of a landed proprietor, he studied briefly at Göttingen, bought an estate, and spent the remainder of his life developing economic theories applying to agriculture. His work *Der Isolierte Staat* (The Isolated State) is important because of its method. The basis of the study is a hypothetical community entirely free from external contacts. However, the basic facts and figures were drawn from the practical management of his own estate. To develop his theories, von Thünen introduced new elements (for example, increments in population) while holding all other factors constant. Then, by objective analysis of his observations, he evolved the principles governing the observed effects.

It was by this method that his theory of rent was deduced. Arranging the tillable area surrounding the community into concentric circles, and assuming for the most part equal productivity, he showed that, at a given price for grain, the costs of transportation made production beyond a certain distance from the town unprofitable. This leads directly to his theory of rent. He maintained that some capital is always expended on farm land. After deducting interest on capital and other costs of production and transportation, the remainder of the earnings is rent. Thus the price of grain is an important element in rent. In order to get the necessary amount of corn, the price the community is willing to pay must cover the costs of production and transportation from the most distant source necessary to provide the required quantity. Since the price paid for grain to the nearest and the farthest producers will be the same, the surplus going to the nearest producer is rent. Extending his analysis to cover not only the disadvantages of distance but of fertility as well, he said that rent arose from the advantages which a piece of land possessed over the worst farms. Von Thünen obviously interpreted value in terms of marginal qualities. This is apparent in his discussion of interest and wages as well as rent.

CRITICS OF RICARDO   The critics of the Ricardian theory of rent have been numerous. Most have been concerned with the impracticality of the theory; others have questioned its basic assumptions. Of the latter, the most important are Carey and Bastiat, representatives of the "optimistic school" of economics as opposed to the "pessimistic school" identified with Malthus and Ricardo. An American economist, Henry Carey (1793–1879), was led to discard two of the foundation stones upon which Ricardo erected his theory of rent. He denied that the law of diminishing returns applied to agriculture, and he protested the Malthusian doctrine of population increasing more rapidly than the food supply. By a vast collection of data on the original settlements of communities, Carey was able to show that the most fertile land is not settled first. Settlers tend to congregate on bare spaces, hilltops, and hillsides, rather than on fertile land, which requires clearing of forests and underbrush and draining of valleys, thus necessitating capital expenditure and years of toil. Consequently, the price of grain is likely to decline instead of rise as new lands are brought into cultivation. Obviously, Carey was writing of a recently opened country where free land was to be had for the clearing. Ricardo was writing of an old established country which had long since placed every bit of available land under the plough. Moreover, in criticizing Ricardo, Carey seems to have misinterpreted the significant points of the theory. Its validity does not depend upon the chronological order in which the land is tilled but on the differences in fertility later manifest at any given time.

Although not very clearly described, Carey's other point is this: Instead of diminishing returns, land, when properly cared for, will yield a continually increasing rate of return for the capital and labor expended. Moreover, an increasing number of births should be considered not only as an increase in the number of mouths to be fed but as an increase in the number of producers. All these arguments taken together allowed Carey to reverse the order of Malthus and Ricardo, so that the future instead of being plagued by wars, disease, and famine because of overpopulation, might well be a period of greater satisfaction for more people. But what is rent, if this is the case? It only comes as a payment for the past expenditure of labor in draining, clearing, and maintaining fertility.

Frédéric Bastiat (1801–1850) remained an obscure farmer until late in life when the free trade vs. protection controversy gave him opportunity to exercise his latent journalistic powers and to participate in local politics. His *Harmonies économiques*, published in 1850, is the vehicle for his optimistic analysis of economic principles. His basic contention is that commodities possess utility contributed by two agencies, nature and labor. The first is free; the second requires payment. But the essence of progress is that the expenses of nature decline, and man ultimately enjoys more of nature's free gifts with less toil and expense. Agricultural products should be sold at a price which covers the cost of the labor necessary to produce them. Rent is payment for the labor and capital expense involved in rendering the land suitable for cultivation. The landowner is simply an intermediary between natural resources and the consumer, who through toil puts land into a condition so that its produce can be utilized.

While there is more hope than logic in the ideas of Bastiat and Carey, both in a measure foresaw the modifications which ultimately were applied to the ideas of Ricardo and Malthus. A long line of economists beginning with Nassau Senior and including among others Jean Baptiste Say, John Stuart Mill, F. A. Walker, Karl Menger, and Alfred Marshall, saw no reason for confining the idea of rent to the surplus over and above what could be earned by the least fertile unit of land. As Say very early pointed out, it was not the higher costs on the less fertile land which produced rent on the more fertile, but the fact that demand for the commodity had so raised the price that after all costs of production had been met, a surplus remained. However, this was true of the product of a machine as well as of land. Finally, these later writers held that it was impossible to separate the return due the land itself and the return on the capital investment made on the land in order to put it in cultivation. Consequently, rent could be discussed just as the return upon an investment of any other type. Old ideas of the limited amount of land and its indestructibility which at first were considered sufficient reason for discussing rents as a separate and unique economic factor have been proved untenable. Land is no more limited than machinery, since both are derived from the substance of the earth; and the fertility of the soil as well as the soil itself can be destroyed.

Modifications of Malthus came mainly from those writers on population who held that increases in population can be supported if an improved technique of production is introduced. For example, the change from handicraft to machine technology enabled the economic system to produce additional food to support a phenomenal increase in the population of western Europe and America during the last two centuries. The more radical economists maintain that the ultimate capacity of the productive system of the world has never been taxed; if the distribution of our national income were more equitable, there would be more than enough to support large increases in population.

Two developments since World War II have led to a re-emphasis upon Mathusian ideas about population growth. In the first place, despite efforts to improve agricultural and industrial development in third world countries, principally in Africa, Asia, and Central America, population growth continues to match and even exceed increases in food supply; thus, living standards remain unchanged and poverty is widespread. Second, worldwide increases in population, combined with industrial growth in North America, Europe, and Japan, have put such pressure on natural resources that some of the most valuable of these are approaching the point of exhaustion. Moreover, increasing population has so polluted air, lakes, rivers, and surface areas, that the law of diminishing returns means existence at any given level has become more costly. Though Malthus could not, of course, foresee the present-day complex relationship of land and people, the essence of his idea was sound: The aggregation of more people on limited areas of land might lead to increased total production; but the amount of output per person diminished, so that each person was poorer. Consideration of such factors has given rise to new political movements to reduce population growth and preserve the environment even at the expense of less rapid development of technology.

3. LABOR AND WAGES

PLATO · ARISTOTLE · AQUINAS · CALVIN · THE
MERCANTILISTS ·THE PHYSIOCRATS · SMITH · MALTHUS ·
RICARDO · MILL ·MARX · BAKUNIN · SOREL · VEBLEN ·
WALKER · TAYLOR · THE WEBBS · CLARK · TAWNEY

*Why do people work? Does man have greater dignity when
he works, or when he is wealthy enough to spend his time
in leisure? Why do some occupations demean an individual
and others make a man or woman more respectable? What
determines how much a person receives for his labor? What
effect does increase in population have upon wages? Does
it pay a worker to increase his output? Are wages paid out
of capital? What is the relative bargaining power of labor
and employers? Do trade unions increase wages?*

THE EXPLORATION OF the possibility of a world where all might
live without working has been left to the makers of dreams. Even
utopians consider work an essential part of their cities in the sun,
if only for the moral benefit of citizens. For nearly all people, work
sooner or later becomes an unescapable reality. However, it is not
with the sweat and toil of the individual that the economist has
been concerned, but with labor as a general factor in economic
activity.

INCENTIVES TO WORK

The question of why people work is perhaps more aptly addressed
in the literature of psychology, but the fact is economists have felt

it necessary to make some assumptions on this issue, even though they have little scientifically established data.

IDEAS OF PLATO AND ARISTOTLE The systems of economy, proposed by Plato and Aristotle, take for granted that when faced with certain conditions, man will respond in certain ways. Plato expressed an ideal concept when, in *Republic*, he asked man to merge himself with the state and accept his place in it according to some judgment outside himself. The communism of the *Republic* assumes such a perfect adjustment to life that each man, in doing what he is best fitted to do, ceases to be stimulated by personal ambitions. Aristotle was more realistic. He opposed Plato's communistic state on the grounds that as an incentive to industry and care of property, self-interest was more dependable than interest in common good.

RELIGIOUS DOCTRINES OF AQUINAS AND CALVIN Thomas Aquinas, writing much later from the perspective of a medieval Christian, agreed with Aristotle's principle that a man who was guaranteed the fruits of his labor would be more industrious and conscientious in his work. In this concept, Aquinas departed radically from the Greek philosophers, who regarded menial work and the affairs of the marketplace as undignified. Even buying and selling were acceptable activities to Aquinas, provided the merchant was aware that in his occupation opportunities for the unrighteous accumulation of wealth were to be guarded against.

It was in the theological writings of John Calvin (1509–1564) that the religious incentive to work reached its most compelling form. Calvin was a Swiss religious reformer who became the intellectual leader of the Reformation. While Christian tradition had long recognized work as necessary and dignified, as nearly all of its leaders had themselves worked, it was not until Calvin that work became a Christian obligation. To labor industriously in a calling was God's command to man. A calling was not to be chosen because of the riches to be obtained; but once in a calling, the worker should not be unmindful of the wealth to be obtained by a close application to duty, since an increase in wealth could be used for Christian purposes. People were admonished to shun luxury and be thrifty. Finally, while salvation came only to the predestined elect, worldly success was accepted as a mark of God's favor. It followed that, since no one knew beforehand who was predestined for salvation, such success was perceived as a confirmation that one had been called by God. It is thus understandable why several authors, notably Max Weber, described Calvinism as a powerful stimulus to the evolution of modern capitalism, if not its cause. The writings of R. H. Tawney in England and Werner Sombart in Germany turned this thesis around, however, by considering the rise of modern capitalism in northern Europe as the cause of the Reformation and the reason for its ready acceptance.

INDIVIDUALISTIC VIEWS   The strong individualistic doctrine of the Reformation was taken over by the less religious philosophers and economists of succeeding generations. Though they accepted individualism as a fact of the world in which they lived, these scholars needed some other justification for it than the favor of God or the salvation of the soul. One school founded a doctrine on the premise that it was instinctive for man to seek his own self-interest. (This had been affirmed by philosophers as far back as Plato and Aristotle.) Where they fell short, however, was in failing to understand that the powerful drive of self-interest had to have a sense of direction other than the individual's own happiness. Plato and Aristotle subordinated the individual to the state; Aquinas deferred to custom developed by man's God-given reason; Calvinism implied control in its moral admonitions and its doctrine of salvation; but the utilitarians found no such control save the sensitivity of man himself.

THE PURSUIT OF SELF-INTEREST: ADAM SMITH   Adam Smith in *The Theory of Moral Sentiments* (1759) and *An Inquiry into the Nature and Causes of the Wealth of Nations* (1776) appears to have two views of incentives to work. This may be due to the fact that in one book he was speaking as a philosopher and in the other as an economist. Smith, in his earlier writings, emphasized the force of vanity in human action. Men strive for more than they need and for more than brings satisfaction simply to secure the approval of their fellows. The riches themselves are not only useless but harmful to the individual, and usually the rich man finds that the happiness he anticipated from them is an illusion. Nevertheless, nature uses these characteristics of man to inspire him to work. In the end man produces useful things for the benefit of others. At the time of writing *The Wealth of Nations*, Smith had no criticism to offer against the pursuit of wealth, apparently assuming that wealth was universally beneficial. Furthermore, it was the individual search for wealth, and not vanity, which spurred men to work. Smith was consistent throughout in the belief that nature can and will direct the selfish actions of men toward the social good. An all-pervading force somehow correlates all the individual pursuits of self-interest into patterns that are socially beneficial.

Smith, rightly or wrongly, is given credit for the creation of the concept of the *economic man*. This is merely a short way of saying that the average person seeks his own economic self-interest. And as his chief motivating force is to secure wealth with the least effort, he seeks the cheapest market in which to buy and the dearest in which to sell. The followers of Smith accepted the psychological theories of *The Wealth of Nations* and overlooked the teachings of *The Theory of Moral Sentiments*. They expanded the identification of wealth with happiness which Smith's earlier book had denied.

The chief innovations of the classical writers were the recognition of differences in intensity of desire; the law of diminishing utility; the importance of custom in determining the nature of the expression of self-interest; and the necessity of balancing wealth-getting with the pain of so doing. All of these, in one way or another, were modifications of certain characteristics of the *economic man*. However, they continued to believe that man's self-interest led him to seek wealth.

It was because they refused to accept the definition of wealth proposed by Smith that economists like Lauderdale, Rae, and those of the Austrian school broke with the classical tradition. They agreed that man's self-interest and his search for wealth were axiomatic, but they wanted the definition of wealth to include more than mere material goods, or objects with value in exchange.

THE PSYCHOLOGICAL APPROACH: VEBLEN   Not until late in the nineteenth century did an economist appear who shared Smith's idea as set forth in *The Theory of Moral Sentiments*. It was an American, Thorstein Veblen (1857–1929), who hit upon the same idea—that vanity is the motivating force behind labor. With this interpretation, Veblen gave new life to the search for the psychological basis of human action, and at the same time undermined the abstract methods of classical and neo-classical economic theory. In defense of the classical position, Alfred Marshall and his followers turned from the psychological aspects of economic behavior altogether, contending that their only legitimate interest was in the objective facts of the marketplace. Such a retreat was unsatisfactory to Veblen and the institutional economists. The underlying theory of this growing school was that by research into the economic behavior of people throughout the ages, valid conclusions might be drawn as to the persistent psychological factors which motivate human behavior. They believed that not only was it possible to make valid assumptions about these psycho-social drives, but that it was impossible for economics to exist without making these assumptions. Herein lies the significance of Veblen's work.

By investigations of the behavior of primitive people and moderns, Veblen concluded that in the simple life of early man the basic drive was the production of things useful to the common good. Men got social approval and satisfaction through the exercise of their skill. The advancement of civilization brought a division of labor into warlike pursuits and peaceful, industrial pursuits. Success in the former gradually made the latter secondary. Prestige and power resulting from personal exploit became wholly desirable. The symbols of success were the trophies of forceful acquisition. Instinctively conscientious labor, even the most skilled, brought little commendation. The change to a commercial, money-making society altered standards of achievement. Predatory behavior was transferred to great industrial undertakings while ordinary labor remained undignified. Symbols of success were now possession of property, opportunity for leisure, and the ability to consume conspicuously vast quantities of wealth. A characteristic of every age is emulation. Those things which bring the respect and approval of one's fellows are sought after with all the energy one can muster. Usually this means imitation of those who are already respected and honored. The spirit of imitation is not always a pleasant competitive attitude; it becomes, in modern society, a bitter, envious thing Veblen called "invidious comparison." Since wealth, leisure, and conspicuous consumption are the marks of success in our commercial-industrial civilization, the pursuit of these things becomes the dominant motive of human behavior. But what has happened to the instinct of workmanship? Temporarily, at least, it is buried beneath the acquired characteristics of our time. But it shows itself in the dissatisfaction and restlessness which mark even the most successful persons according to the world's present standards.

CONCLUSION   To the problems raised by this examination of incentives to work, there are as yet no final answers. One thing seems clear: We know very little about the motivating forces which compel individuals to work. Although the concept of an *economic man* whose chief aim in life is to acquire the greatest amount of wealth with the least possible effort now seems woefully narrow and inadequate, we have no other concept which permits an analytical approach to economic activity.

WAGES

The practical man of affairs seldom troubled himself about the theory of what makes men work. If he paid his workers enough, he knew they would work. If he paid them enough! Here is a point at which businessmen and economists share a deep interest. Even more than rent, the issue of *wages* has been the battle ground of social reform. Laws of wages at various times have supplied the slogans for social upheavals and the placid justification for preserving the status quo.

Wage labor is a relatively new development in economic history.

In societies of the past, menial and laborious tasks were the work of slaves or serfs. Only the artisan had the dignity of freedom, and the privilege of selling the product of his labor for a price. Of course, special forms of contractual relationship appeared frequently, but on the whole only a few persons participated in the system. Since the beginning of the seventeenth century, in western Europe most workers have been free to sell their labor to whoever would buy, at a mutually agreeable price. This system, combining freedom and wage labor, has been one of the most prominent characteristics of our economic order.

The use of the wage system is coincidental with the rise of modern capitalism. In the evolution from the legal and economic semi-bondage of Feudalism, the intellect, labor, business enterprise, and government all were freed from the restrictions set by custom, law, theology, and absolute monarchs. The change was not instantaneous. In England following the Black Death in the fourteenth century, wages were, for many years, regulated by law. Gradually these controls disappeared, and men assumed responsibility for determining their own wage scales. Under the new freedom where men worked for others with someone else's tools and raw materials, the old wage formula of a just wage according to one's social status, expounded by Aquinas, no longer sufficed. New explanations were sought, and the result was an array of theories.

EARLY HYPOTHESES: MERCANTILISTS AND PHYSIOCRATS   On most issues the Mercantilists and Physiocrats differed greatly, but they held the same views on wages. Both agreed that wages were set at the subsistence level of the laborer. It is an exaggeration to say that the Mercantilists formulated a definite theory of wages. That they accepted such a theory without question is inferred from their writings on taxation and foreign trade. For example, Charles Davenant (1656–1714), in his discussion of foreign trade, pointed out how a rise in the price of foodstuffs would cause a rise in the wages of workers producing goods for export, thus shifting the advantage to England's competitors.

The Physiocrats stated the theory a little more positively. Quesnay believed wage earners received only a subsistence wage because the pressure of competition reduced wages to a minimum. Turgot said that in all cases the industrial worker was paid only what was necessary in order for him to secure subsistence, although the worker on the soil was not so restricted. The low level was due, he believed, as Quesnay had said, to the severe competition among workmen.

THE SUBSISTENCE THEORY   Adam Smith appears to have accepted the subsistence theory of wages, but his discussion was more suggestive of alternate theories and possible modifications of the "iron law" (as Lassalle later called it) than it was a definite statement of it. The low standard of living, he declared, was not a cause but an effect of low wages. Fundamentally, the subsistence of the worker and his family set the bottom limit to wages. A rise in wages, therefore, did not so much improve the lot of the wage earner as allow him to bring more children to adulthood. Hence high wages increased the number of workers, and low wages reduced the supply. Wages were never absolute in amount at a given time; there was room for bargaining to take place. The discrepancies in the bargaining power of the wage earners and the employers were clearly described. On the one hand, employers were few, no restrictions were set upon their organization, and tacit agreements existed among them as to wage policies. On the other hand, the opposite conditions applied to the wage earners.

Variations in the statement of the subsistence theory of wages continued to arise, even from those who have been regarded as its staunchest advocates. Malthus, basing his theory of wages on his theory of population, followed a supply and demand thesis, advocating the restraint of marriages as a means of decreasing the supply of wage earners and thus raising the standard of wages. The subsistence level does set the level of wages, but it is a subsistence level governed by custom. Malthus defined it as "that amount of those necessaries and conveniences without which they would not consent to keep up their numbers." Therefore wages could not fall below this level for the various classes of people without a fall in the labor supply and a consequent increase in the rate of wages.

Ricardo's contribution to this doctrine was the theory of the natural wage and the market wage, the natural wage being the wage that enabled the laborers to subsist and perpetuate their class without change. But, he added, the subsistence level was determined by custom for the various strata of society. Ricardo, of course, merely transferred his general theory of value to a theory of wages. Since value is the labor cost of production, wages are the cost of reproducing the same quantity of labor. Variations in the supply of laborers or changes in the demand for the product may change market wages, but in the long run they will tend to conform to the natural wage. There is also the admission that market wages might continue for an indefinite period above natural wages. One must draw the logical inference that an increase in market wages raises the customary standard of living. Does the new wage become the natural wage? Ricardo anticipated aspects of the wage problem that are still plaguing economists. In an expanding economy, Ricardo was well aware, things may act quite differently than they do in a static period.

The Socialists fastened upon Ricardian theories and used them as a justification for the overthrow of the capitalist system. According to Ricardo, labor is the only source of value. He also said that wages tended to be just sufficient to provide for subsistence and reproduction on a given customary standard of life. It takes no imagination to foresee the socialist line of reasoning from this point on. Labor has created ample value for a decent existence; in return labor has received a subsistence wage. Obviously, value has been taken from labor by those who had no right to it since it was the creation of labor.

In the hands of Marx these ideas were worked out as the theory of surplus value and the doctrine of increasing misery of the working class. The last is an embellishment of a process of change first explained by J. K. Rodbertus (1805–1875) but given currency by Marx in the *Communist Manifesto*. Briefly, Marx said that as the productivity of labor increased through division of labor and use of machines, the variation in wage levels tended to disappear; since skilled workers were reduced to unskilled, all wages fell toward the barest minimum of subsistence. Consequently an increasing disproportion appeared between wages paid to the laborer and the value he created.

MILL'S WAGES-FUND THEORY   The credit for formulating another theory of wages, complementary to, rather than a replacement for, the subsistence theory, goes to John Stuart Mill. The theory, known as the wages-fund theory, was first suggested by Adam Smith when he intimated that a store of funds was available out of which wages could be paid. J. R. McCulloch, James Mill, Nassau Senior, Malthus, and Ricardo all found the concept of a wages-fund acceptable as an explanation for the level of wages. Wages, according to this theory, depended upon the relationship between the supply of population and the capital available to employ workers. Mill was forced to add qualifications to the concepts of population and capital. By the former he meant those members of the working population who offered their services for hire; and by the latter, the amount of capital to be used for the payment of wages and any amounts incidental to the hire of laborers Thus the funds available for wages were fixed at any given time, and the only way to increase wages was to reduce the number of wages to be paid or to increase the capital funds available. The theory had important bearing upon the relation of trade unions and legislation to wages. At best, the effect of either alternative would be merely the shifting of a share of wages from one group of wage earners to another, since no absolute increase in the total wages paid was possible. That there was no fundamental contradiction between the subsistence and the wages-fund theories is clearly demonstrated by the fact that the strongest advocates of the subsistence theory also accepted the wages-fund theory without criticism.

Mill had influential supporters for his theory in Henry Fawcett and John Elliot Cairnes To their credit it must be admitted that a modicum of truth appears in the general idea that wages are paid in part out of capital. This does not validate the general theory, as a glance at some of the fundamental criticisms will show; but it does relieve it of some of the stigma of being a distinct capitalist class doctrine.

Criticism of the wages-fund theory came from a variety of sources. Several decades before the final statement of the theory, F. B. von Hermann in Germany had raised objections to it. Later, Francis Walker, Francis Longe, and W. T. Thornton pointed out such errors and impracticalities that the theory failed to survive. These writers noted that it was the consumers who set the demand for labor, and workers might be provided for out of current income as well as from capital. Also, there was no specific fund for wages which was separable from other funds to be used in production. The "fund" was really a matter of the employer's discretion as to how much he would provide for wages.

THE RESIDUAL CLAIMANT THEORY   In countering the wages-fund theory of Mill, an alternative known as the residual claimant theory was proposed. Adam Smith and others before him had intimated that rent and profits were deductions from the produce of labor. William Stanley Jevons first stated the theory positively in 1862, but the analysis of Francis Walker twenty years later is usually referred to. The essence of it is that portions of the product are first deducted for rent, interest, and profits. The remainder is the property of labor. The validity of the theory rests upon the independent determination of, and limitations upon, the shares of these three prior claimants. These being assumed, further economies in production or increased production would enlarge the share remaining for wages. The difficulty lies in establishing the independent determination of rent, interest, and profits.

THE BARGAINING THEORY   Also implied in Smith's *Wealth of Nations* was the possibility of a bargaining theory of wages. His statement of the employer's advantage in bargaining as against the employee's disadvantage sounds modern. He also noted the great variation in wage rates from community to community and from occupation to occupation. Similarly, W. T. Thornton took into account the adverse bargaining condition of wage earners. John Davidson and Maurice Dobb, American economists writing in 1898 and 1938 respectively, became dissatisfied with previous theories which tried to isolate one single determinant of wages. They contended that a variety of factors, not at all equally or consistently, influence wages. Furthermore, there was competition among the various claimants for the larger shares in the total product. The limits within which bargaining can take place are a maximum at the top beyond which the employer cannot stay in business, and a minimum below which the employee will not work. A great many factors will determine the point, within these limits, at which an agreement will be made—not the least of which is the organized bargaining power of the employer and employee.

The chief criticisms of this hypothesis are as follows. First, the theory really begs the question. For what really determines the limits of the employer's and employee's power? It might easily be subsistence modified by custom on the one hand and the sum of the claims of rent, interest, and profits on the other. And second, the theory seems to have its real application in organized industries, which actually account for only a minority of employees and industries.

NEOCLASSICAL THEORY   The marginal productivity theory of wages has been widely accepted in modern times. Once again, it is to Adam Smith that we turn for the first mention of such a thesis. He stated without explanation—possibly without much thought—that the produce of labor was the wages of labor. A fuller statement occurred in Johann Heinrich von Thünen's *Der Isolierte Staat* in 1826. The best exponent was John Bates Clark (1847–1938), Professor of Economics at Columbia University. As analyzed by Clark, the marginal productivity theory is really the explanation for the payment of rent, interest, profit, and price. Essentially the theory is this: The price of labor is determined by its marginal utility to the employer. Each unit of labor hired by the employer contributes to the value of the product, but the amount which each successive unit contributes is less than that of the one preceding; when the point is reached at which the contribution of the worker most recently hired just equals the wages he receives, the employer will no longer hire additional workers. The price of every other worker can be no greater than that of the last hired, who stands ready to replace any of the preceding workers. The wages paid, then, are equal to the productivity of the last worker hired, or to the marginal productivity of the labor force.

CRITICISMS OF THE NEOCLASSICAL THEORY   The required assumptions and the impracticality of the theory have undermined its popularity. It assumes a state of perfect competition which of course does not exist. The lack of knowledge of the market, the immobility of labor, and the presence of trade unions make it unrealistic. Moreover, the difficulty of separating the productivity of labor from that of capital seems insurmountable. On the whole, while such authorities as Alfred Marshall supported the theory, with reservations, the peak of its popularity has passed.

Though neoclassical wage theory remains the dominant tool of analysis, intensive study of wage behavior in various segments of the economy and under defined conditions has raised serious doubts about how realistic the classical concepts of wage determination are. Of equal importance, the facts regarding wage determination have proved false the basic Marxian prediction that working-class impoverishment increases as monopolies develop and ownership of the means of production becomes more concentrated.

Recent economic trends have posed new problems concerning wage determination. Since World War II real wages increased steadily until 1979 when double-digit inflation challenged the historic ability of the U.S. economy to support an ever-rising standard of living. Wage differentials among the various segments of the population have persisted, but differentials among the skilled and unskilled have narrowed. The achievement of an acceptable balance among such important factors as economic growth, wage levels, price levels, and employment has proved elusive. Because of the critical roles of wages and employment in determining the health of the economy, there has been much experimentation with what is widely known as "incomes policy." This refers to a combination of governmental programs—social insurance, training and placement programs, wage and price guidelines (or controls), food and energy subsidies, and the removal of discrimination in employment, for example—designed to keep prices, employment, and wages in balance. Neo-Keynesians supplement their fiscal and monetary controls with an incomes policy to "fine tune" the economy so that growth will be achieved without abnormal inflation (more than 6 percent) or excessive unemployment (more than 5 percent).

THE DIVISION OF LABOR

In the first chapter of *The Wealth of Nations* Adam Smith propounded an idea that seems commonplace, yet is the basic theory of all modern economics. This is the theory of the subdivision of labor. The idea did not originate with Smith. Plato, in his *Republic*, claimed that the formation of society itself was due to the benefits achieved through specialization. Articles of consumption were produced better, more easily, and more abundantly "when one man does that thing which is natural to him . . ." The Physiocrats, likewise, were aware of the advantages of specialization, but their emphasis was on the unproductiveness of some labor and the productiveness of other. Agricultural labor produced all value from the land; other labor was sterile and drew its reward from the original value created by agriculture.

Smith took a different view. Labor was the source of wealth. Not just some types of labor, but all labor. At great length Smith described the tremendous amount of cooperation necessary to provide a nation with the things it desires. The true source of the increase of the wealth of nations lies in the subdivision of labor and the system of automatic exchange which enables specialization to take place. The increase in total production is exemplified by the pin industry, said Smith. One man working alone could produce from one to twenty straight pins a day; through specialization and subdivision of labor each worker could make the equivalent of more than one pound per day. The reasons for these great advantages were stated clearly: Learning one job well saved the time usually absorbed in changes from job to job, and the close acquaintance with a single job led to the invention of new techniques. In further describing the division of labor he saw only two limits to its gradual increase: the extent of the market and the supply of capital. The former was a limitation because specialization required the presence of a large market in which to exchange the increasing quantities of the product. The latter was a limitation because subdivision required increased investments for space, materials, machinery, and advances for wages. These factors are not clearly defined by Smith but seem to be implicit in his description.

The other side of specialization Smith believed would be taken care of by man's "propensity to truck, barter, and exchange one thing for another," and the beneficial effects of each person seeking his own self-interest. In exchanging that part of one's labor which was a surplus for the surplus of another, both were benefited; and through the participation of all, the total wealth of society increased. It is obvious that some of Smith's assumptions, such as a "propensity to truck and barter," were naïve; but these are more than offset by the clarity with which he described the methods and advantages of division of labor and free exchange.

Criticism of the division of labor has come from many sources. Smith himself said that concentration upon a few simple operations for long periods of time might cause the laborer to lose the faculty of exercising intelligent thought. William Graham Sumner (1840–1910), an ardent advocate of many of Smith's theories, noted that the subdivision of labor caused the wage earner to lose all sense of responsibility for the conduct of the business and to lose with it his ability to calculate his own advantage and to foresee opportunities to improve his lot. The chief critics of the subdivision of labor are the Socialists. Marx claimed that machinery and the division of labor had taken from the work of wage earners all individual character, leaving only simple, routine, monotonous jobs which reduced the worker to an unimportant cog in a vast system of production, with his wages lowered to the level of the means of subsistence for propagation of his kind.

SCIENTIFIC MANAGEMENT

From the time of Adam Smith until early in the twentieth century no real advance was made in the theory of labor's use as a productive agent. Then came the farsighted ideas of Frederick Winslow Taylor (1856–1915). He devised a plan called scientific management, or Taylorism, that was the beginning of revolutionary changes in the application of labor to industry. Taylor's aim was to introduce into industry certain "natural laws" which if followed would result in maximum prosperity for employer and worker alike. In general the plan called for the introduction of three new principles of industrial administration: First, to secure greater cooperation of the labor force, the best workmen were hired at wages high enough to guarantee their continued affiliation with the company. Second, to secure greater efficiency, work was standardized and reduced to a routine. Third, to insure the success of larger ventures as well as efficiency in small ones, a system of functional planning was introduced. It was business organized, not by the profit maker but by the engineer.

While the great hopes for prosperity and harmonious industrial relations faded rapidly in the disturbances accompanying World War I, Taylorism set the pattern for the gigantic industrial establishments of today. Labor has opposed scientific management, and employers have abused its programs and purposes; but, like Adam Smith's outline of the division of labor, it presaged something new in the relationship of labor to production.

CLASS STRUGGLE

The economic developments described so clearly by Smith, especially the division of labor, have cut the general population into antagonistic parts, each with its own economic interests, organizations, and political programs. This tendency was described by Marx as the class struggle and elevated to the position of the central factor in human history. Marx described the process in the *Communist Mani-*

festo. In modern society class struggle exhibits itself as the struggle between the propertyless wage earner and the owners of the means of production, that is, the proletariat and the bourgeoisie. The latter group, not satisfied with its economic control, seeks to perpetuate its privileged position by securing control of the government. The wage earner finds the mechanization of his job the cause of declining wages. Women and children are brought in as competitors to do the simple tasks necessitated by machines. Moreover, the wage-earning class is being pushed further down into the ranks of the proletariat. Actually, however, the increasing size of business units brings workers together in larger masses, makes them aware of their common problems, and welds them into a strong revolutionary force. Such is Marx's theory of the progress of labor to a position of power.

LABOR ORGANIZATION

The Webbs, Sidney (1859–1947) and Beatrice (1858–1943), English authorities on labor and social problems, describe in their *Industrial Democracy* (1897) how the organization of labor unions gradually removes freedom from the labor market. Nonetheless, they advocated the complete unionization of wage earners and the direct participation of the organized workers in government through the agency of a labor party whose membership would be identical with the membership of the trade unions. The essential principles of this plan have been achieved in England.

Of quite a different character was the anarchistic theory of Michael Bakunin (1814–1876). He too believed in the strong economic organization of all wage earners, but he was confident that any attempt to achieve political reforms would only lead to a diluting of the basic philosophy of the working men's movement. Economic equality should come first, principally by the confiscation of capital. The method he proposed was international organization of wage earners for revolutionary purposes.

The Syndicalist movement was much stronger in Europe than in America. One of its leading exponents was Georges Sorel (1847–

1922), a one-time Marxist who lost patience with the Socialist movement and allied himself with the more militant Syndicalists. His program depended upon the organization of wage earners into syndicates (associations of workers), not unions. The aim of the movement was not political; there was no intention of taking over the power of the state. General strikes and violence were looked upon as the chief means of securing control of industry, and domination of political institutions would follow automatically.

A less violent form of Syndicalism was advocated by the Guild Socialists. R. H. Tawney (1880–1962) and G. D. H. Cole (1889–1959), noted English economists, were leaders in Guild Socialism. They believed that by gradual, evolutionary means workers organized along industrial lines can assume control of industry without simultaneously controlling political institutions.

Perhaps the most conservative of all labor movements is to be found in the development of the American trade unions. As outlined by Samuel Gompers (1850–1924), founder of the American Federation of Labor, union organization should be confined to the skilled trades, which by the very nature of their control of skill could bring pressure upon employers to achieve their aims. The unions should also control the training of new craftsmen through systems of apprenticeship. The labor unions as a whole would not participate directly in political activity, nor would they become affiliated with any political party. In general their policy was that of "rewarding their friends and punishing their enemies." Their chief weapons were strikes and boycotts. Dissatisfied with the aristocratic type of union, John L. Lewis (1880–1969), president of the United Mine Workers of America, sponsored a new type of labor union called the industrial union. As described by Lewis, every worker in a given industry, regardless of his craft or job, should be united in one union. The strength of such would lie not in the power to withhold essential skills but in the complete organization of all workers in an industry so that a strike could thus cripple an entire industry.

The absence of the names of the theoretical economists from this discussion of labor organization may be surprising. One must realize that the great economists of the past believed that the economic system could operate only under free competition. Labor organizations were unborn or in their infancy at the time. The reaction of the economists, therefore, was either to ignore the existence of trade unions or to look upon them, where they were present, as an evil of more or less consequence. That Adam Smith should have been aware of labor organizations and the problems associated with them, even in his day, is a true measure of his stature. Even Mill, for all his sympathy with the working man, felt that unions were useless. The disappearance of the freely competitive market—if such ever existed save in the minds of economists—made it easier for later writers to discuss the theory of trade union organization as an important aspect of modern economy.

4. Capital, Interest, and Profit

PLATO · ARISTOTLE · AQUINAS · HUME · CANTILLON ·
TURGOT · SMITH · LAUDERDALE · VON HERMANN ·
RICARDO · MILL · VON BÖHM-BAWERK · SAY · SISMONDI ·
MARX · MARSHALL · KEYNES · SCHUMPETER

*What is capital and where does it come from? Is capital
productive? What makes it possible to pay interest on capital?
At what point does legitimate interest cease and usury begin?
Why did early philosophy and religion condemn the taking
of interest? What is profit? Is profit the payment for risk;
for managerial ability; or is it merely theft from the earnings
of labor? Should profitableness or social desirability be the
test of whether or not an enterprise should be started or
continued?*

As GENERALLY DEFINED, capital is an accumulation of wealth used
in production. Land, labor, and capital are regarded as the three
chief elements of production. Of the three, *capital* is the most recent;
before the mid-eighteenth century it was almost completely ignored
in the writings on economic subjects. There is no use of the word
capital in the English language prior to 1600. For the next hundred
years or more, it was only used as a term in the keeping of accounts
or in signifying an investment in a business venture, such as a commercial voyage or the East India Company.

The word *stock* was the predecessor of our word *capital*. Early
discussions of economics referred to an accumulation of stock as
necessary before production could begin. The word seemed to mean

a supply of consumer's goods on which the producer might subsist while preparing or actually producing the final commodity.

CAPITAL

It will be doing the Physiocrats more honor than they deserve to credit them with the first use of the idea of capital. Nevertheless, in their writings, particularly those of Turgot, the concept of circulating wealth was clearly a step in the direction of recognizing capital as an agent of production. The cultivation of the soil from which all value arose was made possible, they said, by advances for tools and seed and for the maintenance of the worker while crops were growing.

ADAM SMITH AND HIS EARLY CRITICS Adam Smith was the first to produce an analysis of the place of capital in production. His ideas were vague and indefinite, yet he grasped the essentials of the use of capital. Although he believed that labor was the source of all value, he also said that the productivity of the worker increased with the subdivision of labor, this in turn being dependent upon the quantity of capital available. Furthermore, the number of workers could not be increased except by the augmentation of capital. In his opinion, capital was accumulated by the savings of individuals, not as a social contribution but in the pursuit of self-interest. However, one who saved was a public asset; a spender was a liability. It is impossible to discover what Smith believed to be the source of capital's productivity or its relative contribution to the value of the total product. As with so many other questions, Smith left his followers to debate the point and find explanations.

Criticisms of Smith as well as alternative explanations of the function of capital came from Lauderdale who, in 1804, published *An Inquiry into the Nature and Origin of Public Wealth and into the Nature and Causes of Its Increase*. He argued that Smith had not really given capital its due as a factor in production. He then proceeded to analyze capital as an independent factor, productive in itself. Capital, as he saw it, either supplanted a certain amount of labor, or performed services which labor could not do. Pursuing this point further, he showed that not only were industry and labor limited by capital, but that it was also possible for a country to be oversupplied with capital. This resulted in Lauderdale's belief in a potential overproduction of consumer's goods. Parsimony, or saving, as a source of capital was denied in favor of labor itself as a source.

F. B. W. von Hermann (1795–1868) published in 1832 *Staatswirtschaftliche Untersuchungen*, in which he criticized Smith's discussion of capital on two points: first, that it did not go deeply enough into the nature, operation, and interrelations of capital, and second, that capital was not treated consistently throughout. Hermann defined capital as "all producers of income which have durability and exchange value." Capital was divided into *use capital* and *industrial capital*, the latter being further broken down into loan and productive capital. His unique contribution to the theory of capital was that land, being a durable source of income, was capital.

Ricardo's point of view on capital was thoroughly in line with his labor theory of value: Capital was stored-up labor. That he was never completely satisfied with such a definition was borne out by his correspondence with McCulloch, and by his belief that value might be increased without labor. Of two objects brought to the market, each requiring the same expenditure of labor, the superior price of one which arrived later was due to the longer period for which profits were withheld. This was obviously payment for waiting time. The idea was given more careful treatment by Nassau Senior, who is credited with the formation of the abstinence theory of capital accumulation. He believed that land and labor were the primary factors in production, but unless tools were used the productive capacity of a people remained on a low level. In order to provide tools it was necessary to abstain from present consumption (unproductive consumption) in favor of using the resources available to produce more commodities (productive consumption). Abstinence was the term he gave capital; more elaborately defined, capital was wealth produced by labor to be used in the production of more wealth.

John Stuart Mill described with facility the ideas of the classical school. He seemed to consider capital as the maintenance for workers advanced during periods of activity until such time as they could get the benefit of their labor. This was not only the essence of the earliest ideas of capital as stock, but also it was a necessary ingredient of Mill's wages-fund exposition of wages. In his more practical sections, his conceptions of capital appear similar to the stored-up-labor theory of Ricardo.

BÖHM-BAWERK'S TIME-PREFERENCE THEORY One of the most extensive works on capital is found in the writings of Eugen von Böhm-Bawerk. His *Kapital und Kapitalzins* is a description and critique of the history of theories of capital and interest and a presentation of his own understanding of these subjects. His theory is known as the time-preference concept. Men, he said, fail to calculate fully their future wants; therefore goods in the present are of more value than the same goods in the future. He also believed that present goods had greater value because capital was productive. The addition of more capital, however, had the effect of postponing the enjoyment of benefits for increasingly longer periods. Therefore, the value of capital must be judged by its ability to make up the loss between the present consumption and future consumption of the goods which were turned into capital. By incorporating into his own theory von Thünen's ideas on diminishing returns, Böhm-Bawerk provided the basis for much of our current thought on capital.

THE SOCIALISTS Theories of capital play an important part in the teachings of the exponents of socialist doctrines. One of the first to complain about the effects of capital was Sismondi (1773–1840), who in many instances used the theories of Adam Smith as a starting point in making his analysis of capital. Sismondi believed that the division of labor was the principal cause of the increased powers of production. This, however, was dependent upon an ever-increasing quantity of circulating capital. The machines and the expensive establishments in which they were housed required a first cost which was returned only over long periods of time. This presupposes a quantity of capital which can be spared from present use "in order to establish a permanent kind of rent." Sismondi contended that the introduction of new machinery should serve a social purpose such as creating a new demand for labor or putting goods within the reach of new consumers. If it did not achieve this purpose, it should at least not displace or render useless a certain number of producers, whether native or foreign. But he saw no way to control inventions at home, much less abroad, and he concluded that economic life was a war of machines against man.

The views of Karl Marx were in the same direction, but better grounded in theoretical economics. Modern capital came into being in the sixteenth century in the form of money to be used for commercial purposes. Through the process of appropriating the surplus value produced by the worker in the form of goods, which were then sold on the market for cash, the employer was able to purchase additional means of production. This process is continued "by incorporating living labor with their dead substance," and the employer continues to convert a "materialized and dead labor into capital . . . a live monster that is fruitful and multiplies." This new capital is then used to exploit labor further. As additional machinery is added from the surplus value already appropriated by the employer, the productivity of labor is increased. The worker does not share in it, as we have noted before, for his wages can never rise above a subsistence level. The net result of this process is the increasing impoverishment of the working class and the increase of capital (the means of production) in the hands of the employer. Marx did not condemn capital as such, only the fact of private ownership, which enabled the employer to appropriate for himself surplus value created by labor with the aid of capital. There is no doubt that Marxian capital was the old Ricardian concept of stored-up labor.

KEYNES AND THE REVOLT AGAINST CLASSICAL DOCTRINE John Maynard Keynes (1883–1946) was not only a theoretical economist of great stature, he was also a civil servant. In Keynes's view, economic theory should be an instrument of public policy. He devoted his energies in the two decades following World War I to explaining the depressed state of England's economy, the shattering effect of the Versailles Treaty on business throughout the world, and last, in developing an economic theory to achieve full employment and higher living standards. His *General Theory of Employment, Interest and Money* (1936) is a masterful analysis of the role played by saving and investment in promoting economic well-being. The basic thesis was simply that in the aggregate, as with individuals, the higher the income, the greater will be the propensity to save—a factor not directly related to interest rates. While the classical economist assumed that savings were equivalent to investment and thus re-entered the economy as expenditures, this equilibrium in fact did not always occur. Investments were made by people other than the savers, and frequently savings exceeded what entrepreneurs were ready to invest; thus a decline in consumption made even the current capital excessive. Underemployment was therefore the result of low rates of consumption brought on by saving more than plans for investment in new plant and equipment demanded. On the other hand, an infusion of purchasing power into the economy by government spending had a multiplier effect. That is, if the propensity to save was 10 percent, then each dollar of government expenditure generated another 90 cents of expenditure, and that in turn resulted in 81 cents of expenditure; thus as the government dollar circulated through the economy, the impact was nine or ten times the original expenditure.

INTEREST

This discussion has from time to time bordered upon the related field of the theory of interest and profit. In fact, no discussion of capital would be complete without an analysis of these two subjects which have proved to be among the most controversial in economic theory.

EARLY THEORIES: FROM ETHICS TO ECONOMICS Much of the early literature on interest was concerned with its ethical rather than economic aspects. Plato condemned interest as it applied to loans. Aristotle, investigating the various aspects of economic life more deeply than Plato, also condemned it on the ground that money was barren and could not reproduce itself. To require payment over and above the value of the thing itself when it had produced nothing, he believed, was unjust. The early Christian fathers declared that usury was sinful, citing biblical teaching for their objection. It remained for Aquinas to modify the earlier Christian doctrine in the face of clearly observed conditions and practices in his own time. He divided material wealth into those articles which were consumed in use and those which were used without consuming. The first could not be loaned but only purchased outright; the second could be leased for use and returned. Money, somewhat illogically it seems to us moderns, was looked upon as of the former variety. Hence Aquinas sided with Aristotle in condemning the practice of requiring more than its face value as the sale price of money. Nevertheless, interest could be paid to professional usurers (who were usually not controlled by Christian doctrine) if the borrowers desired the money for good purposes.

Two general conditions prevailed during the Middle Ages when payment of interest might be considered legitimate. One, *damnum emergens*, occurred when the owner realized a loss because of having loaned the money. The second, *lucrum cessans*, was the occasion of the owner losing an opportunity for profit while his money was loaned to another. Christian doctrine approved the first but raised doubts against the second. The final break in religious objections came when Calvin took a positive view on the legitimacy of interest, with only minor reservations. For a time following the Reformation, usury laws setting a maximum rate of interest existed. Then, finally, under the attacks of men like Bentham the laws were abolished. Bentham's point of view was that the usury laws made it easy for the old, settled business enterprises to get money, but new industries which involved risk, but which also were the origins of progress, could not borrow because no lender would assume so great a risk at such a low rate of interest.

INTEREST AND THE PRODUCTIVITY OF CAPITAL Concern for the economic aspects of interest dates from the late seventeenth century when a pamphlet debate engaged in by Sir Josiah Child brought forth the theory that the wealth of a country was a cause and not an effect of a low interest rate. Locke proposed that the interest rate could be determined by the ratio of ready money to the "whole trade of the kingdom," by which he probably meant business transactions. John Law also took the position that if the quantity of available money increased the interest rate would fall. Sir William Petty, in opposing attempts to restrict the rate of interest, protested that such a course was impossible since interest rates were set by the quantity of money, which was beyond Parliament's control.

David Hume, writing in 1752, subscribed to the *quantity of money* theory as a temporary factor in interest rates. Using Spain as an illustration, he showed how the influx of gold and silver from the New World caused prices and interest to rise temporarily, only to subside again to normal levels. But he believed that the quantity of money was not the true cause of variation in interest rates. He claimed that the interest rate was set by supply and demand. If society was composed mainly of poor persons who were always wanting to borrow, interest rates would be high; should society have an abundance of wealthy individuals seeking profitable places to lend money, the competition among them would tend to drive down interest rates. He added a significant factor, that interest rates were also influenced by the profit to be secured from commerce. High profits meant less money to lend, therefore high interest rates, and vice versa.

Richard Cantillon, in a book published in 1755 (although written much earlier), also objected to the quantity of money theory of interest. He held that though an increase of money might raise prices, it would not necessarily raise interest rates. He believed that a change in the class status of borrowers and lenders influenced the rate. For example, in the Middle Ages when borrowing was by persons in dire need, interest hinged upon the degree of necessity of the borrower and the unscrupulous nature of the lender. At the time Cantillon was writing, borrowing was for business enterprise, and the interest rate rose in direct relation to the number of such enterprises. He claimed that the prodigality of nobles and war also caused a rise in interest rates by increasing the activity of business enterprises. He made a unique contribution to interest theory by describing the importance of a person's social class upon the rate of interest.

Upon the simple foundations laid by Hume and Cantillon, Turgot built a more elaborate concept of interest. He accepted the supply and demand theory. To this he added the new idea that increasing supplies of "movable riches" were constantly being provided out of savings from previous incomes and profits. He believed that a greater amount of saving would lower the interest rate if the number of borrowers remained constant. Turgot also claimed that interest was the price of an advance of money. Although this last observation seemed obvious, it began a never-ending series of speculations on the question of why interest was paid at all.

The more formal statement of the theories expounded by Hume and Turgot came from Jean Baptiste Say. His reduction of all prices to a matter of supply and demand was directly applied to interest. By dividing capital into disposable capital and production capital he made a notable advance in the understanding of interest. Only the former influenced interest rates, he claimed, for since the latter was already incorporated into enterprise there was no way it could affect the supply of disposable capital. Say also introduced the idea that many factors may influence interest rates, including risk and liquidity, i.e., the ease with which the loan can be converted into cash.

Another class of interest theories has been called the *indirect productivity* theories. The basis of these theories is the fact that the addition of capital enables a worker to produce in greater quantities. Therefore the one who supplies the capital is entitled to a share of the increase. Lauderdale was one of the first supporters of such a theory. He believed in the independent productivity of capital. Although he did not distinguish between interest and profit, his argument showed that both would naturally come from the earnings of capital. Von Thünen in *Der Isolierte Staat* applied his theory of diminishing returns to the general productivity idea and proposed that the interest rate would be determined by the productivity of the marginal unit of capital, that is, by the unit whose cost just equaled the amount it could produce. He went on to explain that the interest rate could not reflect the total increase in production derived from the use of the capital, since competition tended to reduce the price of capital to the amounts paid by those who could profit by the capital least.

Ricardo said that the interest on money is determined by the rate of profit which can be made by the employment of capital. Add the idea of diminishing returns, and the theory is not materially different from von Thünen's.

THE PAYMENT FOR WAITING: TIME PREFERENCE   Developed at the same time as the productivity theory was another theory with which it was later linked to provide the most popular explanation of interest and interest rates. This was the *time-preference* theory, based on the contention that because present goods possess superior value over future goods a payment must be made for waiting. In his definition of capital as abstinence, Nassau Senior turned attention to the factor of waiting. In order to create capital it was necessary to abstain from present consumption. Abstinence was not pleasant; therefore payment was necessary in order to cause persons to endure the discomfort. No distinction was made among English economists between interest and profit; consequently it was assumed that waiting might be responsible for either one or the other or both.

It was von Böhm-Bawerk who made the synthesis of the time-preference and the productivity theories of interest. He accepted the proposition that man generally prefers present to future values, although this inclination might be greatly modified by the character of the individual and the security of the environment. He claimed, in addition, an economic reason for present values being greater. Since the function of capital is to increase the productivity of labor, an article made today will have greater value than the same article in the future, as its cost of production is greater today. People were willing to pay extra for the use of goods in the present, rather than waiting until the future, and those who abstained from the use of goods until the future felt the need for compensation. But added to these considerations was the diminishing productivity of capital. Consequently, interest rates tended to be set at a point where the payment people were willing to make for present values against future values equaled the productivity of the last unit of capital added. This was not materially different from the von Thünen analysis, except that the demand for capital was analyzed with regard to the time-preference theory. One might draw the valid conclusion that this was merely another manifestation of the process of synthesizing utility on the one hand with cost of production on the other, a relationship so frequently made in other theories.

Modifications of von Böhm-Bawerk, in the sense of elaborations of and deductions from his theory, have appeared in vast quantity since his original work. General support for the theory came from such writers as the American economist Irving Fisher (1867–1947). Although using different approaches, the general idea of Fisher was similar to that of von Böhm-Bawerk. The interest rate was set when the marginal utility of the capital to the borrower, which consisted of both the psychological factor of time preference and the marginal productivity of the sum borrowed, was thought to balance the lender's time preference and his estimate of the opportunity for investment. The general criticism leveled against this analysis was the inability to know what the psychological factors of borrowing and lending were and how they worked. Assumptions on the question could be made, but they provided a very artificial base on which to establish a theory. Furthermore, the assumption that time preference led one to prefer present to future values had so many obvious exceptions that it seemed unwise to believe that it applied generally.

MARSHALL AND KEYNES   As opposed to the complicated analysis of von Böhm-Bawerk, there was a tendency to return to simpler formulae for explaining interest and interest rates. Alfred Marshall, although he developed no systematic treatment of interest, made several observations on the subject which may be briefly summarized. He believed that the interest rate was set by the supply of the money stock balanced against the demand for capital. In small localities the equilibrium would remain fairly constant because supplies of capital might be drawn from outside communities. In larger areas, however, the demand for capital could not be met immediately because saving required time; hence, a rise in the interest rate would be inevitable until equilibrium was re-established by the withdrawal from the market of those persons to whom the marginal utility of the added capital would not warrant the payment of the added cost. He indicated acceptance of the Say doctrine that previously invested capital did not affect the interest rate, since by no consideration could it enter the supply of money available for loans.

John Maynard Keynes assumed, with some justice as far as our own society was concerned, that most people invest not because of the interest rate but because of the prospective yield or, in other words, the increase in value of the original investment. However, it was also true that a large number of persons would save even if there were no interest rate. Fundamentally, the interest rates in vogue were a result of custom on the one hand and liquidity preference on the other. This line of reasoning dealt a mortal blow to classical theory, which was based, in the long run, upon supply and demand for capital.

PROFIT

At many points the theory of interest coincided with the theory of profits. Indeed, some authors discussed them interchangeably, and others found that interest rates and profit rates were determined by the same factor—the earning power of capital. There are, however, a number of different theories as to the meaning, the origin, and the rate of profit.

THE CLASSICAL TRADITION The early writers, prior to Adam Smith, made no clear distinction between interest and profit, although it is obvious that businessmen of the time, conducting their affairs many times on borrowed capital, must of necessity have paid interest and considered profit as the residue. The Physiocrats and Mercantilists generally failed to note any difference between interest and profit. Adam Smith tried to clarify the meaning of these terms. He pointed out that profits were not wages paid for any kind of supervisory labor, but were a distinct income derived solely from capital or *stock*, as he called it. He was careful to caution against an error quite common even today, that of lumping both the earnings of capital and the wages of proprietorship as "profits" when a business enterprise was conducted by a person who furnished his own capital. This point was elaborated by J. B. Say, a close follower of Smith's theories. Although Say's terms *profits of industry* and *profits of capital* were in themselves somewhat confusing, he tried to separate the wages of the entrepreneur from his returns as an investor. Profits of industry, he said, included wages paid to common labor and to the supervisors and directors of the enterprise, whereas profits of capital included elements of interest and payment for risk. When the rate of profit in relation to the risk and the length of waiting time was low, capital would neglect such ventures in favor of more lucrative ones. This withdrawal would cause the competition to slacken (due to the lack of new ventures and the failure of old ones). A rise in profits would follow until risk and waiting were well enough rewarded to encourage the investment of new capital.

Ricardo is never very clear on the meaning of profit. In some instances it was discussed as a residual amount after labor was paid. Since the subsistence theory of wages implied a stable amount for this factor, the increase or decrease in the total income would affect profits. In other discussions he stated that the return on capital was payment for past labor. It is always well to keep in mind that Ricardo speaks usually of long-term principles, under systems of perfect competition (although occasionally the peculiar movements of the present broke into his exposition). Certainly the reward of capital as payment for the labor necessary to produce it was a "natural" payment, as Ricardo saw it, modified at any given time by the short-term conditions of the market.

Both Mill and Ricardo were interested in the effect of population movements on profits. They believed that the increase in population resulted in use of the less productive land; and capital, earnings, and, of course, profits would fall, tending to approach zero. Advances in civilization, however, of which inventions were an important part, would go a long way to preserving a substantial rate of profit.

In his discussion of the relation of profits to other forms of income, Mill incorporated some of the ideas of J. B. Say. He advised that the returns on business enterprise should be broken down into the return on the use of capital, a payment for risk, and wages to the entrepreneur. Just which of these should constitute true profit, Mill did not say.

MODERN VIEWS   This discussion of the elements which constitute profit has continued on into the twentieth century. Alfred Marshall and J. B. Clark proposed solutions to the difficulty. Marshall believed that profits were made up of the divisions described by Mill, but added the idea of profits as combination earnings. This was an aspect of profit which appeared only as large-scale industry began to take shape. Whereas, in earlier days the owner of a business enterprise invested his own capital, managed the business, and assumed the risk, in modern times each of these services could be and was frequently performed by a specialized group for a fee established by market conditions. Profit, then, would be the result of the skill with which these factors were brought into combination in a particular branch of industry. This seemed to have certain advantages from a quantitative standpoint. If, as in large corporations, all the traditional elements of profit, even risk, could be bought at a stipulated sum, the surplus over and above all costs could be nothing more than the earnings of an intangible aspect of the business enterprise best characterized as the skill in integrating the factors of production, at a certain time, for a certain purpose.

Not content with this explanation, Marshall and Clark separately proposed that profit be considered as the product of market disequilibrium. They assumed a hypothetical situation in which perfect competition and the free application of supply and demand brought all aspects of the economic process into balance. Under such a circumstance there would be no profit. Such a situation could never exist; however it was theoretically possible and interesting. The fact that it did not materialize was an indication of the operation of such unpredictable forces as unexpected shortages, losses, and demands. Marshall coined the term *quasi-rent* to cover the short-term earnings of the forces of production which arose because of the unbalance in the economic process.

Joseph A. Schumpeter (1883–1950) was born in Moravia and spent most of his early life in Vienna. Although later a severe critic of Böhm-Bawerk, he owed his early training in economics to that exponent of classical economic theory. Schumpeter argued that basic economic forces are most clearly identified in a static society. Profit and interest, which he regarded as relatively interchangeable, gravitated to zero as the economy approached the static position. It was innovators, supported by entrepreneurs, who galvanized the economy into action and encouraged prospective lenders to anticipate a high rate of return. Savings were inadequate to finance such new economic adventures; therefore, bankers (particularly investment bankers) played a major part in financing new businesses and setting in motion the forces producing a new upward thrust in the business cycle.

Contemporary economists have delved deeply into the elements of profit, hoping to grasp a factor which would seem to give a fairly adequate explanation of profit for the modern type of business enterprise. When, as in many industries, all of the constituents of profit, such as wages of an entrepreneur, return on invested capital, and payment for risk-bearing, are met in advance for a definite sum, the source of profit becomes an elusive and complicated factor indeed.

5. FOREIGN AND DOMESTIC TRADE

MUN · PETTY · NORTH · QUESNAY · TURGOT · HUME · SMITH · SAY · RICARDO · MILL · MALTHUS · BASTIAT · MÜLLER · LIST · HAMILTON · CAREY · PATTEN · COURNOT

Is the policy of "sell more than you buy" as valid for nations as for the individual businessman? Is money or useful goods the better measure of an individual's wealth? Of a nation's wealth? Will free trade or government-protected business produce the most profitable economic relations? Are there stages in economic development when protection is more advantageous than free trade? What are the modern methods used by business to control the "market"?

THE STORY OF the transition from the self-sufficient manor of the Middle Ages to the great national-economy systems of the modern world is largely the story of the rebirth and maturing of foreign and domestic trade. It is difficult, if not impossible, to differentiate cause and effect in historical sequences. Was it the Arab control of the Near East which caused the western voyages of Columbus? Was it Watt's application of steam to hand tools which set in motion the industrial revolution? One cannot give an unqualified answer to questions such as these. Evidence is ample, however, to show that behind the economic activity of the latter days of the Middle Ages and the centuries which followed lay the continually expanding markets at home and abroad, spurring on the increasing productivity of farm and factory. Without a market for goods, few of the revolutionizing inventions of the past centuries would have become so well known or so widely accepted. Thus it is first of all to trade that we must turn if we are to understand the driving power and the organizing genius which guides and motivates our economy.

Trade, of course, never ceased, even in the most static period of the Middle Ages. Enterprising craftsmen became merchants who bought articles in one part of Europe to sell to another. The expansion of markets called forth new forms of manufactures. By the fifteenth century and lasting through the seventeenth century, trade was carried out mainly in the form of monopoly.

MERCANTILISM

When Adam Smith was searching for a name to identify the body of generally accepted economic ideas in the century or two before he wrote, he called it Mercantilism, because of the emphasis placed upon trade. In earlier chapters we have already encountered the outstanding representatives of this general theory of economic life: Mun, Petty, Steuart, Montchrétien, and von Hornick.

Briefly stated, the Mercantile doctrine identified wealth with money. It therefore emphasized the necessity of a community so conducting its affairs as to acquire an abundance of precious metals. The surest method of doing this, especially for those countries without mines, was to export the utmost quantity of its own manufactures, and to import the absolute minimum from other nations. The excess of exports over imports would be paid for in gold and silver. A favorable balance of trade (that is, when more coin is received than paid out) was considered the only satisfactory condition of commerce. The establishment and maintenance of such a favorable balance was not the sole responsibility of individual merchants; the government carried a heavy obligation as well. It was agreed that by prohibitions against foreign goods, subsidization of exports, restriction upon the export of precious metals, and the creation of monopolies among the trading companies, the government might assure the nation of a steady influx of gold—the means of making the state strong and powerful.

While most economists of the period must be classed as Mercantilists, not all of them would subscribe to the above summary of their doctrine. Many of them were too clear-sighted to be trapped by certain obvious errors in the Mercantilist line of reasoning. However, the Mercantilists were in a sense merely expressing abstractly what was the actual practice of the times. In spite of variations, similar conditions gave birth to similar ideas. The growth of commerce and discoveries of the New World led to the rapid development of a common medium of exchange. Feudalism, with its barter system and general self-sufficiency, gave way to an economy where buying and selling was important and money was always in demand. The more of it one had, the more goods one could control. Money would last. Tomorrow, or the next day, or years hence, money represented the power to acquire goods. The formation of great states, with powerful governments, large armies, luxurious courts, and hosts of officials, required the expenditure of vast sums of money. Dense populations and industry seemed better able to produce revenue-getting conditions than sparsely settled regions dependent upon agriculture. Hence industry and trade received the favors of government, while agriculture was left to seek its own survival. Colonies were sought as markets for goods, while severe laws restricted their economic freedom and made them dependent upon the grudging purchases of the mother country alone for commerce and trade. Duties on imports, barriers to the export of gold, and great trading monopolies were characteristic of every nation. These things were not theories; they were the most important facts of the times. The economists either summarized what was happening and found reasons to justify, it, or they took issue with the turn of events and suggested alternatives. Such ideas compose the theory of Mercantilism.

Thomas Mun (1571–1641), perhaps the ablest exponent of Mercantilism, began his explanation of that doctrine while endeavoring to justify the practices of the East India Company, of which he was a director, against attacks by anti-Mercantilists. *A Discourse of Trade from England into the East Indies* (1621), Mun's first work, was a polemic against attacks on his company, with an abundance of charges and counter charges and a minimum of considered thought. It was in his *England's Treasure by Forraign Trade, or The Balance of Our Forraign Trade Is the Rule of Our Treasure,* written about 1630 but published posthumously by his son in 1664, that Mun gave his most lucid explanation of the mercantile philosophy and presented a comprehensive plan to increase the wealth and treasure of England. The merchant, according to Mun, was a most important figure in the community since he was responsible for enriching the kingdom, for providing the king with revenue and maintaining his treasure. Although an academic education was not necessary for the merchant, he should be well versed in language and skilled in ship building and navigation. Mun accepted in principle the mercantile idea of a favorable balance of trade.

> The ordinary means therefore to increase our wealth and treasure is by *Forraign Trade,* wherein we must observe this rule; to sell more to strangers yearly than wee consume of theirs in value . . . because that part of our stock which is not returned to us in wares must necessarily be brought home in treasure.

How clearly dependent the nation's welfare was upon foreign trade in Mun's opinion was indicated in the closing pages of his book.

> So much Treasure only will be brought in or carried out of a commonwealth as the Forraign Trade doth over or under ballance in value. . . . Behold then the true form and worth of forraign Trade, which is the great Revenue of the King, The honor of the Kingdom, The noble profession of the merchant, The School of our Arts, The supply of our wants, The Employment of our poor, The Improvement of our Lands, The Nurcery of our Mariners, The walls of the Kingdoms, the means of our Treasure, The Sinnews of wars, The terror of our Enemies.

For Mun's practical suggestions as to how a favorable balance was to be maintained see Chapter 1.

Thomas Mun was not uncritical of the system he so well described. For example, his proposal for the export of bullion was not readily accepted by his contemporaries. In their view, no bullion should leave the country save in payment of debts. Mun saw beyond the immediate present. He believed that the use of bullion to foster a carrying trade established by Englishmen abroad was a legitimate excuse for shipping gold out of the country, since a prosperous trade would in time return more bullion to the country than was taken out. The analogy Mun used to drive home his point has become famous: A farmer viewed only at seed time, when he scatters his seed over the ground, seems wasteful; but when his harvest is considered, the worth of his action becomes apparent. Thus at this early date Mun pleaded the cause of all foreign investors. The economic history of England amply proved his point.

On other aspects of mercantile theory and practices Mun was in advance of his time. He did not fall into the fallacy of thinking that wealth and money were identical. It was what money could buy that was important. Furthermore, he denied the idea that in order to secure a favorable balance of trade it was essential for each merchant to have a favorable balance. The sum total of exports and imports for a given period was the important consideration. It was a hundred years or more before this last consideration led to a complete reappraisal of the idea of foreign trade.

There was great similarity between Mun's exposition of Mercantilism and that presented by Philipp von Hornick, an Austrian whose works appeared a half-century later. His *Oesterreich Über Alles, Wann Es Nur Will* (Austria Above All Others, If It Wants to Be), published in 1684, indicates the interest in national self-sufficiency and power that pervaded his work.

A great many writers in one way or another accepted the idea of a favorable balance of trade being essential to national strength. A number of 'them are noted for the new lines of thought they opened up, and have consequently been discussed in other chapters. Sir William Petty emphasized the monetary aspect of foreign trade; Sir Josiah Child, who venerated Dutch industry and Dutch moral character, saw economic success as dependent upon low interest rates; Sir James Steuart, whose excellent *Inquiry into the Principles of Political Economy* had the misfortune of supporting a moderate mercantilism just nine years before *The Wealth of Nations* by Adam Smith appeared, nevertheless contributed greatly to later theories of value and population.

CRITICS OF MERCANTILISM: DEVELOPMENT OF THE FREE-TRADE DOCTRINE

Some writers of economic history look upon Petty, Locke, and North as the authors who laid the foundations for the revolutionary doctrine of *freedom in trade*. Although Petty is usually classified as a Mercantilist because of his general acceptance of this philosophy, his greatest contribution was a destruction of the mercantile theory of money and prices, hence his inclusion among the forerunners of free trade. He understood that a nation needed money; but he believed there could be too much or too little of it, thus affecting price levels. Although the idea of an automatic control of the quantity of money in a nation was not yet developed, Petty advocated the removal of all restrictions upon the export of money. His statistical work on the commerce of Ireland showed that an abundance of exports under certain circumstances was actually harmful, and that other things than goods and money influenced a nation's economic position.

For purely economic criticism of mercantilist ideas of trade no one in the seventeenth century surpassed the directness and forcefulness of the writings of Sir Dudley North (1641–1691). In his *Discourse upon Trade* (1691), he showed that wealth could exist independently of gold or silver. Agriculture and industry were the true sources of wealth. Money, he conceded, was one element of wealth, and it performed invaluable services in facilitating the exchange of goods. The quantity of money in a country might be in excess or less than the requirements of the nation's trade, but this was something which would regulate itself without human interference. North condemned the practice of granting business privileges and concessions to one particular group of merchants, saying that every such exclusive privilege was to the public's disadvantage. He stands out as an independent thinker, as a herald of the new economic era that was ushered in nearly a century later by Adam Smith.

The names of Roger Coke, Nicholas Barbon, and Charles Davenant should be added to the list of critics of Mercantilism. Their
work kept aflame the smoldering fires of discontent that were threat-
ening to destroy the doctrine of foreign trade operated under government control for the sake of more metal. Coke pointed out the
probable reaction of foreign nations to the tight-fisted money policy.
He foresaw the diminution of England's foreign trade as rival countries refused to trade with a nation that would not reciprocate,
just as he foresaw the stagnation of domestic industries when freed
from competition. Barbon showed how trade might increase rather
than diminish if restrictions against imports were removed. Davenant
expressed the opinion that trade was self-regulating and would prosper better if freed from control.

The reaction against Mercantilism was particularly strong in
France where the evils of an exaggerated mercantilist policy had
brought financial ruin to the country. The unrest among the people,
oppressive taxes, and a depressed condition of agriculture led to
violent protests against the financial administration of Jean Baptiste
Colbert. Unwittingly, Colbert had become the chief exponent of
Mercantilism in Europe to such an extent that the system became
known on the continent as *Colbertism*. The extravagant demands
of Louis XIV forced Colbert to find new and fruitful sources of
revenue. He developed the pattern of Mercantilism in France not
as a studied purpose but as the inevitable result of hundreds of
independent moves to increase the revenues of the state.

THE PHYSIOCRATS   Credit for the final destruction of mercantile
principles both in theory and practice, as far as France was concerned, goes to those economists known popularly as the Physiocrats.
Quesnay and Turgot were representative leaders of this school of
thought. Their attitude toward trade was a direct outgrowth of
their basic concept of a natural law which applied to all nature:
The individual had a right to whatever natural enjoyments he could
procure through his labor. The right to hold and transfer property
was therefore undeniable. Once having granted these assumptions,

it followed that competition should not be restricted by law, by the creation of monopolies, or by the granting of special privileges. On the other hand, Quesnay considered commerce as unproductive labor. The mere exchange of wealth, he claimed, was not the same as the production of wealth. The gain made by merchants was at the expense of the agriculturalists, who alone were the producers of all value. He denied the value of a favorable balance of trade since its effect would be to raise prices, and held the wealth of a state could not be judged by the quantity of money it possessed since money had no value in itself except as it effected an exchange of commodities. To conduct commerce at the expense of another nation was impossible, since commerce can only take place as long as there exist reciprocal advantages. Nevertheless, the Physiocrat defense of free trade cannot be accepted as evidence of high estimate of its worth. Just the opposite was the case. Foreign trade was a liability since the expenses of it were deducted from the real production of agriculture. Domestic trade at least kept all true values within the nation. Turgot modified some details of Quesnay's ideas. For example, in emphasizing the obligation of the state to prevent monopoly and special privilege to the extent of preserving natural liberty, he objected to extending the state's responsibility to the degree of a paternalistic care of the careless, lazy, or indifferent.

DAVID HUME The work of the philosophers during this period of transition to a new economic society was of incalculable value. They attacked existing ideas from an objective viewpoint, clarifying the economic issues and indicating the probable direction of future developments. No systematic analysis of economic life was attempted by them. This job they left for economists, who benefited, however, from their philosophic work. This essentially describes the relation which existed between David Hume and Adam Smith. Hume (1711–1776) was a learned man, able to write on many subjects with lively style and penetrating insight. His writings in economics consist of a few scattered essays. In the main these writings attacked the mercantilist ideas on the value of money and the importance of foreign trade. Hume denied that a nation's wealth was dependent upon the accumulation of bullion. In fact, he went so far as to state that regardless of the quantity of money, trade could be carried on effectively, for prices tended to adjust to the quantity of money in circulation. On the other hand, he contended, a nation's wealth consisted of its people and its industry; a nation would by natural forces and without effort get the money it required for its economic activity. One of his most amazing statements was that England's economic success depended upon the growing prosperity of countries in Europe, since only if they were prosperous could English merchants sell them goods. The basis for this doctrine was Hume's idea of a territorial division of labor; consequently he condemned any artificial barriers to trade.

ADAM SMITH   It is Adam Smith who stands forth as the great critic of Mercantilism and the chief exponent of the doctrine of individual freedom in trade. It has often been said that there was more than coincidence in the fact that both the Declaration of Independence and *The Wealth of Nations* were given to the world in 1776. One was a declaration of political freedom; the other proclaimed industrial and commercial independence. Certainly, strong ties bound the two together. Very little that Adam Smith said on the subject of trade was new, most of it had been said before; but the scope of Smith's work, the completeness of his analysis and the timeliness of its appearance all conspired to make *The Wealth of Nations* a landmark in economic thought.

The ideas expressed by Smith on the subject of trade were rooted in his beliefs concerning the nature of man and society. Each individual, he said, was more understanding than any other as to his own needs and desires. If each were allowed to seek his own welfare, he would in the long run contribute most to the common good. Natural law, better than government restraint, would serve to prevent abuses of this freedom. It was self-interest, in the course of human history, which led to the subdivision of labor. The cooperation and exchange which naturally followed were responsible for the world's economic progress, and therein lay the road to future achievements.

It is obvious that Adam Smith favored free trade. Any restriction upon domestic or foreign commerce he believed unwise since it hampered the operation of natural law and prevented the increase in benefits that further exchange would undoubtedly bring. A large part of *The Wealth of Nations* is devoted to an attack on the principles of Mercantilism. That Smith's ideas of Mercantilism tended to exaggerate its evils is of small moment today. His work served to bring public confidence in the practices associated with mercantile policy to an end. He demonstrated that all forms of government interference, whether the granting of monopolies, subsidizing exports, restricting imports, regulating wages, or the effort to acquire a stock of money, hampered the natural growth of economic activity. It was, however, in his portrayal of the advantages of specialization by regions and nations that Smith secured his most general support. "It is the maxim of every prudent master of a family never to attempt to make at home what it will cost him more to make than to buy." Beginning with such reasoning, Smith showed how each nation would be far better off economically by concentrating on the thing it could do best, rather than following the Mercantilist doctrine of national self-sufficiency.

The new economic society which Smith proposed was to be regulated by competition. Economic privileges and monopolies were to be destroyed. Competition assured that each man and each nation would do the thing it was best fitted to do, and it thus assured to each individual the full reward of his services and the maximum contribution to the common good. One important function of government in relation to the business life of the community was to preserve competition.

Adam Smith's position on the question of government regulation was not absolute. He could be counted upon under most circumstances to defend free trade, but there were conditions which in his opinion required government action. For example, he did not believe that complete freedom in foreign trade could be achieved in England. He admitted that for political reasons the government might regulate trade. The Navigation Acts, requiring the use of English vessels to transport goods to and from England, Smith believed were necessary to safeguard the marine service as a matter of national defense. He was willing to compromise on the laws prohibiting the export of wool, accepting a tax instead of a full embargo. Although he disliked the use of counter restrictions to secure the reduction of barriers raised against English goods by foreign countries, he thought their use should be determined by the estimate of their success. Further departure from an absolute free-trade position was apparent in Smith's suggestion that gradual steps should be used in restoring freedom to large industries heretofore maintained by government concessions and that risky ventures from which the public would later benefit might be granted privileges of monopoly.

In spite of his defense of the *laissez-faire* policy, Smith saw vast opportunities for a positive contribution by the government to its people. Necessary projects which were too large for private enterprise or for the voluntary efforts of a small section of the population should be undertaken by public authority. All institutions and works related to public defense and justice (especially the enforcement of contracts and the protection of property) were government business. He believed that education, licensing of professions and trades as a protection to the public, perhaps even the financial sup port of religious institutions, fell within the sphere of government action.

The effect of *The Wealth of Nations* on the thoughts and actions of the people was extraordinary. The ready acceptance of Smith's ideas seems to indicate that the people were waiting expectantly for his message even though the Napoleonic wars prevented direct application of these ideas to foreign trade for nearly forty years. As Eric Roll pointed out, Smith's analysis of trade gave businessmen a significant place in history: it justified their pursuit of profit; it gave them a social respectability as a class; and identified them with great national destiny. In particular, Smith voiced the ideas shared by many that opportunities for trade were practically unlimited if legal restrictions and government privileges were removed. *The Wealth of Nations* quickened a trend toward a new era in trade which was already well along but had thus far remained unobserved.

LATER EXPONENTS OF FREE TRADE   The arguments for and against free trade following the death of Adam Smith were carried on by men whose names stand high in the ranks of great economists. J. B. Say in France was the first continental follower of Adam Smith to give widespread circulation to Smith's ideas. In addition to popularizing *The Wealth of Nations*, Say made some clear observations of his own on the question of trade and the functions of markets. To him, as to Smith, money merely facilitated exchange of goods. It had no value in itself and it created none. Consequently, trade was really an exchange of goods for goods, and every supply of goods gave rise to a demand. Thus trade could be fostered if each nation would increase its own surpluses. An oversupply of goods he generally believed impossible, although scarcity and abundance might occur in particular commodities.

The protection of trade as a government policy died slowly in England, but many aspects of the theory of free trade were worked out in the controversies that accompanied every change in existing legislation. Ricardo clearly stated his position on free trade through his participation in the protest against the Corn Laws. Before Adam Smith a common principle of the anti-mercantilists was "that it pays to import commodities from abroad whenever they can be obtained in exchange for exports at a smaller real cost than their production at home would entail." This seems almost a truism. Obviously a nation is not going to engage in trade unless it seems less costly than to produce the commodities at home. Nevertheless, it is usually a different matter to convince a nation that this principle is worth following.

Ricardo, in developing an idea known in economics as the *doctrine of comparative costs*, was merely restating and amplifying a rule of trade developed much earlier. To make the idea clearer, Ricardo employed an illustration which has continued in use ever since. In speaking of trade between England and Portugal he said that if Portugal could produce cloth with the labor of 90 men and wine with the labor of 80 men, and England could produce the same quantity of cloth with 100 men and wine with 120, it would be advantageous to exchange English cloth for Portuguese wine. For by concentrating on the thing each nation could do with the least effort each had a greater comparative advantage. Thus each nation had more wine and more cloth than it could have had by producing each commodity independently without the benefit of exchange. Ricardo used another illustration to drive home this same point:

> Two men can both make shoes and hats, and one is superior to the other in both employments; but in making hats, he can only exceed his competitor by one-fifth or 20 percent—and in making shoes he can exceed him by one-third or 33 percent;—will it not be for the interest of both, that the superior man should employ himself exclusively in making shoes, and the inferior man in making hats?

It was Ricardo's contention, however, that imports could be profitable to a nation even though that nation could produce the imported article at a lower cost. Consequently, it was not true, as some of the early economists had believed, that under free trade each commodity would be produced by that country which produced it at the lowest real cost. Ricardo had a great deal more to say on the subject of trade; but since his ideas were concerned with the money aspects of trade, they will be discussed in the following chapter.

Further elaboration of this method of calculating the advantages of foreign trade was made by John Stuart Mill. In *Essays on Some Unsettled Questions of Political Economy*, he discussed the quantities of goods which would be exchanged under a system of free trade. He showed that prices of commodities in exchange would adjust themselves so that the quantities of each article imported would be just sufficient to pay for the article exported. No nation would give more units of commodity A for commodity B than it could produce at a cost equal to that at which it could produce B. Thus the law of comparative costs, while indicating the advantage of exchange, also indicated the limits beyond which exchange was unprofitable.

One of the most tantalizing problems connected with foreign trade was the degree of specialization that would bring the greatest economic advantage. Mill at first held that under free trade complete specialization would take place, but he later modified this idea to take account of the fact that facilities of the producing countries might be such that one country would have to make up for a deficiency of supply by domestic production. Ricardo had also made allowance for the fact that complete specialization might not be possible. He claimed that partial specialization might still be profitable. Economists have had extensive discussions on this point, many of them holding Ricardo in error.

Practical applications of the principles of free trade began to appear in England with the close of the Napoleonic wars. At the beginning of the Corn Law controversy, Thomas Malthus made keen observations as to the effect of high duties upon imported corn. He said that the restriction upon imports caused a greater expense of raising corn in England due in a large part to the "necessity of yearly cultivating and improving more poor land to provide for the demands of an increasing population; which land must, of course, require more labor and dressing and expense of all kinds of cultivation." While this argument was used by agriculturalists to secure greater protection, the net effect was to open the minds of the people to the need for importing cheaper corn. Richard Cobden and John Bright, the recognized leaders of the so-called Manchester school of economic thought, several years later formed the Anti-Corn Law League to combat not only the Corn Laws but trade restrictions generally. Using Malthus's arguments, they were able to show a greater advantage to England by allowing foreign corn to enter, which would lower living costs, therefore eventually lower costs of production through lower wages, and which would allow the concentration of land and men to industrial uses in which England had recognized superiority. The Corn Laws were repealed in 1846, the Navigation Acts were abolished a year later, and by 1860 protection was completely removed from English economic practice.

The English economists took the lead in the battle for free trade, but they received able support at times from Europe. Frédéric Bastiat (1801–1850), a French politician who gave serious attention to economic matters, advocated the adoption of free trade as a government policy. His best-known work on this subject was a satirical pamphlet purporting to be a petition of manufacturers of candles and wax lights against the sun. Since the sun was the lighting industry's chief competitor flooding the market with light at cheap prices, the petitioners advised the passing of laws requiring the closing of all openings through which sunlight was accustomed to pass. Bastiat introduced a sly dig at the unreasonable animosity toward England when he intimated that England had encouraged the sun to shine so brilliantly on France as contrasted with the circumspection the sun "displays toward that haughty island." The early writing of Bastiat indicated a thorough-going support of free trade and opposition to government intervention of any kind save in the interests of justice. His final work, *Harmonies Economiques*, showed him to be less certain as to the degree of freedom from government control that was desirable.

PROTECTIONISM

The opposite of free trade is protection, which is usually achieved through the instrument of a tariff, or duty, on imports. Exports in the modern day have seldom been subject to duty; indeed, the American Constitution forbids such imposts. Free traders as a rule do not object to a tariff for revenue purposes only, that is, as long as it is low enough to allow for competition of foreign goods with domestic products. Protection means a tariff high enough to make the sale price of foreign goods prohibitive in the domestic market.

THE GERMAN NATIONALISTS   Among the first to oppose Smith's trade were the so-called nationalists. These were for the most part German economists who believed that the individual's wealth was secondary to that of the state, and that the state should safeguard its own economic and political power by whatever means seemed expedient. The explanation for the rise of economic nationalism in the Germanic countries is not far to seek. First of all, *The Wealth of Nations* grew out of English economic conditions and it was designed primarily for England. It naturally spoke of situations and propounded ideas which had little application to continental conditions. Furthermore, the Central European nations were not so far advanced commercially and industrially as England. Germany was predominantly agricultural. An unfavorable geographic position had prevented the development of mercantile pursuits in Germany when the center of trade passed from the North Sea and the Mediterranean to the Atlantic. The lack of political unity, and the accompanying petty jealousies of minor sovereigns hampered the growth of an extensive internal trade or common economic policy among the German states. Finally, a philosophical idealization, to which both Fichte and Hegel gave expression, of the all-pervading influence of the state permeated German thought and allowed no development of individualism.

Adam Müller (1779–1829), who is known in economic thought as a German Romanticist, was one of the first to oppose the individualistic, free-trade doctrine of Adam Smith. He advocated the foundation of a national economic order. Home industry was to be protected, and, wherever necessary, imports and exports were to be prohibited as a means of stimulating national feeling. To him, the individual pursuit of economic gain was a disrupting force in society.

In the writings of Friedrich List (1789–1846), however, the emphasis upon a distinctly national economy was given its strongest expression. The English title of List's most important work, *The National System of Political Economy* (1841), is clear evidence of the character of the author's thought. The original plan for this work called for three volumes. Only the first was finished, and this dealt almost exclusively with the evolution of national economy and with trade. The economic development of a country passed through five stages, List said: (1) a hunting and fishing stage; (2) a pastoral stage (tending domestic herds); (3) a settled agricultural stage; (4) an agricultural and manufacturing stage; and (5) a stage consisting of agriculture, manufacturing, and world trade. As nations pass through these various stages different measures are required for their development. List's criticism of Adam Smith was that Smith had written as though his principles were universally applicable, whereas they were only useful for England, which had reached the last stage of economic development, or for some imaginary group of nations living in guaranteed peace and harmony. List, having lived in Germany, and then from 1820 to 1832 in America, believed that these two nations were at the fourth stage, and therefore must of necessity follow a more controlled economic policy until such time as their manufacturing had reached a position to compete with that of any other country. In analyzing world economic activities he came to two basic conclusions. The first was that the most desirable economic state of a nation could be achieved by arriving at a balance of its agricultural and manufacturing resources so that no interruption of exchange was possible. The second was that since some tropical nations have little adaptability to manufacturing but produce agricultural commodities which cannot be produced elsewhere, the manufacturing nations of the temperate zones should bind these purely agricultural communities to themselves to the mutual benefit of both.

Following this line of reasoning, it was desirable for a nation such as Germany, or any nation which had the necessary requisites of a manufacturing nation, to adopt a policy of protection. Duties should be introduced gradually and reasonably, so as to achieve the maximum benefit. Agricultural products and raw materials should be exempt. After a reasonable number of years, if an industry did not give evidence of being able to survive on a minimum of protection (List suggested 20 to 30 percent) it was evidence that the industry was not adapted to the country and all protection should be removed from it.

It is quite obvious that the ideas of List found fertile soil in Germany. The economic development of the German nation followed closely the general outline he developed, and later economists and statesmen of that nation turned to him for the basic principles of a strong national economy.

JOHN STUART MILL'S COMPROMISE   Protectionism as a policy of international trade was not confined to the outspoken opponents of classical theory. Yet most of the other economists who supported protection against free trade tried to stay within the general bounds of classical tradition as outlined by Smith. John Stuart Mill, in spite of his adherence to classical economy, found certain instances where he believed protection was justified. For example, since the superiority of industries in older nations may merely be that of time, it is necessary to protect a new industry in a young nation during the formative period when it is adapting itself to the new conditions and gaining strength to compete against the well-established foreign firms. Mill warned, however, that a duty on imports should not be conceived as a permanent subsidy to an industry unfitted by nature to its new location or extended beyond the time necessary for the industry to be fairly established. For the most part Mill defended the doctrine of free trade against the arguments of the protectionists. He especially challenged the ideas of Henry Carey, who advocated a thorough-going nationalistic policy for America.

AMERICAN IDEAS America seemed more fruitful soil for the growth of protectionism than England. From the earliest days of the United States there were sponsors for protectionist views. The burning resentment felt for the mercantilist policies adopted by England in the seventeenth and eighteenth centuries did not prevent several great Americans from supporting a paternalistic attitude of government toward industry. The economic ideas of Alexander Hamilton (1757–1804) were born out of his efforts to stabilize the financial structure of the new United States, not that the ideas were original, for many of them had appeared centuries earlier in the writings of the English economists. Nevertheless, Hamilton wrote in the face of the growing popularity of the doctrine of free trade and the disappearance of protection as a national policy in England. As the first Secretary of the Treasury in the U.S. government, Hamilton was asked to assume the economic leadership of the new nation. He expected to exercise authority comparable to that of the English Chancellor of the Exchequer, but American political organization prevented the settling of such important powers outside the national legislature proper. In spite of this rebuff Hamilton continued to advocate programs of national policy in reports such as the one on manufacturers submitted to the House of Representatives in

1791. He was concerned over the fact that restrictions in foreign markets curtailed the demand for American goods, while at the same time, the American market was completely open. The need, as he saw it, was for a program that would ensure more of the American market for American manufacturers. Moreover, Hamilton saw the possibility of developing new industries in America to the advantage of the people of the United States.

Hamilton was well acquainted with the arguments of Adam Smith in favor of agriculture and against protection, just as he knew the objections and distrust of his fellow citizens against any government participation in economic activity. Nevertheless, he fought for a protective tariff to retain the domestic market for those industries which were just beginning and a government subsidy to start enterprises that seemed desirable. The use of the protective tariff and subsidy was not to be an indiscriminate matter: first, a careful analysis of the industries to be assisted was necessary to see if American conditions would support the industry; and second, if the demand for the article warranted the effort, and third, if the industry contributed to national defense.

Henry C. Carey (1793–1879) was one of the first American economists to stand as an ardent advocate of protection. His success in managing a family publishing business enabled him to retire with a comfortable fortune at the age of thirty-five. From then on he devoted himself to writing on economic subjects. His most important work was *Principles of Social Science* (1857–1860) in which his system of social organization was outlined. It was in one of his earlier works, *The Harmony of Interests, Agricultural, Manufacturing, and Commercial* (1851), that he presented his views on industry and trade.

In general outline Carey's arguments were similar to those of Hamilton and List, but at various points he differed and took a more extreme position. Manufacturing was a socializing and a civilizing force, while agriculture held a population in ignorance and semibarbarism. Furthermore, Carey believed that agriculture without a neighboring market could not survive; the cost of transporting produce to distant markets would more than consume the farmer's profit. But through protection the people of the nation would be knit closer together and the value of natural resources which America possessed would be retained by the people. Protection would increase the diversification of occupations in America, bringing about cooperation and exchange among various elements of the population, and consequently the intellectual development of the nation as a whole. On the second point, Carey had a peculiar notion. Selling agricultural products and raw materials abroad took out of the earth its valuable qualities and left the people of America poorer. Produce sold within the nation was returned at least in part to the earth as fertilizers. It is difficult to follow this argument, for the sale of agricultural products would enable the people to import goods they considered more valuable than cereals or dairy products. If necessary, fertilizer could be artificially created or imported, as John Stuart Mill pointed out in his criticisms of Carey.

A later writer, however, took pains to clarify this point. Simon N. Patten (1852–1922), a well-known economist at the University of Pennsylvania, followed Carey in the defense of protectionism. Patten believed that economic prosperity depended upon building a market for goods in the immediate vicinity where they were produced. And, in the same vein as Carey, he also believed that free trade would lead to the exhaustion of American raw materials, since without the protection necessary to produce manufactured goods these would be the chief source of money income to the country. Exportation of natural resources would lead to exhaustion of soil and mineral wealth. The history of the American southern states where the tremendous export trade in cotton led to most severe cases of soil exhaustion gives strong support to this idea. Finally, while subscribing to the "infant industry" argument as a bona fide reason for protection, he pointed out that a nation would have "infant industries" as long as it continued a dynamic economic existence. There would always be efforts to start new manufactures after their successful introduction in a foreign country. Thus protective tariff for that reason alone would be ever present.

ADDITIONAL ARGUMENTS IN THE FREE TRADE VS. PROTECTIONISM CONTROVERSY

The question of free trade vs. protection has been a perennial one in American politics. The arguments for and against have become so commonplace that it is impossible to find the original authors of many of them. Some of the arguments are interesting in themselves, even though originators remain in doubt. The modern defense of protection frequently begins with the Mercantilist idea that a nation must sell more than it buys in order to have a favorable balance of trade and an annual influx of gold. In spite of its age and its obvious fallacies, this reasoning continues to be used. The most widely cited argument for protection is that cheap foreign products must be kept out of the country in order to maintain high wage scales and full employment. If foreign goods, made by workers who get half the wages of domestic workers and who live on a much lower standard, were allowed to enter the country, one of two things would happen: either the domestic workers would have to accept lower wages so that the domestic product could compete with the foreign product, or the industry would shut down and the workers would be unemployed. Economists such as Ricardo and Malthus answered this argument long ago by showing that high wages and consequently high standards of living of wage earners could be traced to superior skill, machinery, and capital, or advantages in the character and abundance of raw materials or both. Consequently, the question of protection has little bearing on wages. As to employment, Ricardo's analysis of the values of international trade showed that by free trade each nation would gain most by concentrating upon the production of those items in which it had an advantage and exchanging such items for other necessities. On the other hand, Augustin Cournot (1801–1877) made it clear that the question of unemployment could not be dismissed unless both labor and capital could adapt themselves immediately to other pursuits, which in many instances would not be the case. Adam Smith, however, foresaw this type of difficulty and agreed that protection should be removed from any privileged industry by gradual stages so that severe dislocation might be avoided.

THE ROLE OF GOVERNMENT TODAY

Another important procedure by which governments have interfered with freedom of trade has been the subsidy for manufacturing or farm produce that is sold abroad. Such subsidies can take many different forms, making detection almost impossible. For example, governments can lease land at no cost, grant loans for purchases of equipment at artificially low interest rates, give rebates on taxes, make up the difference between a guaranteed price and the price at which a product can be sold abroad, and use many other indirect methods of reducing costs of production or meeting price competition so that goods can be sold abroad and create a favorable balance of trade.

The contemporary phenomenon of prosperity in Japan and West Germany, two nations defeated in World War II and prohibited from rebuilding a military establishment, has caused serious rethinking of the principles of foreign trade. This apparently has come about not alone from the expertise of German and Japanese businessmen, engineers, and workers but also from government economic and monetary policy on the whole question of industrial growth with reference to foreign markets. The experience of these two nations makes it clear, contrary to most critics of capitalism, that a prosperous economy can be maintained without the stimulus of vast government expenditures for armaments.

There is one argument for protection for which there is no rebuttal, except a change in outlook of the peoples of the world toward each other. It is simply this: that protection is essential in order to assure the nation of a full supply of all necessary materials in time of war or international tension. List was a realist; he saw the virtues of free trade in a world in which order was guaranteed by a universal association or federation of all nations as a guarantee of perpetual peace. But he felt that as long as nations competed with the view of resorting to war to settle disputes, tariff protection would be needed.

Oil shortages in the United States, Western Europe, and Japan during the 1970s posed a different problem in international trade. The most abundant supplies of oil upon which the world depends are located in the Arab countries of the Middle East, Venezuela, Indonesia, and certain areas of Africa. Beginning in 1970, the oil-rich nations, joining efforts as OPEC (Organization of Petroleum Exporting Countries), decreed price increases that by 1979 were more than ten times the 1970 price and controlled production both to ensure their own economic stability and to create political leverage in international conflicts, such as the Arab-Israeli dispute, and in a variety of Third World programs. Efforts to counter the power of OPEC by an organization of oil-consuming nations has had little effect. Strenuous measures have been taken in the United States to conserve oil and encourage the development and use of alternate forms of energy in order to make the United States independent of foreign energy supplies.

6. COMPETITION, SUPPLY AND DEMAND, AND PRICE

AQUINAS · PETTY · CANTILLON · STEUART · SMITH · SAY ·
RICARDO · SENIOR · MILL · SISMONDI · COURNOT · GOSSEN ·
JEVONS · WALRAS · MARSHALL · PARETO · VEBLEN ·
SCHUMPETER · GALBRAITH · VON NEUMANN

*How are prices determined? Why will the same article cost
more or less tomorrow than it did yesterday? Is the law of
supply and demand really important in determining price? Is
competition beneficial to the consumer? Does competition give
the consumer better goods at lower cost than a government
system of price fixing? What is utility? How does the utility
of a good affect consumer choices? Why is it that perfect
competition never exists in fact? What does the economist
mean by imperfect or monopolistic competition? What are
advantageous prices? What causes inflation? What is game
theory?*

BUYING AND SELLING are such commonplace activities that the many
economic processes involved in the simple exchange of goods are
ignored. Suppose, for example, a customer went to a grocery store
on Saturday morning and, after inquiring the price of eggs, bought
a dozen at ninety-five cents, commenting that the price was a bit
higher than the week before. But why were eggs ninety-five cents
a dozen and not ninety or eighty-five? Why were they higher this
week than last? Who or what sets the price of eggs anyway? Economists have devoted no small amount of effort to find the answers
to these questions.

SOME EARLY VIEWS

In the days of Thomas Aquinas conceptions of price could be summarized by the words *just price*. Aquinas lived in an age when small units of population were largely self-sufficient. Exchange was little known and there was almost no competition among producers and sellers. In the absence of a market for goods there were no "economic" forces to determine price. Therefore, the price of an article could logically be determined only by the amount of labor time required to make it. This did not mean that every laborer's time was equal; the social status of the laborer determined his standard of living. A just price was one which enabled the maker of the goods to maintain his accustomed standard. Economically speaking, the medieval period was comparatively unchanging, consequently such social facts as custom, status, and inheritance were of utmost importance.

Regardless of the teachings of ecclesiastics and the power of guilds, the market had to be reckoned as a force controlling prices. Droughts, wars, and disease were natural factors which influenced both the supply and the demand for goods. The tendency for prices to rise or fall as a consequence of any of these could not be denied. For example, the Black Death, occurring about 1350, so decreased the working force that wages rose precipitously. Local magistrates were empowered to set wages and to enforce the terms of existing contracts. In spite of legal restrictions and the heavy penalties inflicted for violation, wages and the prices of commodities continued to rise. The information available on the general course of agricultural prices from the thirteenth to the eighteenth centuries indicates that prices were continually fluctuating. Devaluations in currency brought about by monarchs in their efforts to increase the state's revenue also affected the price level, causing prices to rise several hundred percent during the course of a few centuries.

In the seventeenth century, Sir William Petty introduced several ideas of price which indicated the trends of thought in future years. He suggested first of all that the price of a commodity would, in the long run, tend to remain equal to the amount of silver that a man could mine if he worked as long as it was necessary for another man to produce a unit of the commodity in question. This is how Petty himself explained it:

> Let another man go travel into a country where is Silver, there Dig it, Refine it, bring it to the same place where the other man planted his Corn; Coyne it, etc., the same person, all the while of his working for Silver, gathering also food for his necessary livelihood, and procuring for himself covering, etc. I say, the Silver of the one, must be esteemed of equal value with the Corn of the other: the one being perhaps twenty Ounces and the other twenty Bushels. From whence it follows that the price of a Bushel of this Corn to be an Ounce of Silver.

Hence labor, in Petty's thinking, was the basis of value, or true price. The political price, or worth in exchange, was dependent upon a number of factors: excessive competition among those supplying goods to the market; an abundance of substitute commodities; custom; and the general relationship of supply to demand.

Some references to the influence of both money and the law of supply and demand on prices were made by Cantillon in his famous *Essai sur la Nature du Commerce en Général*. He said, by way of illustration:

> Suppose the Butchers on one side and the Buyers on the other side. The price of Meat will be settled after some altercations, and a pound of Beef will be in value to a piece of silver pretty nearly as the whole Beef offered for sale in the Market is to all the silver brought there to buy Beef. This proportion is come at by bargaining. The Butcher keeps up his Price According to the number of Buyers he sees; the Buyers on their side, offer less according as they think the Butcher will have less sale; the price set by some is usually followed by others. Some are more clever in puffing up their wares, others in running them down. Though this method of fixing Market prices has no exact or geometrical foundation, since it often depends upon the eagerness or easy temperament of a few buyers or Sellers, it does not seem that it could be done in a more convenient way. It is clear that the quantity of Produce or of Merchandise offered for sale, in proportion to the demand or number of Buyers, is the basis on which is fixed or always supposed to be fixed the Market Prices.

Through the influence of price, he believed that supply and demand equalized themselves. Another illustration showed a farmer with a surplus of corn and not enough wool. Reversing the ratios next year the farmer found himself with too much wool and not enough corn. This alternation continued until the farmer found the correct proportion. The criterion of oversupply and undersupply is price, for the farmer with an oversupply finds his money income too small to pay his rent.

Sir James Steuart was another who anticipated the work of Adam Smith by developing a theory of price based upon supply and demand. If supply and demand balance, the resulting price will be relatively fixed, he claimed. But the balance might be disturbed by any one of a number of factors. If an oversupply existed, seller's competition would reduce prices. If an undersupply appeared, buyer's competition would raise prices. Under ordinary circumstances, Steuart believed, the activity of merchants themselves would maintain a price equilibrium. Should any unusual change occur, however, he maintained that the Government should intervene.

ADAM SMITH AND THE CLASSICAL SCHOOL

All these writers were laying foundations for the first major statement concerning price. The main points emphasized by Adam Smith, in the last quarter of the eighteenth century, differed little from those of Cantillon; but in greater detail, completeness of analysis, and abundance of interrelationship described, Smith's work was outstanding. "The real price of everything, what everything really costs to the man who wants to acquire it, is the toil and trouble of acquiring it." Thus Smith stated his theory of value. He went on to show that while the real value of all commodities was the amount of labor necessary to produce them, their value in exchange was seldom estimated by it, because of the difficulties of equating two different quantities of labor. Thus the process of exchange was carried on by the "higgling and bargaining of the market," in which money was the common unit of measurement.

Smith demonstrated that a number of factors influenced the formation of nominal or money price. The value of money itself fluctuated, since the amount of labor necessary to produce a given quantity of metal varied. This in turn depended upon the productivity of mines. To illustrate, Smith used as an example the increased production of gold from the mines in America, and showed how this additional supply of gold caused a tremendous increase in prices throughout Europe. Likewise, debasement of currency caused an increase in prices; because values were normally equivalent to a quantity of gold, if coins included less gold at one time than at another, they would purchase less goods, or in other words, cause an increase in price.

Smith said that the true price of any commodity included the true price of all the factors making the commodity. "In the price of corn, for example, one part pays the rent of the landlord, another pays the wages or maintenance of labourers, and labouring cattle employed in producing it, and a third part pays the profit of the farmer. . . . When the price of any commodity is neither more nor less than what is sufficient to pay the rent of land, the wages of labour, and the profits of stock employed in raising, preparing, and bringing it to market, according to their natural rates, the commodity is then sold for what may be called its natural price. The commodity is then sold precisely for what it is worth, or for what it really costs the person who brings it to market . . ." However, "the actual price at which any commodity is commonly sold is called the market price. It may either be above, or below, or exactly the same with its natural price."

How then is the market price determined? Smith went on to explain. The market price is regulated by the quantity which is actually brought to the market and the demand of those who are willing to pay the whole of the natural price. Smith was careful to point out that the effective demand is the important consideration, not the absolute demand. The former is the expressed desire for goods plus the ability and willingness to buy them; the latter is the desire of all persons for an article whether they have the ability to buy or not.

When a quantity less than the effective demand is brought to the market, rather than do without, some of the prospective buyers will offer to pay more than the natural price. Competition among buyers tends to increase the price. Where buyers of some wealth exist, a shortage results in exceedingly high prices if the acquisition of the commodity is of more or less importance to the prospective buyers. On the other hand, when the quantity of a good brought to the market exceeds the demand, it cannot all be sold to those willing to pay the natural price. "Some part must be sold to those who are willing to pay less, and the low price which they give for it must reduce the price of the whole." The degree to which the market price sinks below the natural price depends upon the extent to which the excess supply increases the competition of the sellers. The perishable nature of the commodity also affects the price; since sellers are more anxious to get rid of perishable goods quickly, competition among them increases.

It is to the benefit of all that the supply and demand balance one another. The natural price is then paid, covering all costs; all those exercising an effective demand are satisfied; and there is no excess of supply to lower the market price. The natural price, therefore, is, as it were, the central price to which the prices of all commodities are continually gravitating. Different accidents may sometimes keep them suspended a good deal above it, and sometimes force them down even somewhat below it, "but whatever may be the obstacles which hinder them from settling in this center of repose and continuance, they are constantly tending towards it."

Smith was well aware that sellers might seek to maintain a high price by artificial means. He knew that when a market price was established far above the natural price the producers tended to keep the matter a secret in order not to attract additional competitors. Processes which tend to cut costs, if retained secretly by a small group of producers, may keep prices from falling to the natural level. When the effective demand exceeds the total productive capacity of the country, as in the case of some vineyards in France, to use Smith's illustration, the price may be sustained indefinitely above the natural price. Monopolies, too, exert the same influence as a trade secret or a commodity naturally limited. Monopoly prices differ from freely competitive or natural prices in that the former are "the highest which can be got" while the latter are "the lowest which can be taken." All kinds of monopolistic conditions prevent the free interplay of supply and demand, and may for years maintain a price above or below the natural price. While prices might be kept above a normal level almost indefinitely, it would be impossible to keep prices below the natural price for more than a very short period, for persons who suffered loss would reduce the amount of produce they brought to the market, or withdraw from production altogether.

It is obvious that Smith's ideas on price assumed a freely competitive market as the ideal or natural market. As a consequence, he was extremely critical of any monopolistic or regulatory force, whether it came about as a result of the normal self-interest of individuals or the arbitrary extension of governmental power. However, he recognized the tendency for workers and employers to organize into combinations. Since their interests were by no means the same, Smith said, "The workmen desire to get as much, the masters to give as little, as possible." The tendency toward combination was less hampered among employers than among workers. There were fewer employers, and no acts of parliament forbade their organization as in the case of workers. Consequently they were always found in a sort of tacit agreement concerning wages and prices. Smith also recognized that the employers were likely to call on the agencies of government for assistance in their competitive struggle with organized workers. This tendency of combination was noted in what has since become a classic quotation from Adam Smith: "People of the same trade seldom meet together," he said, "even for merriment and diversion, but the conversation ends in a conspiracy against the public, or in some contrivance to raise prices."

SMITH'S FOLLOWERS

Of the general acceptance of Adam Smith's ideas on the importance of freedom of business enterprise and the effectiveness of competition as a regulator of economic activity there can be little doubt.

Smith's followers in the nineteenth century were innumerable. However, even those who claimed adherence to the classical ideas modified and pointed out inconsistencies in the generally accepted thought. J. B. Say in France never tired of defending the importance of supply and demand in determining price. He was even less tolerant than Smith of government intervention and other obstruction to the free play of economic forces. Nevertheless, in his emphasis upon the importance of the utility of an object as a consideration in price determination he unquestionably turned the emphasis away from cost of production and supply in the direction of utility and demand.

RICARDO   Few persons reflect the character of their times as clearly as did David Ricardo (1772–1823). He lived in a period when free competition in economic matters was nearer perfection than it had been or would ever be again. Legislation restricting foreign trade enacted in the full glory of Mercantilism was unenforced, only the first of the factory acts had been passed, and trade unions were still held illegal by the courts. The market was in reality almost free. It was Ricardo's method to examine carefully a concrete fact and then, with unusual intellectual daring, to draw general conclusions from it. Ricardo contended that these conclusions were not directed to temporary effects, but to the long-run and fundamental factors, or as he preferred to call them, the natural factors controlling economic behavior. Consequently, his belief in the power of competition to regulate production and distribution is not merely an unquestioning acceptance of an assumption made by Adam Smith; it is the result of keen observation of the economic activity of his own times.

In the long run, Ricardo believed that the power of competition alone would determine prices, wages, profits, and rent. Further, under a system of free trade each country would devote its labor and capital to those pursuits which were most beneficial. Likewise, the abolition of taxes on the transfer of land would tend to place land in the hands of those best able to use it.

Some authors contend that Ricardo accepted so fully his postulate of free competition as the basis of his analysis that he failed to concern himself with the economic problems which arose because of the absence of competition. He did note the effects of government intervention, of wars, and of the immobility of capital and labor; but these obstructions he characterized as short-run effects which delayed but did not prevent the operation of economic forces. Moreover, he advocated the direct interference of government in the regulation of money, drugs, physicians, and the issue of credit.

In addition to his assumption of free competition, Ricardo emphasized the importance of exchange value in the organization of the economic system. Briefly stated, Ricardo believed that the exchange value of any commodity was determined by the quantity of the commodity which a given amount of labor could produce in a given amount of time as related to the amount of another commodity produced by the same labor in the same time. This was different from Ricardo's concept of market price, which he believed was essentially the result of the operation of the laws of supply and demand. Throughout Ricardo's work the same confusion exists between natural value and exchange value on the one hand and market price on the other. This fact is noticeable in his discussions of wages and rent. However, if one could assume—as Ricardo did— a freely competitive market, natural value, exchange value, and market price would tend to coincide.

SENIOR   Nassau Senior (1790–1864) also supported the classical ideas of competition, supply and demand, and price. But just as Say had unconsciously emphasized the "demand-utility" aspects of price, Senior emphasized the "supply-cost of production" side. The limitation of supply, he said, was by far the most important consideration in the determination of price. Whereas Ricardo referred to labor as the sole source of value, allowing little or nothing for the contribution of natural resources and capital, Senior rearranged these factors. He believed that supply was affected by the three elements of production: labor, abstinence (Senior's term for capital), and the forces of nature. The supply of any commodity was "limited by the difficulty of finding persons ready to submit to the labour and abstinence necessary" to its production. Hence the cost of production limited supply. When the supply of raw materials was accessible to all—that is, where free competition existed—prices would tend to equal the cost of production. Senior was aware that the forces of supply and demand could not cause an instantaneous adjustment of price; but he thought that gradually, barring some interference, the net effect of supply and demand would be to equalize price and cost of production.

A bit more realism entered the writings of Senior than those of his predecessors, for he acknowledged the presence of monopoly and attempted to show how it influenced price. The first class of monopolists, he said, were those who had control of the use of some special facility in production but not of production itself. Hence, the producer could expand but could not limit the supply. Nor could he set the price above the cost of production of his competitors who were producing without the use of the special facility which he possessed. The tendency of such a producer would be to set the prices below that of his competitors but above his own cost, and to expect thereby to increase his own sales. Except for the fact that exclusive rights to the new device might be guaranteed to the producer by patent, the conditions of free competition and the laws of supply and demand were not set aside in this instance. Indeed, the interests of the producer and of the consumer were identical.

In the second type of monopoly, although the monopolist was in complete control of supply, increase in supply was impossible. The lower limit of price would be set by the cost of production and while the monopolist might set his price at any point he desired, he had to recognize that the laws of supply and demand would ultimately determine the amount of sales and the market price. A third form of monopoly existed in which the monopolist had complete control of the supply and he had power to increase or decrease it at will. On the whole, in spite of the absence of an upper limit to the price the monopolist could charge, the tendency would be to increase production, and expand sales at a lower price.

Then a fourth and final situation appeared in which the monopolist while not the only producer had peculiar facilities for production which tended to disappear with increased production. Thus as long as he produced small quantities, he could set his price just below that of his most efficient competitor; but if he expanded production, the peculiar circumstances which enabled him to produce a small quantity cheaply would not apply and his cost would mount. A piece of extremely fertile land, for example, would produce a certain quantity of grain with a minimum of labor and fertilizer, but productivity of the soil would decrease with each additional application of labor and fertilizer. Price under such circumstances would be set at the cost of that unit whose production was most expensive.

The work of Senior stands as a realistic application of the principles of Smith and Ricardo, especially the latter. The emphasis is upon supply and the factors which influence it. While demand is recognized as the counter force to supply, Senior makes no attempt to analyze it.

MILL

MILL   John Stuart Mill (1806–1873) recognized the idea of free competition for what it was worth—an abstract ideal accepted merely for use in logical analysis. Whereas Smith, Ricardo, and Senior had believed in free competition as a state which existed and asserted itself in the long run—even though various obstacles hindered the free play of economic forces—Mill understood that this process of reasoning did not fit actual conditions, and should not, therefore, be used as a guide to political or social behavior. Said he, "Assume competition to be their [economic affairs'] exclusive regulator, and principles of broad generality and scientific precision may be laid down . . . but it would be a great misconception of the actual course of human affairs to suppose that competition exercises in fact this unlimited sway." Mill conceded that competition was modified in matters of price by monopoly and custom, the latter being far more important than generally recognized. One of his more important contentions was that the laws governing production and exchange were in the nature of physical laws, while the conditions of distribution were man-made. Therefore, free competition should be promoted in connection with production, while common sense and sound judgment should apply to the problems of distribution. Of course, such a rigid distinction between production and distribution is unfounded. There is such a clear dependency of one upon the other that any law which applies to one must of necessity influence the other.

In his discussion of the law of supply and demand Mill was able to show that previous interpretations of its operations were incomplete. Generally speaking, the law meant that supply and demand determined price; that is, an increase in supply caused the price to fall, an increase in demand caused it to rise. Mill said that while supply and demand controlled price, price also caused variations in supply and demand. Price was, for example, the guide to the producer. Falling prices warned him to turn his efforts in another direction. Rising prices indicated that supplies were insufficient and that greater profits could be gained by entering the field or by increasing output. Variations in price guided consumers' purchases, though not with the directness or in the same degree that had been usually assumed. Mill attempted to restate the law of supply and demand to take account of this process of action and reaction. "The law is that the demand for a commodity varies as its value, and that the value adjusts itself so that the demand shall be equal to the supply." In Mill's exposition, the law of supply and demand applied directly and completely only to objects absolutely limited in supply. For other objects whose quantity could be increased by the expenditure of labor and capital, the cost of production represented a natural value below which the market value would not fall. The force that caused prices (market value) to fall to the level of the cost of production but not below was competition; for if the market value was greater than the cost of production, producers would increase the supply so as to increase their profit and new producers would enter the field. Except for the restatement of some points, Mill does not add greatly to the general ideas of price expressed by Ricardo and Senior. His emphasis was upon supply and demand, as influenced by various factors of supply. Apparently Mill felt that demand was more or less fixed, for he devoted little or no time to an investigation of it.

CRITICS OF COMPETITION AND THE LAWS OF THE MARKET

There were few critics of the classical ideas of competition during the early decades of the nineteenth century. Most writers agreed that the economic system could regulate itself, at least within the borders of the nation if not in international trade. Yet there were some who at first subscribed to classical doctrine and later became severe critics of it.

SISMONDI   Although a sincere admirer of Adam Smith, the Swiss economist Simonde de Sismondi was impressed by the poverty and the economic crises that accompanied the advance of industrialization. Sismondi re-examined the assumptions which formed the foundation of classical doctrine, and for all of his admiration he eventually challenged the fundamental ideas of the master.

First of all, Sismondi was impressed by the immobility of labor and capital. It was all very well for the economist to claim that an oversupply of a product and a falling price would result in a decrease in supply until price was stabilized and supply and demand were equal. But looking at the human factor, the process was not so simple. The workers were likely to accept lower pay and work longer hours in order to hold on to their jobs. Competition became more bitter, wages were further reduced, and a lower standard of living became fixed. The owners reacted in much the same way. It is not easy to give up a business in which a major share of one's fortune has been invested, and to which years of effort have been given. Under certain circumstances the owner would not be able to withdraw his capital even if he wanted to. Consequently, the owners of the business would continue to produce, cutting costs, piling up debts, and finally abandoning their enterprises when ruin overtook them. This was the course of events as Sismondi saw them. He believed that equilibrium, that is a balance of supply and demand, was achieved in the long run, but only at the cost of great suffering and hardship.

Sismondi was extremely fearful of an increased production that was not preceded by an increased demand. He could not accept the idea widely held today that an increase in production might easily create its own market. Thus competition was beneficial only when it encouraged an increased production in response to an increased demand. If it encouraged production in advance of demand the result was distress and impoverishment for workers and manufacturers alike, for only by emphasizing cheapness could any manufacturer survive. But the pursuit of cheapness meant lower wages, lengthened hours of toil, and the exploitive employment of women and children. Sismondi asks, Of what value are increased production and lowered price, if the net result is a poor and unhealthy class of workers?

There was justice in much of Sismondi's criticism. As he said, his eye was not fixed either upon the long-run effects or the mechanical perfection of competition and supply and demand as regulators of the market; it was fastened upon the obvious human consequences of the period of transition from a society based upon agriculture and commerce to one founded upon large-scale industry. He was likewise concerned with what Sumner Slichter in the twentieth century called the human costs as related to the money costs of economic activity. Whereas Adam Smith had applied the doctrine of free competition to production and judged it good because of the abundance of goods produced, Sismondi applied the doctrine to distribution and found its effect bad when judged from its human consequences.

Sismondi was not a Socialist, even though his writings frequently sound like the Socialist denunciation of capitalism. He justified the return to the landowner and the manufacturer, and his alternatives to modern capitalism have little in common with socialistic programs. Yet it should be noted that he advocated the intervention of the state to safeguard human welfare.

THE SOCIALISTS   Sismondi's criticism of competition and the reliance upon the law of supply and demand to determine price set the pattern for later socialistic writing on this subject. Briefly stated, the Socialists contend that when prices are set by the freely operating forces of the market, and when wages and employment are left to the competitive self-interest of employers, the result is exploitation and impoverishment of the wage-earning population. Marx went even further; he maintained that the disparity between what the employee receives for his work and the value he actually produces is confiscated by the employer. This process is the result of competition coupled with the institution of private property, and leads directly to recurring economic crises.

List As leader of the nationalist school, Friedrich List (1789–1846) rejected the whole concept of free competition and dependence upon the law of supply and demand. Since industrial development was a source of national strength and enrichment, it could not be left to the free play of economic forces. The government, in the national interest, must regulate industry. While competitive enterprise might yield a greater abundance at present, the nation must bear the sacrifices necessary to increase the national productive capacity. There obviously is little room in List's economic system for free private enterprise, at least in the stage of economic development which he assumed applied to the Germany of his day.

Cournot Another continental economist is credited with a criticism of the classical emphasis upon free competition which, although milder in form, did much to shake the faith of modern economists in the ability of competition and the law of supply and demand to preserve equilibrium in the economic order. Augustin Cournot (1801–1877) was a French economist who attempted to describe economic behavior in mathematical or quantitative terms. He is looked upon by many authorities as the herald of the mathematical school if not its actual founder. Cournot questioned the ability of competition to guide the activity and set the goals of the economic system. He very fairly asked, What was the social good to which competition was leading? In his opinion neither the classical school nor any other group of thinkers knew what the social good really was. Since the question of the final good could not be answered,

Cournot doubted the view of classical economists that competition would inevitably produce this undefined good. He did not, however, despair of all improvement. He believed changes for the better could be introduced in various parts of the economic structure one at a time and with care not to disturb other related parts of the system. To achieve such a purpose, state intervention would almost certainly be necessary.

Another of Cournot's important innovations was concentration upon exchange value, or price, as the truly significant aspect of economics. He disregarded the relation of utility to demand and emphasized only the visible aspects of supply. He did not say that utility had no bearing upon demand, but he assumed that investigation of it was impossible, and that the important items to be considered were the concrete data of the market. Cournot accepted completely the operation of the law of supply and demand; but instead of starting with the assumption of free competition, he recognized the imperfections of the market. He first analyzed price when it was determined in a market controlled by one seller, or monopoly; then in a market controlled by two sellers, or duopoly; and finally in a perfectly competitive market. It had been the contention of Smith, Ricardo, and Mill that the forces of supply and demand would in the long run produce equilibrium, when the forces themselves just balanced. In other words, a price would be set at which the effective demand would be satisfied and the supply taken from the market. Cournot showed that when a manufacturer was able to expand his production and at the same time reduce his cost of production per unit, no stability was possible; for the producer was under compulsion to increase his output, lower his cost, and thus increase his profit. While not fully developed, Cournot's ideas did much to turn the attention of economists who followed him toward a more realistic analysis of the processes of exchange.

THE MARGINAL UTILITY SCHOOL

Before completing the development of the thought of those economists who held with Cournot that a controlled market was more usual than a freely competitive market, we need to take note of another school of thought which influenced the consideration of competition, supply and demand, and price. This is known as the *marginal utility* school. Briefly stated this school claims that utility is the fundamental characteristic of value, and as such its influence upon price and exchange is paramount. Hermann Heinrich Gossen (1810–1858) is credited with one of the first clear formulations of the concept of marginal utility. Gossen's basic conceptions were formulated in two economic laws. The first stated: "The amount of one and the same enjoyment diminishes continuously as we proceed with that enjoyment without interruption, until satiety is reached." The second law stated: "In order to obtain the maximum sum of enjoyment, an individual who has a choice between a number of enjoyments, but insufficient time to procure all completely, is obliged—however much the absolute amount of individual enjoyments may differ—to procure all partially, even before he has completed the greatest of them. The relation between them must be such that at the moment when they are discontinued, the amounts of all enjoyments are equal." According to Gossen then, while it is impossible to satisfy all wants, the greatest satisfaction can be achieved by keeping the intensity of all wants at about the same level.

The development of the idea of utility was carried on by William Stanley Jevons, Léon Walras, and Karl Menger. Our interest lies not so much in an exhaustive examination of their theories of utility as in discovering how they evaluated competition and the law of supply and demand as part of the economic process. The law of supply and demand is unquestioned in the writings of these economists. They assumed its validity and set themselves tasks, first of expressing these forces of the market in quantitative terms and second of reducing demand to the psychological factors of which it was composed. Although Jevons labored over the relation of price to subjective utility and set the stage for later theories of marginal utility, his statements remained cumbersome and vague. He is best known for his formulation of the law of indifference, which is, briefly, that where there are two or more identical articles on sale at the same time, it is a matter of indifference to the buyer which he chooses. Therefore there can be only one price at a given time for identical articles.

Menger and Walras began with Gossen's idea that the desire to maximize utility, or to increase the sum total of satisfaction, was the basis for exchange. The utility of every commodity to the purchaser sets the upper limit to the price he is willing to pay. Each prospective purchaser will put a quantitative measure upon the utility of the commodity to be purchased. This will express not only the desirability of the article alone, but its desirability in relation to a known number of other things which also have utility. Menger proceeded to analyze price under different economic situations. In isolated exchange the price will be set somewhere between the buyer's and the seller's quantitative expression of the utility of the object. Price may be said to be indeterminate between these limits. In the case of monopoly the seller will set the price at a point just above the price offered by that buyer who is necessary to clear the market, that is, the marginal buyer. However, the monopolist may choose to make individual bargains with each buyer.

Walras went more deeply into the processes determining market price, although he used the same concepts and much the same terminology as previous writers of the marginal utility school. To Walras, however, we owe the idea of scarcity as it applies to goods. It is the utility of a good accompanied by the fact of scarcity which gives an object value. Price, therefore, is the quantitative expression of utility and limited supply. When supply and demand are equal as a result of competition, the price will be what Walras termed the *called price*—that is a price set by competitive bidding at an auction. Walras developed the concept of general market equilibrium and he defended not only the freely competitive market but the doctrine of *laissez-faire*.

In summary, whereas previous economists had been concerned with cost of production and supply, adherents of the marginal utility school dealt with subjective utility and value in exchange. Thus there was common agreement on the importance of supply and demand and competition; but there was nevertheless a growing realization of the importance of external control of the market as found for example in monopoly.

THE NEOCLASSICAL SCHOOL: ALFRED MARSHALL

By 1890, all the essential fields of inquiry and criticism concerning the assumptions made by Smith and Ricardo as to competition and the law of supply and demand had been more or less catalogued. Some had been fully explored. There was first of all the socialist criticism that unbridled competition was detrimental, not beneficial. There was a clear indication that some writers believed that a controlled market rather than a freely competitive market was typical, and that supply and demand never achieved or never continued in equilibrium. There were some who said that cost of production and supply were the chief forces in determining price, while others took the opposite view, saying that utility and demand were most important.

The materials for a restatement of the basic ideas in economics were present. They waited only for a mind with the breadth and skill to weave them into a comprehensive pattern. That individual appeared in the figure of Alfred Marshall (1842–1924). An English economist of the classical tradition, he brought together the best thought of his time into a description and explanation of economic processes which served as a model for economic thought in England for several decades. As of Ricardo, it can be said of Marshall: He was the most representative figure of the economic activity of his times. That many of his ideas have lost their popularity is testimony to the changed character of the times rather than to the shortcomings of Marshall's ideas. In most cases, even his severest critics found their inspiration in something he said or hinted.

On the question of competition itself as a means of organizing the economic order, Marshall had some very definite opinions. He assumed that competition would produce those forms of business enterprise best adapted to their environment. This did not mean, however, that they were most beneficial to their environment. In fact, Marshall said that he did not doubt that an economic order operated by virtuous men cooperating actively with one another would be superior to the best forms of competition. His question was whether such a cooperative ideal could thrive in the present environment. Competition, in the sense that Marshall used the term, allowed for certain forms of business cooperation and for some intervention on the part of government. As a matter of fact, he believed that enlightened government intervention might enlarge the scope of economic freedom. It is well to note, however, that such competition was not the perfect competition of the early economists, which assumed perfect knowledge of the market and perfect mobility of the factors of production. Free competition in Marshall's opinion required only the exercise of faculties possessed by the average well-informed person and a reasonable mobility of labor and capital. Marshall was well aware of the forces tending to restrict the operation of economic forces. These were law, custom, trade union regulation, inertia, and sentimental attachments. Nevertheless, competition and economic freedom were continuous and all-pervading.

In his discussion of the effects of competition upon the process of exchange, Marshall noted all kinds of different markets, each with its own peculiar characteristics. For example, at the two extremes there were world markets and isolated markets; and between, with innumerable variations, lay the majority of markets with which businessmen normally must deal.

The relation of competition to supply and demand, especially the former, was one of the chief points of Marshall's work. As we have noted, the willingness of a producer to increase his supply depended upon his costs of production, i.e., whether they were increasing, decreasing, or constant. Whereas the early economists assumed that all costs were constant, Marshall knew that costs varied greatly. The producer with increasing costs would expand his output only if an unusual demand so far outran the normal supply as to keep the price above the increased cost. Constant or decreasing cost represented sources of instability since an increase in supply might prove quite profitable if some obstruction prevented the operation of freely competitive forces. But there were other modifications that required attention. One situation Marshall noted was the time required for a change in the market, especially as time affected the supply of goods. Marshall said, in speaking of exchange value: "As a general rule, the shorter the period we are considering, the greater must be the share of our attention which is given to the influence of demand on value; and the longer the period, the more important will be the influence of the cost of production on value." Marshall knew that with the tremendous amounts of fixed capital tied up in business enterprises, variations in supply to meet short-run changes in market price or demand were unlikely. Businessmen frequently continued to operate at a loss rather than retire from business and lose the large original investment. Realizing the importance of long-term trends, Marshall expressed his price formula in terms of cost of production. He said that prices tended to be set at the cost of production of the most expensive unit necessary to meet the existing demand. That is, if the most efficient producers could not supply the demand, less efficient producers would be encouraged to enter production, and the market price would be set at the cost of production of that one of the less efficient producers whose addition to the supply just met the demand.

When Marshall turned his attention to the effects of monopoly on the market, he made some rather striking comments. The rapid increase in capital and the intense drive toward greater specialization he knew constituted real threats to freedom of economic action. Yet he held that there was an element of monopoly in every competitive business, and that the power of monopolies was of "uncertain tenure; consequently every monopoly must give attention to the factors of present or latent competition if it intended to survive." In spite of the encroachment of monopolies and other forces seeking control of the markets, Marshall believed that such tendencies were counteracted by the development of new instruments of competition. Government intervention was one; greater consumer information was another; the increase of small investors a third; new emphasis upon trade morality, and a diminution of trade secrecy through newly developed avenues of publicity were others. Throughout, the net effect of Marshall's work is to emphasize the continuing power of competition as a regulator of economic activity. Consequently, in spite of his emphasis upon the imperfect nature of competition, he remains in the classical tradition by accepting a freely competitive market as a starting point for his investigations and in his confidence that the power of competition would in the end establish equilibrium between the forces of production and consumption.

THE THEORY OF IMPERFECT COMPETITION

The importance which Marshall attributed to competition as a regulator of the market and a determinant of price was not shared by all his followers. The current trend in economic thought is unquestionably toward the analysis of exchange under conditions of monopoly and imperfect competition. It was the force of actual conditions which turned the attention of economists away from Marshall's ideas of a competitive market toward the uncertainties of the controlled market. The selling of goods is such an integral part of large-scale production that business cannot afford to trust the control of a freely competitive market. Consequently, tremendous efforts have been made to devise methods of maximizing money value of sales and guaranteeing an adequate market. Devices such as class price and the use of advertising to break down consumer indifference, as in trade names, are now commonplace. E. Chamberlin's *The Theory of Monopolistic Competition* and J. Robinson's *The Economics of Imperfect Competition* ushered in new concepts of analysis. The new line of investigation abandoned the assumption of competition as a regulator of the market through the forces of supply and demand; instead, it attempted to analyze the effective methods of control of the market now in practice, usually expressing the results of such control in quantitative terms. The emphasis placed upon mathematical formulae can be traced to the influence of Walras and the Italian economist Vilfredo Pareto (1848–1923), Walras's successor at the University of Lausanne, and to a revival of interest in the work of Cournot.

The goal of the newer school of economic thought is to establish a theory of price determination that will be applicable for both competitive and noncompetitive markets. The initial formulations of the new doctrine were derived from an analysis of prices in monopoly markets; it was necessary only to expand the scope of the analysis so as to include a greater number of sellers while continuing to use exactly the same assumptions and methods. Extensive research continues in the behavior of prices in oligopolistic markets, usually by means of refinements in the neoclassical concepts of Alfred Marshall.

Thorstein Veblen

The assumptions of free competition and the control of market forces emphasized by the classical economists came under attack from yet another source. Thorstein Veblen (1857–1929), father of institutional economics (which holds that man's economic behavior is greatly influenced by his social and political environment), believed that the fallacies of previous economists lay not in their logic but in their premises, for even the critics of classical economics accepted generally the basic assumptions of the school. According to Veblen these basic assumptions were: (1) that man inevitably sought pleasure and avoided pain; (2) that each man thought the pursuit of self-interest (i.e., pecuniary gain, subject only to control by competition) contributed to the well-being of the community; and (3) that because of self-interest and competition, society inexorably ascended to greater heights of happiness. The facts of living, as found among primitive peoples and in historical civilizations, denied these assumptions, said Veblen. His principal works were devoted primarily to the accumulation of data to prove his contention. He believed that man is endowed with certain instinctive tendencies which condition his behavior, but that in every age the established customs and traditions of a society determine the specific direction such instinctive tendencies will take. In order to understand the economic activity in any age, therefore, one must study the interaction between man's instinctive tendencies and the institutional form in which they find expression.

The most important of human instincts, in Veblen's treatment of the subject, is the *instinct of workmanship*. This innate force causes men to use care in the development of those material objects, especially tools, which enable them to exploit nature more completely and adapt it to their own needs. The institution of private property, however, which began in either fraud or force in the predatory stages of social evolution, subordinated the instinct of workmanship to the accumulation of property. With the outset of modern industrialism two new aspects of social organization became apparent. The first was a division of society into two classes: those who lived in ease and luxury off the accumulation of property and those who labored at routine tasks for a bare existence. The second aspect was the existence of envy and jealousy among members of society, especially in matters of money and property. Veblen saw modern society as a seething mass of individuals, each striving to outdo the individuals just above him in the accumulation and display of wealth. Veblen coined terms to designate this characteristic of contemporary life. *Pecuniary emulation* (imitation in the accumulation and use of money and property) and *invidious comparison* (the envious comparison of one man's social position with that of his neighbor) have become familiar words in economic literature.

Thus with Veblen, as well as with later members of the institutional school of economic thought, competition was a prominent feature of economic behavior. It was, however, competition for property, place, and power and not merely competition in the buying and selling of goods. Competition, as Veblen understood it, has far more serious implications for society than the competition of the marketplace. To demonstrate his superiority over his competitors, the modern businessman does not confine his efforts to producing better articles more efficiently to sell at a cheaper price; indeed, the pursuit of wealth and power leads the entrepreneur to undermine the competitive conditions of the market by perfecting his control over all the factors of production and distribution. He strives to obtain a monopoly of raw materials; he seeks to restrict the use of the peculiar types of machinery necessary for production; he limits production in the interest of higher prices; he tries to make wage earners dependent upon him alone for employment at wages he is willing to pay; he reaches out to control the wholesale and retail agencies responsible for the sale of his product; and through the use of trademarks, brand names, and advertising, he seeks to determine the choices of the consumer.

It is obvious that Veblen would seek some other explanation of price than the operation of supply and demand in a competitive market. Whereas the classical economists believed competition to be the natural or normal state of the market from which monopolistic practices were but occasional and temporary deviations, Veblen held that free competition was impossible in an industrial society. Every successful business, he believed, was to some degree marked by monopolistic practices. Indeed, he held that the only source of profit in modern industry was the interference on the part of the businessman with the natural efficiency of business enterprise, that is, a "conscientious withdrawal of efficiency" from economic activity. Thus, the setting of prices was not a matter of the free play of market forces, but the result of innumerable controls exercised over the factors of production and distribution.

CONTEMPORARY VIEWS

A popular and widely read analyst and critic of the increasing size and power of business units is John Kenneth Galbraith (1908–). In his study *American Capitalism* (1954) Galbraith coined the term *countervailing power* to describe the fact that giant economic units, although exercising widespread controls over production and price, were themselves checked by other powerful units in areas where they were competitive: i.e., for labor, labor unions; for raw materials, private or quasi-public monopolies controlling such resources as tin, bauxite, or sulphur; and for energy, nations and giant corporations controlling oil. As these giant organizations endeavor to assure their own continued existence and growth, a new managerial class develops possessing skill in administration, science, and technology. This group constitutes a new dimension in social organization which Galbraith labeled the technostructure (*The New Industrial State*, 1967).

Joseph A. Schumpeter (1883–1950), a critic of Keynes, took a rather benign view of monopolies (*Theory of Economic Develop-*

ment, 1912). Monopolies were checked, in his view, by innovations that gave rise to newer business enterprises which challenged the old through competing products or superior processes. Moreover, monopolies led the way in improving conditions of employment. At best, monopolies were only temporary, and, although they interfered with the operation of the market, in the long run they could not control it. Nevertheless, large-scale monopolistic production and distribution would bring about the destruction of capitalism, because (anticipating Galbraith) bureaucratic administration in giant business enterprises stifled innovation and growth which was essential to the continued success of capitalism as an economic system (*Capitalism, Socialism and Democracy*, 1942; *Business Cycles*, 1939).

Game theory, as developed by the joint efforts of John von Neumann (1903–1957) and Oskar Morgenstern (1902–   ) and expressed in *Theory of Games and Economic Behavior* has its application in both oligopolistic pricing and income distribution. The theory of games presupposes two or more units competing with one another. Each is free to choose a strategy, but without accurate knowledge of what choices the competitor will make. Each then chooses that course of action which, in relation to a series of choices open to the competitor, will result in the combination of least potential loss with maximum potential gain. Game theory has succeeded in exposing some of the unrealistic elements of classical analysis and directing research to economic activities which are not well understood. It has not, however, displaced classical analysis.

7. MONEY, CREDIT, AND BANKING

AQUINAS · GRESHAM · BODIN · MUN · MISSELDEN · POTTER ·
LAW · PETTY · SMITH · MALTHUS · RICARDO · MILL · OWEN ·
PROUDHON · KEYNES · FISHER · FRIEDMAN · SAMUELSON

*Why is money so important in modern society? Why have
gold and silver been accepted as standard money? What gives
paper money its value? Does it matter how much money there
is in circulation? Is a nation more or less wealthy if it has a
large quantity of money in circulation? Do banks create money?
What is inflation? What determines the value of money? Would
business be aided if the government changed the value of
money to suit price levels? How does demand-pull inflation
differ from cost-push inflation?*

THE TWENTIETH CENTURY is frequently referred to by economists
as a period of *money economy*. In contrast to the self-sufficiency
of the early agricultural communities, people today make directly
or completely very few if any of the things they use. The adage
that men must work for a living has changed. People work for
money to buy a living, and there is no other way in modern society
to live and do the things which they want to do.

MONEY

As Adam Smith pointed out so forcefully, although he was not
the first to do so, money originated as the counterpart of specializa-

tion. When people ceased to make everything they needed and began to emphasize production in which they had special ability, exchange became an important aspect of economic life. As long as group A could exchange its grain for meat produced by group B in quantities satisfactory to both, ordinary *barter* was sufficient. When direct exchange was not possible, the next best arrangement was for group A and group B to exchange their grain and meat with other groups for some one item that was generally desired by most people. Suppose, for example, it was skins. Groups A and B then would hold the skins they got for their meat and grain until they could be exchanged for other commodities which they desired to use. In that way skins, while having some value in use, actually would be in greater demand because they had become a medium of exchange, or money. This explains the origin and—as Othmar Spann suggests—perhaps the fundamental nature of money. Some objects are better adapted to this function than others. Perishable and bulky commodities would not do. In the inevitable weeding-out process, objects such as shells, cattle, skins, tobacco, and beads proved serviceable. Due to their greater convenience modern society has grown accustomed to the use of metal and paper for money.

AQUINAS'S VIEWS   The moral relationships associated with money have, naturally, been paramount in all religious teachings. In Thomas Aquinas we can recognize the influence of the essential teachings both of early religion and the Greek philosophers. The admonition of St. Paul that love of money was the root of all evil very clearly restricted the thinking of Aquinas, as did the principles laid down by the Mosaic law. Money and trade were perhaps necessary, but they were both spiritually dangerous since they led to the search for wealth for its own sake. Following Aristotle, Aquinas believed that money was barren and could not reproduce itself; hence to require interest was taking from another what one had not earned. Allowance was made, however, for some compensation for loans in exceptional cases. Prices were the money expressions of fair value, or as Aquinas interpreted it, the value of a man's labor according to his station in life.

THE DEVELOPMENT OF NEW IDEAS DURING THE LATER MIDDLE AGES   What Aquinas had to say on economic matters was largely in the nature of ethical recommendation rather than a critical description of economic processes. The stability and self-sufficiency of the feudal period might have found the just-price concept and non-interest-bearing loans sufficiently practical to serve as working principles; but in the very century in which Aquinas lived, the thirteenth, commerce and trade with their demands for money and credit were swinging into a rapid tempo. In spite of the toll houses, the laws against trade, the opposition of the Church, and the arbitrary restrictions of feudal lords, the small band of traders who moved across Europe during the Middle Ages now swelled into a mighty throng of merchants. Strangely enough, conditions which at first retarded the flow of commerce were in the end responsible for many of the instruments of trade now held indispensable.

The need for an abundant supply of money led to the rapid growth of money-lending agencies, and, according to tradition, the Christian prohibitions against lending at interest had the effect of giving to Jewish trade this economic function. Buying and selling between cities lacking a common currency and adequate police to give the merchants protection led to the revival of the bill of exchange. Although its origin is unknown, the bill of exchange was used in the Italian commercial cities before the invading Arabs destroyed their sea-borne trade with the cities of the Eastern Mediterranean. Once brought back into use by the development of European trade, it has continued as an essential element of modern business.

The operation of a bill of exchange was simple; it required only that persons of wealth in different cities be known to each other and agree to act in mutual trust and confidence. Suppose a buyer of merchandise wishes to journey to a distant city to purchase goods. Since police protection is meager and restrictions against the exportation of money numerous, the merchant would rather not risk carrying a large sum of money on his person. He therefore goes to a resident of his city known to have acquaintances in the city to which he is going. Paying the necessary money, the traveller receives a letter authorizing a wealthy friend to give the traveller a similar sum when he calls for it. This essentially is the way a bill of exchange operates. Of course, the settlement between the two friends, or bankers, is an important matter, but it does not need to be described here. Suffice it to say that since the relationship between the bankers is reciprocal, many of their transactions over a period of time will cancel out, leaving only a small balance, if any, to be settled in cash.

The increase of commerce and its demand for money found the monetary situation in Europe chaotic. Kings, nobles, and cities issued coins differing in weight, stamp, and name. The lack of a common unit made the function of the money-changer important. Added to this were two tendencies which caused increased difficulty. Since coin was so scarce, every independent state and barony established restrictions against the exportation of metal. Within the state the content of the monetary unit was frequently changed, either by the process of devaluation instigated by the rulers in their desire for more funds, or by citizens who habitually reduced the content of the coins which fell into their hands by scraping, cutting, or chipping.

Henry VIII of England, for example, was exceedingly hard pressed for money. On several occasions he lowered the gold content of the English monetary unit in order to increase his own revenues. Henry had also borrowed large sums of money abroad, principally from Dutch bankers. When he was on the point of repaying his indebtedness he found that English currency had lost much of its value in foreign exchange and only coins of poor value were circulating in England. His financial advisor at the time was Sir Thomas Gresham. In order to offset the disadvantage in English money, he required English merchants who sold English wool abroad to pay the King's debts with the money they received for their wool. The King reimbursed them in debased English coins when they arrived home. Experiences such as this made Gresham a staunch advocate of sound money. He saw clearly that where two kinds of money were in circulation—one of full gold value and the other of only part of the stated gold value—the people would hoard the good money and spend only the bad money. Although Gresham did not originate this principle it became known as Gresham's law. It states briefly, that bad money will drive good money out of circulation and even out of the country.

MERCANTILIST THEORIES   A few Mercantilists, including Mun, Davenant, Petty, and Steuart, clearly distinguished between wealth and money, but most either considered the two identical or avoided a clear statement of their relationship. It seems fair to say, however, that the complete identification of money with wealth was an extreme position of mercantilist thought, exaggerated by critics of Mercantilism.

Although the assumption that wealth consisted in an abundance of money may now appear unreasonable, strong arguments were offered to support it. The financial stability of the state in those days depended largely upon a ready supply of precious metals. Since public borrowing was still undeveloped, and taxation was not as flexible as it is today, the security of a government was naturally assumed to lie in an accumulated reserve of coin and bullion. Thomas Mun, writing on this subject, admitted the necessity of such a reserve but urged the heads of state to restrict their accumulations annually to the excess of exports over imports so that the people would have sufficient money for commercial transactions. However, Mun also advised that ships, stores of grain, war supplies, and loans to the people for use in production should be considered desirable employment for the state's reserve.

Not a little of the desirability of a store of money was directly traceable to the use of mercenaries in warfare. Even more than today, money was considered the sinews of war. Only a ready supply of cash could provide armies, ships, and munitions. An empty state treasury was frank admission of military impotence.

Although none of the Mercantilists could explain clearly the relationship between the quantity of money in circulation and the price level, a few of them at least were aware that such a relationship existed and openly subscribed to an increase in the money supply in order to increase trade. The value of the circulation of money was usually derived from and frequently explained in terms of William Harvey's discovery of the circulation of the blood in the early seventeenth century.

Edward Misselden was a staunch advocate of the idea that to increase money was to increase trade. Misselden's two works, *Free Trade* and *The Circle of Commerce*, were published during the severe depression in English industry in the early 1620s. He believed firmly that money was the "vital spirit of trade." His suggestion that the state should increase the money in circulation by depreciating the value of the coins is quite out of line with the sound money ideas of classical economics, but recent events give the plan a very modern cast. He saw no danger in the rising prices such tactics would bring on, indeed he felt that the stimulation of trade and the increase of money resulting therefrom would more than compensate for the high prices.

William Potter, whose contribution to economic thought has been largely overlooked, said in his *Key to Wealth* (1650) that an increased quantity of money would result in greater sales and hence in greater trade. To make available a larger quantity of money he advocated the issuance of paper currency backed by land and other property. He argued that the only barrier to foreign trade was an artificial dependence upon gold and silver for money; therefore, if some purely domestic standard of currency were established, concern over foreign trade and export restrictions upon gold could be abolished.

CLASSICAL THEORIES   Although many Mercantilists deviated at various points from the traditional pattern of mercantilist thought, none gave clearer indication of the changes in the fundamental ideas of money that were to come than did Sir William Petty (1623–1687). When most of his contemporaries were advocating stronger control of the exportation of money, he maintained that without governmental regulation a nation might achieve a sufficient quantity of money to meet its internal needs by lending excesses at interest and creating a bank to make up for deficiencies by means of credit. He also gave some intimation that the quantity of money in circulation affected prices.

It was David Hume (1711–1776), however, who made the first comprehensive attack upon the idea that the measure of a nation's economic and political welfare was the size of its stock of precious metal. Hume put an end to the hold of Mercantilism on English economic thought. His exposition of the fallacies of the *bullionist* position and his advocacy of automatic regulation of the flow of money is still outstanding for its clarity of reasoning and excellence of style. Good partial discussions of the self-regulation of trade and the flow of money are found in the writings of John Locke, Sir Dudley North, Isaac Gervaise, and Jacob Vanderlint; but it was Hume who, in his *Political Discourses* (1752), assembled the several points of discussion and wove them into a masterful analysis of the total idea.

The essence of Hume's theory is that the monetary supply of a country is self-regulating and the best interests of the country will be served without government attempts to secure a favorable balance of trade or to prohibit the export of bullion. A decline in the quantity of money in England will cause a decline in the price of goods; thus foreign buyers will buy English goods and pay for them in money until the quantity of money in England is equal to that of other countries. If money should increase, prices will rise, foreign buyers will seek other markets, and imports will exceed exports until the level of money in the trading countries is once again equal. The flow of metal is also influenced by the rates of exchange between countries which act as forces similar to price levels operating to restore monetary equilibrium. Hume, it appears, believed in a direct and equal relationship between the quantity of money and the price level. The actual quantity of money, he said, made little difference since it was the quantity of money as related to the amount of goods available which determined the price. There was, of course, a temporary advantage from an increase in money: since prices did not react immediately to increases in money, there was a brief period of adjustment when at the same prices the nation possessing more money could demand more goods.

In John Stuart Mill's discussion of this topic there is a general acceptance of the Hume point of view, with one important innovation: The increase of money in one country actually increased that country's demand for its own and foreign goods. The effect of this was not only to increase the prices of domestic goods, which turned away foreign traders, but also to start the flow of foreign goods into the country, thus sooner or later bringing about an equilibrium.

Adam Smith made no changes in the basic ideas of money that his predecessors had propounded. Explaining how the origin of money was due to the necessity of exchange arising from a subdivision of labor, he proceeded to show how the quantity of money in circulation was regulated. He conceived of money as both a medium of exchange and a measure of value, but he denied that it had any value in itself other than that of facilitating exchange. Because of this factor, the greater economy in its use the better. To this end the use of paper money was eminently desirable, for this increased the quantity of coin which was available for purchases of instruments of production abroad without decreasing the supply for domestic use. Money was a commodity, Smith believed, and like any commodity the amount of it would be regulated by necessity. If a greater quantity was available than domestic trade required, the excess would be used for purchases abroad. In the case of paper money issued by banks an excess would be attended by a rise in prices, and foreign purchasing would result, requiring the exchange of bank notes for coin with which to make foreign payments. Thus Smith's real contribution to the theory of money seems to have been his emphasis upon the value of paper money as an aid to economic activity.

In a general way, the monetary views of David Ricardo follow closely the pattern of Adam Smith. Regarding the movement of bullion and the effect of the quantity of money on prices in international trade he subscribed to the quantity theory and supported the self-regulating mechanism, adding the significant point that even before commodity prices the price of bills of exchange seemed to reverse the course of trade in the direction of equilibrium between nations. Ricardo's name became closely associated with the efforts to solve the monetary problems of his day; in fact he is looked upon as the best exponent of the bullionist position. Economic crises, the suspension of specie payments for two decades, and price inflation, all occurred during his lifetime. In his pamphlet, *The High Price of Bullion* (1809), Ricardo attempted to explain the monetary instability as an effect of poorly regulated paper currency. Although he believed, as did Adam Smith, that paper money should be substituted for coin wherever possible, he was convinced that in order to bring about economic stability the amount of paper currency should be reduced to conform to the quantity of specie on hand. On the other hand, he advocated as a long-term policy the issuance of paper currency rather than specie to meet the demands of increased population and increased business activity. The banking legislation of Great Britain for the first half of the nineteenth century reflects the monetary theories of Ricardo, testifying not so much to his originality or the validity of his ideas as to the energy and clarity with which he presented them. There was one subject that emphasized Ricardo's adherence to Adam Smith's ideas and the classical tradition. While the value of money was primarily determined by the supply and the demand for it as a medium of exchange, Ricardo thought that the cost of production of gold and silver also influenced the value of money just as the cost of production tended to influence the value of other commodities. It was at this point that Ricardo's ideas seem most confused. Nevertheless, classical economists of later years tended to follow the same line of reasoning without criticism.

The idea that the value of metal money was determined by its cost of production was taken up and elaborated by John Stuart Mill. He was concerned with showing that the value of money could be affected both by its quantity combined with rapidity of circulation, and by its cost of production. In the case of the former the effect was immediate; the effect of the latter would be felt only over long periods of time. Obviously, said Mill, the law of supply and demand operated more quickly on money than on other commodities; but since the cost of production ultimately affected the supply of money, it must be considered as influencing value.

THE QUANTITY THEORY OF MONEY   No idea has been more important in economic thought than what the economist calls the *quantity* *theory* of money. In the writings of such economists as Law, Petty, Vanderlint, and Hume, the question of the influence of the quantity of money in circulation upon the price level was continually referred to.

One of the earliest writers to be concerned specifically with the function of money and its effect upon prices was Jean Bodin (1530–1590). His explanation of the advance in prices in *Réponse aux Paradoxes de Malestroit* (1569) was far in advance of his time. He ascribed current price changes to the abundance of gold and silver, scarcity caused by effort, and the debasement of currency, and he cited historical facts to support his contentions. There is no doubt that he had a fair understanding of the relation of the quantity and value of money to prices.

To John Locke (1632–1704), however, goes the credit for the first formulation of the quantity theory of money. He claimed that the value of any commodity, money included, was determined by the relation of the supply to the demand. As long as the quantity of money remained the same, any alterations in price were due to changes in the supply and demand for commodities in terms of each other. If, however, the quantity of money was altered and the amount of trade remained the same, any change in price could be traced directly to the change in the quantity of money. Locke was aware that some consideration had to be given to the speed of circulation, since a coin used several times would count for more than the same coin used only once in the same period of time.

Subsequent additions to the quantity theory were in the nature of refinements of detail. For example, Cantillon showed that the increase in money due to the exploitation of mines first affected prices of goods used in the process of mining and then affected the prices of goods used by those whose incomes were increased as a direct result of the increased mining activity. A general rise in prices would follow sooner or later throughout the country, the net effect of which was the dislocation of domestic industry through a development of foreign buying.

The earliest statements of the quantity theory of money were made when the chief circulating medium was coin. During the years which followed, first paper money, then bank credit were introduced, and they quickly pushed metal money into obscurity. For a time paper money was the chief medium of exchange for business transactions, but since the middle of the nineteenth century bank credit alone has kept pace with the rapid expansion of business enterprise. These innovations have made the quantity theory of money more difficult to observe in practice, but they have not changed the basic principle. Until the 1930s, it was generally understood that a nation's currency would be backed by precious metals which would be used to settle balances in international trade. The dislocations of international economic life and the practices of most nations in controlling both credit and note issue with little regard to the quantity of precious metals on hand made this commonly accepted rule inoperative. Today, in the determination of the quantity of money on hand at a given time, bank credit, note issue, and international monetary units are more important than metal.

TWENTIETH-CENTURY VIEWS   In the early decades of the twentieth century, Irving Fisher (1867–1947) was considered the best exponent of monetary theory. (Many of Fisher's ideas ran parallel to those of J. G. Knut Wicksell [1851–1926], a Swedish economist who became internationally known for his application of mathematics to the analysis of money and the business cycle.) Fisher's equation, and refinements of it, dominated thinking about the relationship of money to prices. He claimed that the quantity of money in circulation, including currency and bank deposits (M), and the velocity with which money and deposits turned over (V), if divided by the number of business transactions, would determine the price level. This price level was represented by a number which, when compared to similar numbers applicable at different times, indicated the exact amount of change in the price level.

John Maynard Keynes is noted for his analysis of the place and importance of money in the operation of modern economic life. In both *A Treatise on Money* (1930) and *The General Theory of Employment Interest and Money* (1936), he emphasized the fact that money had unique characteristics. While the volume of most commodities can be almost indefinitely increased by the application of labor and capital, that is not so with money. Money can be increased, but the amount of increase is a matter of arbitrary decision by government authority and is not self-regulated by production costs and selling price as are other commodities. And when the exchange value of other commodities rises, substitute products usually are available; but there is no substitute for money. Further, money holds a liquidity preference higher than any other commodity. It is the one commodity for which there is always a market. And, finally, Keynes claimed that the importance of money lay in its being the link between present and future values. As a general statement of relationship, Keynes accepted Fisher's formula, but he added so many possible variables—such as the demand for money, labor factors, and physical factors determining the rate of diminishing returns in production—that the simple formula for him had very little meaning and could be used only in relatively artificial situations where one of the variables arbitrarily was held constant.

In the long run the effect of the changing quantity of money on prices has never been allowed to operate. The normal trend of prices and wage rates has been upward. If by chance a deficiency of the supply of money caused a decline in prices and wage rates, the increasing burden of the debt structure which followed such changes was too painful to tolerate. Measures of debt relief and changes in the monetary unit were introduced by the state to curb the deflationary trend. Keynes's investigations into the role of money and its effect upon interest and employment resulted in a recommendation that departed from the whole classical tradition.

Keynes was pessimistic about the possibility of a free market lifting itself out of a static condition in which general equilibrium was achieved with a persistence of widespread unemployment. But his analysis of the relationships of money, saving, investment, and interest suggested the ingredients for economic control and the means to combat economic depressions by administratively changing the amount of money in circulation. Neo-Keynesians believe that with the carefully timed use of such devices as government spending, control of interest rates, and alteration of money supply, the arcs of the business cycle can be flattened so that unemployment does not rise or fall significantly from a base line figure of 4 to 5 percent. The multiplier effect which Keynes developed, primarily in connection with his studies of the impact of investment on income and employment, has been expanded by his disciples to apply, often in accentuated form, to other infusions into the economy. Keynes was able to show that, depending upon the propensity to consume, one dollar of investment might result in several times one dollar, because each person who received the dollar in exchange for capital equipment or raw material would in turn spend that proportion of the dollar not saved. Such a theory, especially when related to another economic phenomenon (developed by Paul Samuelson) called the accelerator, provided a powerful force for managing the economy through various forms of government intervention.

Banking and Credit

The great economic achievements of the Dutch in the fifteenth and sixteenth centuries were a source of envy to many commercially minded Englishmen. Naturally, they tried to ferret out some explanation of Dutch prosperity. It is not strange that many concluded that the source of the Dutch commercial success rested in the fact that a bank was operating successfully in Amsterdam, while none as yet had been started in England. Sir William Petty and Sir Dudley North, seventeenth-century writers, both advocated the formation of a bank in England which might issue credit, though they were somewhat vague as to what banks could and could not do. North's idea was that a bank should be created to lend money to the government; and as a matter of fact that was the chief reason for chartering the Bank of England. Banks served as repositories for coin which could be put out at interest, but the ideas of note issue and commercial credit were scarcely known, even on the Continent, in the seventeenth century.

Early Banks   The banks at Amsterdam and Hamburg were not banks in the modern sense of the word; they were places where money could be exchanged into currency of recognized and standard value. Because of the variety of coins circulating in Europe at the time, and because the weight and fineness of the metal coins varied so much from that which was claimed by the state issuing them, some reliable method of testing coin and calculating exchange was essential to the conduct of trade. The increasing amount of commerce passing through Amsterdam and Hamburg made these cities natural places for the establishment of exchange banks. They weighed and assayed the coin which traders brought them; and in exchange, they gave coins of certified weight and fineness or certificates of deposit. Banks of this type needed no capital of their own, since they exchanged value for value and were rewarded by the small charge they made for the service they rendered.

Banks created primarily for the purpose of accepting deposits and making loans were organized in the commercial city of Venice as early as the fourteenth century. These private banks were required by the laws of Venice to hold coin as security for their depositors. Public banks were established during the next two centuries to accept deposits from citizens, make loans—especially to the government— and to issue bank notes on government authority.

When the Bank of England was founded in 1694 it was designed to create a market for government loans. It was a period of financial instability. With new monarchs on the throne (William and Mary, 1688) and part of the population disgruntled at the change, it was not easy to secure money for public purposes. The bank accepted money from private citizens which it immediately loaned to the government.

The Bank of England was the first bank in England to have government authorization, and it was the first of national importance; but private banking activity had been carried on for a century and more before by the goldsmiths of England and Scotland, some of whose names are still attached to private banks now operating. The goldsmiths accepted money for deposit and paid interest at a stated percent. Their guarantees of security, easy withdrawal, and interest brought forth abundant money which heretofore had been hoarded or lent at interest on personal security.

A further extension of the goldsmiths' banking activities came when the certificates of deposit were accepted in payment for financial obligations. These deposit receipts, at first merely the holder's evidence for his deposit and his right to withdraw the amount stated, soon began to circulate as currency. As long as the reputation of the bank and the depositor were good, people had no fear of accepting deposit slips instead of cash. This issue of certificates was followed by the issuance of notes, and then in 1781, by a book of checks.

SPECULATIVE SCHEMES The immediate effect of the organization of the Bank of England was the stabilization of public finance, but the long-run effect was a serious inflation of currency and credit. Specie disappeared, the mint closed because no one brought bullion to be coined, and devaluation of the currency was advocated. John Locke (1632–1709) opposed devaluation, and in his essay *Further Considerations Concerning Raising the Value of Money*, he argued for a sound money policy. He believed it unjust to deprive blameless citizens of one-fifth of their estates and income. Many, he said, would be glad to give a much larger proportion of their estates if they were assured the nation would benefit; but to take from some and give to others less deserving (the debtors) did not help the state at all. Furthermore, the function of government was to preserve contracts. How could the government require that some pay less than their contract and others receive less? Such a policy was no more just than requiring men to pay more than they had contracted to pay. Finally, he believed devaluation would undermine public confidence in the government and defraud not only the king but also the Church, the universities, and the hospitals.

Locke's arguments were persuasive, especially to the class of landowners who continued to exercise control over the government. A period of deflation set in, but the hardship which the advocates of devaluation had foreseen never materialized. What might have happened eventually will never be known, for a wave of speculation founded upon colonial enterprises overtook both England and France and brought on a banking crisis in both countries in 1720.

The name of John Law (1671–1729) is closely identified with

this period of speculation, inflation, and subsequent financial crisis, especially in France. Law, the son of a banker (one of the goldsmiths who originated banking practices in Scotland), became an authority if not a genius in economic matters. His ideas were coldly received both in Scotland and England. Because of certain personal misfortunes of a social nature while living in London, he was exiled from England and forced to spend the rest of his life on the Continent. The financial difficulties of France following the extravagant reign of Louis XIV gave Law his opportunity, and in an amazingly short time he had established institutions to put his ideas into practice.

Law's principal work, *Money and Trade Considered, with a Proposal for Supplying the Nation with Money,* was written in 1705 as a plan to relieve Scotland of a severe financial panic following the failure of the Darien colonizing expedition. The plan was never seriously considered in Scotland, but it embodied the basic ideas which Law held on wealth, money, credit and banking, and to which he gave practical expression in France in 1716. Law denied the general contention of Mercantilism that money was wealth. He held that wealth in terms of goods depended upon trade, and both employment and trade depended upon the quantity of money in circulation. Furthermore, he added, credit had all the beneficial effects of money. The quantity of specie need not be increased; but merely by the device of creating a bank, credit could be expanded. The bank which Law proposed was to issue notes backed by land. Credit expansion and note issue would be under rigid control, since the bank would be a state agency and the commission controlling it composed of government officials. The most daring part of the proposal was that foreign trade and public finance would be managed through one gigantic corporation, controlled by the state in the interests of the people, and carrying on business through the issue of an abundant supply of paper currency.

The story of Law's experiments in France reads like an economic fairytale. During his exile he supported himself in luxury mainly through financial speculation and gambling. The chaotic financial situation in which Louis XIV left France on his death baffled the best financial experts of the time. A declaration of national bankruptcy was seriously considered. When an acquaintance of Law's, the Duke of Orléans, became Regent, Law was given an opportunity to submit a plan to stabilize the nation's finances. Opposed by the financial oligarchy in Paris, the plan was tentatively accepted by the Regent. The first step was the establishment of *La Banque Générale* under the immediate direction of Law. The capital of the bank consisted of shares of stock paid for in four installments, one-quarter in currency and three-quarters in the then nearly worthless paper notes of the French state. The privilege of note issue was granted to the new bank, the notes being redeemable in metal by weight on sight. Thus far the plan was a success. The fact that the bank was willing to accept the existing government notes raised the credit of the government; the bank's own notes became a most desirable medium of exchange since they had a fixed value in metal. The use of the notes for industrial transactions in the provinces and the decree making the notes acceptable in payment of taxes created such a demand for the notes that new issues soon followed. It must be remembered that Law saw no difficulty in an unlimited issue of paper currency as long as there was a demand for it and as long as there was good security for it.

The success of the bank earned the immediate confidence of the Regent; consequently Law's request for permission to carry out the other parts of his program met with approval. The Mississippi trading area was not prospering under the management of an incompetent speculator. Law took over the franchise and set up the *Compagnie de la Louisiane ou d'Occident.* Its capital was raised by the sale of shares payable part in cash and part in notes of indebtedness of the French state. The same confidence did not exist in the new company as had obtained for the bank. Consequently, the price of the shares fell below par. Law remedied this by agreeing, as director of the bank (now an official state bank named *La Banque Royale*), to redeem the shares at par with notes guaranteed by the king. The favorable effect on the shares was immediate; their price rose on the exchange to above par. Law's next move was to unite the companies engaged in foreign trade into a single company, *La Compagnie des Indes,* under his own direction. Confidence in Law and the renewed vigor of business enterprise caused every new issue of shares to be grabbed up immediately at fantastic prices. To meet the demand for money caused by the accompanying price rise, the bank issued more paper currency. Finally, the more intelligent investors realized that the earnings of the companies were too meagre at this early date to pay a dividend commensurate with the price of the shares, and they began to sell. With the dictatorial power over French financial matters which he now held, Law introduced measures to check the falling price of shares and the rising price of metal and property. He declared a 40 percent dividend on the shares and he forbade the use of diamonds and the manufacture of gold and silver plate. A virtual embargo was placed upon coin. But the shares still fell. Then Law made his most daring effort to check the downward trend. He ordered the bank to buy and sell the shares of the various trading companies at a fixed price, payable in bank notes. The loss of confidence, which at first affected only the companies, now extended to the bank and to the paper currency. The latter soon became as worthless as the shares. Law was driven from France and the bank notes were incorporated into the debt of France, the total of which was subsequently reduced by more than half. Much criticism has been leveled against Law for his mismanagement of French finances. Mature judgment seems to indicate that while on the whole his plan was admirable it was spoiled first by a fundamental misconception—that paper money could be issued in unlimited quantity—and, second, by a foolish gamble—ordering the bank to buy the discredited shares at a fixed price. Except for the latter action, the bank might have been saved and the credit structure of France maintained. It is not an exaggeration to say that Law's four years of experimentation with his "Mississippi Scheme" stands as one of the most exciting periods in financial history.

While John Law was learning through bitter experience the fallacies of some of his economic ideas, a similar course of events was being pursued in England. In 1711, the South Sea Company was incorporated. This was the first move in a scheme, supposedly originated by Daniel Defoe, to reduce the government's debt and stimulate foreign trade. The South Sea Company agreed to pay the government several million pounds to be applied to the national debt in return for a monopoly on trading rights in South America and the Pacific Islands. The money paid to the government was to be raised by the sale of stock. Within six months the stock had risen almost eight times in value. Companies imitating the plan and organization of the South Sea Company began to appear. Speculation was wild. Then came word of the panic in France, and a similar loss of confidence began in England. The price of shares fell rapidly as insiders, sensing the situation, unloaded huge quantities of stock on the market. By December, not only the South Sea Company stock but securities of sound companies such as the Bank of England and the East India Company went down rapidly, and Parliament was forced to take action. Investigation of the company showed both fraud and bribery and the leaders of the company were brought to trial and imprisoned. Those who had exchanged government obligations for the South Sea Company asked the government to guarantee them their original investment, but they received only half of what was due them before the panic.

With these two major disasters in the background, it is no wonder that the more conservative economists were reluctant to give wholehearted approval to paper money and bank credit during the century which followed. This period was marked by bitter and continued controversies on the question of money and credit especially as they related to banking practices and government control.

RICARDO AND HIS CRITICS   In the midst of money and banking uncertainty, David Ricardo (1772–1823) endeavored to outline the function and methods of modern banking, with the hope that a more general understanding of how and why banks operate would ease the mounting tension. In his *Proposals for an Economical and Secure Currency*, Ricardo described modern banking practices. He said the real advantage of banking begins only when it employs the capital of others as well as its own. This additional money comes from deposits and the notes which it issues. Most of it is loaned to persons whose trustworthiness is assured, who intend to use the funds for business purposes. A small part merely remains in the bank awaiting its depositor's decision to withdraw it. On the money loaned, the bank collects interest; some of the money deposited and some of the original capital may be invested in government bonds or other sound obligations which can be converted into cash on short notice. Another important function of the bank, said Ricardo, was the facility it offered in making payments between merchants in near or distant towns, or foreign countries. Finally, banks could issue notes on the government bonds and specie which they held. The former not only furnished funds to the government but enabled banks to increase the paper money in circulation. The earnings of a bank arise through the interest it collects on loans to the government or individuals, the profits from investments it makes, and the fees it collects for services. With these earnings the bank pays expenses, interest on deposits, and dividends to the holders of shares in the bank.

This outline is a fairly accurate description of conservative banking practices of Ricardo's time. The simplicity of the description belies the problems and debatable issues in connection with it. As a matter of fact, at least two major issues stirred the financial world during Ricardo's lifetime. The first great controversy was between the bullionist and the anti-bullionist positions, noted in the discussion of Ricardo's ideas on money. The uncertain economic situation which could be traced to the almost continuous warfare during the eighteenth and early nineteenth centuries upset normal banking procedures. Specie payments were suspended in England; exchange rates were usually unfavorable; country banks failed; and excessive government demands were made upon the Bank of England. The chief issue throughout the period was the control of paper currency. Ricardo, Whatley, Malthus, and Thornton were the outstanding bullionists. They contended that the constant depreciation of currency was due to the over-issue of paper bank notes, and they advocated in the report of the Bullion Committee, which was largely the work of Ricardo, a return to specie payments.

The anti-bullionist position was presented in speeches and pamphlets by Nicholas Vansittart, Bosanquet, and Trotter. Their argument was that Bank of England statistics did not show that a greater note issue existed in periods when bullion was selling at a premium over paper money; and further, that in the years when large payments in specie were made by the Bank of England to foreign countries the premium of specie over paper was greater. Hence, the anti-bullionists refused to agree that depreciation in the value of paper money was due to over-issue. They believed that rather than set rigid limits to the amount of paper money a bank could issue by setting a fixed ratio to the amount of bullion on hand, the bank itself could control the issue simply by restricting issue when the interest rate began to fall. The anti-bullionist views were accepted until after the Napoleonic Wars, when specie payments were resumed. The immediate effect of the resumption was to set in motion a deflationary process which lowered prices and wages but continued fixed incomes and debts at previous levels. Objection to this economic condition was as outspoken as it had been of the unstable inflationary period which preceded it.

Thus, the fires of controversy were kept burning. Did devaluation and the consequent inflation of currency stimulate business? Was the failure to honor the gold standard a breach of faith on the part of government? Could paper currencies be stable without being tied directly to the quantity of metal money on hand? These and other questions challenged the best minds of the times.

SOCIALIST IDEAS OF MONEY AND BANKING

While the classical economists were bickering over the relative virtues of metal money and specie and ways to control paper money and credit, ideas about money of an altogether different nature were being developed by other schools of economic thought. Robert Owen (1771–1858) in England, for example, was originating a socialist idea of money. His line of reasoning went something like this: The difficulties of modern economy could be traced to profit. Therefore it was necessary to abolish profit. Owen did not believe, as did some of his contemporaries, that through competition profit would gradually be eliminated anyway. He believed that some active force must be found to destroy it. He concluded (reasoning in another direction) that since profit was always expressed in terms of money— that is, the result of buying in the cheapest market and selling in the dearest—if metallic money could be eliminated so could profit. Therefore, he planned to substitute labor notes for currency. In practical terms, if a producer wished to dispose of an article, he received payment in notes according to the number of hours of labor spent in production. Ricardo had said that labor was the true source of value. Owen's plan was calculated to make the *labor theory* of value a reality by making the man-hours of labor the unit of currency.

Owen was not a person to remain content with the expostulation of a theory. He immediately established the National Equitable Labour Exchange in London to test his idea. Each member cooperating with the Exchange brought his produce to the Exchange and received labor notes in payment, according to the time spent in production. This member was then privileged to purchase any other produce on sale by giving the required number of labor notes in exchange. In this way, hours of labor were exchanged for hours of labor directly.

The Labour Exchange opened in 1832. Members numbered 840, and the initial success of the Exchange warranted the establishment of several branches. But difficulties were obvious. Members could not be trusted to state their hours of work correctly. When experts were employed to evaluate articles brought for sale, they did so by setting a money value and dividing it by a standard hourly wage. This, of course, was a reversal of Owen's intention. Furthermore, since the notes could be exchanged with non-members, neighboring merchants exchanged the notes for cash, then by buying the best articles at the exchange for the notes, they were able to realize a handsome profit by reselling in the regular commercial markets. In the face of such obstructions the Exchange soon found it impossible to continue operations.

Owen's failure with the Labour Exchange did not prevent later experiments intended to accomplish the same purpose. The Exchange Bank, initiated by Proudhon in 1849, was the next attempt to adapt socialistic theories to practical reform. His basic assumption was that interest was the cause of economic inequality and oppression. If one could make capital available to the wage earner at no cost, he would control the means of production and his produce, getting full value for the labor expended. To accomplish this purpose Proudhon advocated the establishment of an exchange bank which would issue paper money backed by the finished but unsold produce of those affiliated with the bank. Notes would be issued as a form of credit, and the notes would be acceptable as a medium of exchange among the members of the bank. Only a slight service charge would be made to cover actual operating expenses of the bank. Since the notes in circulation would never exceed the demand for commercial credit, and would represent goods already produced, Proudhon could see no difficulty with his scheme. In two respects, however, he failed to see its consequences. First, the competition of the exchange-bank notes with regular currency backed by gold would limit the circulation of the former and make the bank notes exchangeable with the regular currency only at a heavy premium. Second, there would inevitably be a distinction between the members of the exchange bank who paid cash and those who demanded time, thus creating two different prices, since the use of discounting is merely a method of equating the same payments made now and in the future. In modified form, Proudhon's bank actually came into existence as the People's Bank. After three months of operation the bank closed its doors, due not only to the fallacies of its principles but additionally to the fact that Proudhon was imprisoned for his literary attacks upon Louis Bonaparte. Although the practical experiment failed, Proudhon's basic ideas for an exchange bank have been incorporated into the modern cooperative and mutual credit societies.

The position of Karl Marx (1818–1883) on the subject of money was confined mainly to two ideas. The first was the use of money as capital, and the second was the relationship of money to the operation of his labor theory of value and of surplus value. Marx did not go so far as to condemn money as the source of profit as Owen had done; but it is significant that the economy which Marx proposed made no place for the use of money. Goods were to be distributed according to need, not according to one's ability to pay. Since the state owned and operated all industries, there was no need for credit. In the early days of the Soviet Union, Lenin attempted to operate the state according to the general outlines of communist theory. He soon found, however, that the absence of money was a severe handicap. Consequently, with the introduction of the New Economic Policy, money reappeared, and its use has increased rather than diminished in recent years.

INFLATION

Inflation is not a unique experience for nations. The French fiscal debacle with John Law, described in the preceding pages, and the monetary disaster of Germany in the years following World War I are two extreme examples that have left indelible marks on economic thought. The inflation experienced during the 1960s and 1970s in many major industrial nations cannot be explained by the simple fact of too much money. There is ample evidence of the power of demand-pull inflation, that is, when too much money (that is, currency and bank deposits) is available for the amount of goods and services available. Recently, much more concern has been expressed about cost-push inflation, the situation when a rapid increase in costs for energy, labor, and raw materials requires ever higher prices to cover costs and yield the expected profit.

Paul Samuelson (1915–), the analytical and articulate economist who crystalized the basic concepts of neo-Keynesian economics, has dealt at length with the question of inflation. He has pointed out that demand-push inflation can be controlled by regulating the size of the money supply, reducing government spending, and/or increasing taxes. Cost-push inflation is a much more difficult factor to control. Since such inflation arises as a result of costs (e.g., labor, energy, and raw materials) rising faster than productivity, the inevitable consequence is loss of employment; and if costs continue to rise faster than productivity, year after year, ever-increasing unemployment results, unless the managers of the economy create more consumer income. But this is really not a solution to the problem of inflation. A graphic effort to describe the interrelationship of wages, prices, and unemployment was made by A. W. Phillips (1914–   ) of the London School of Economics, whose "Phillips Curve" shows dramatically how every percent rise in prices is accompanied by a comparable decrease in unemployment, unless productivity somehow increases in the same ratio.

Opposite views concerning the way to counter inflation come from the University of Chicago School of Economics, of whom Milton Friedman (1912–   ) is the most able exponent. In popular terminology, Friedman and his associates are known as libertarians because they espouse a return to basic principles of classical economics. They believe that, except for efforts of central banks to keep money supply in balance with business needs, and with perhaps judicious control to stimulate or cool off the economy as needed, the market should be left to seek its own equilibrium. Unfortunately, rigidities in the market, such as those created by organized labor preventing wages from fluctuating or by protected monopolies maintaining an artificial price structure, prevent the market from keeping economic activity in balance. The government, say the libertarians, should seek ways to remove such obstacles to market operations.

It is fair to say that despite painstaking research on the behavior of prices, critical analyses of economic behavior, and excellent logical systems, the tools to control inflation are elusive. Or perhaps we must recognize that the economies of the world are in such a dynamic state and so interrelated politically that no single economic theory can possibly establish a comprehensive view of all the contingencies.

8. DISTRIBUTION OF WEALTH AND INCOME

QUESNAY · SMITH · SAY · RICARDO · SISMONDI · MILL · RODBERTUS · OWEN · ROCHDALE PIONEERS · MARX · CAREY · BASTIAT · VON WIESER · MARSHALL · CLARK · VEBLEN · WARBASSE · KEYNES · FRIEDMAN ·

Why do such extremes of wealth and poverty exist in modern society? What determines how much of the national income goes to the businessman, the landlord, and the workman? Are there productive and non-productive social classes? Whence do they derive their income? Is each person or each class in society rewarded according to the value of his productive effort in society? Is distribution of wealth the effect of man-made arrangements or of economic laws? Is unequal distribution of wealth wholly or partially responsible for depressions? In the long run is a disproportionate share of national income paid in rent as compared to the amount of wages, interest, and profit? How does Socialism attempt to provide a more equitable distribution of wealth? Why, despite extraordinary efforts to distribute wealth and income more evenly, does the gap between rich and poor individuals and nations continue to widen?

ONE OF THE MOST STRIKING ASPECTS of modern civilization is the inequality in the distribution of wealth. Granted that the difference between rich and poor is as old as the world, poverty has never been quite so apparent as it is today in the midst of such an abundance of material goods. Wealth and poverty are of course relative matters. No one would question the fact that the poorest classes of today have a greater variety of goods at hand than the most favored classes of the Middle Ages. But it is questionable whether there was as great a gap between rich and poor then as now exists. Both the rich and the poor today have greater possessions and a higher standard of living than the rich and poor of 1,000 years ago, but the rate at which the rich increase their wealth is much greater than the rate at which the standard of living of the poor rises. It is these great disparities in economic position that are the source of unrest and discontent.

The problem of great wealth and great poverty is not merely the matter of the rich enjoying more leisure and more luxuries than the poor, though that might raise serious questions of ethics in the minds of some people, but also that wealth today is a source of power. Society is organized economically by those who possess wealth, our judgments are primarily money judgments, and success is evaluated in money terms. (The pecuniary elements in modern society became the chief point of emphasis in Thorstein Veblen's most stimulating analysis of contemporary civilization.)

Closely related to the inequalities in annual income are similar disparities in the distribution of wealth. Generally speaking, economists distinguish two types of distribution. The first type is the distribution of income and wealth to individuals. This is called *personal distribution*. The second type is *functional distribution*, which arises as a result of remuneration paid for the services in production of land, labor, and capital. The different types of income are accordingly: rent, wages, interest, and profit. In popular thought and discussion, however, distribution also refers to the process by which goods and services flow from producer to consumer. The marketing of goods through salesmanship and advertising is big business, and has a great deal to do with the content, if not the level, of our standards of living.

Attention to the problems of distribution appears relatively late in the development of economic thought. While ideas on the production of wealth and the process of exchange found a place in the writings of early philosophers and ecclesiastics, distribution was not so honored. During the Middle Ages, because of the self-sufficiency of the feudal estate and the rigidity of the class lines, questions of distribution were, in a sense, nonexistent.

THE MERCANTILISTS

The expansion of trade, following the breakup of feudalism, had little effect upon the general understanding of distribution. Since the economic ideas of the time were fostered by the Mercantilists, interest was focused upon the money aspects of foreign trade. Production was subordinated to the demand of foreign buyers and restricted by the production costs of foreign competitors. Distribution of the proceeds of commercial transactions was again a matter of politics, since privileges of foreign trade were granted by the sovereign to his favorites at the price of taxing their earnings to support his court. The powers of the state were enlisted to ensure a favorable balance of trade. This obviously was not an atmosphere which encouraged consideration of the problems of either personal or functional distribution. National distribution was all that mattered, and the prevailing ideas on this subject can be stated briefly: In the absence of mines to produce gold from natural sources, a nation could assure itself of political security and economic prosperity by the simple device of always selling more to other nations than it bought from them. In that way the stock of gold, the only source of economic and political strength, would be constantly increased.

THE PHYSIOCRATS

Interest in the distribution of national income and wealth arose as a consequence of the reaction against Mercantilism. The Physiocrats, French economists and philosophers of the eighteenth century, were the first to protest against nationalistic commercial policies. They believed that a nation's wealth was derived from intensification of agriculture rather than from foreign trade. The Physiocrats felt it important to show how this wealth was distributed throughout the population. In their thinking, as Turgot said, the circulation of wealth was the "very life of the body politic."

The investigation of the Physiocrats into the basic principles of distribution was elaborate and pretentious. The *Tableau économique*, developed by François Quesnay (1694–1774), summarizes the ideas of distribution prevailing among the Physiocrats generally. In the *Tableau*, Quesnay described society as consisting of three classes: first, a productive class composed chiefly of agriculturists; second, a class of landowners and other persons who exercised power as a result of landownership who were partly productive; and third, *la classe stérile* (the sterile class), consisting of merchants, manufacturers, and professional men who produced nothing, but drew the necessities of life from the productivity of the agriculturists. Nothing was said of wage earners and laborers. The *Tableau* attempted to trace the circulation of a sum of money from the time of its investment in agricultural pursuits by the productive class until it returned to that class for further use in production. Quesnay estimated the return on the investment at 100 percent. Let the annual return equal the round figure of 100. It will be divided so that 40 is immediately used by the agriculturist to meet the expenses of next year's production, while 40 is paid to the proprietor and to the state in the form of taxes; and the final 20 goes to the sterile class to pay for manufactured goods and services. The amount received by the landlord is the *produit net*. Now the landlord and the sovereign spend their income (40) as follows: half going to the agriculturists (20) and half to the merchants, manufacturers, and professional men (20). The sterile class must also spend their income (20 + 20). And since as a class they are unproductive, the total goes to buy raw materials and foodstuffs directly from the agriculturist. Thus the total income received by others than the agriculturists soon gravitates back to the productive class and is used to increase real production from natural sources. The process continued indefinitely to the advantage of all classes.

The important position accorded to the landlord and the failure to attribute any productive quality to the functions of the wage earner and farm laborer indicate clearly that the Physiocrats believed firmly in private property in land. Indeed, the function of the landowner in preparing the land and in making it available for productive use was worthy of the highest honor, and, in the plan of distribution outlined by Quesnay, the landlord received abundant compensation though he actually lived in idleness. The claim which the landlords had to income was justified because if they had not cleared the land, prepared the soil by cutting trees, removing roots, and setting drains, and had not constructed buildings, the one source of wealth would never have been available for use.

In return for this income and honor, the proprietor was obliged to assume certain duties. First of all, he was required to keep the land up to its maximum efficiency by constantly improving its capital equipment. He was required to see that the *produit net* was adequately distributed and not appropriated for personal use. His leisure was to be spent in services for the general welfare. And finally, landlords, generally, were forced to assume the entire burden of taxation for the upkeep of the state.

At best the Physiocratic scheme of distribution of wealth was a paternalistic ideal. Its manner of operation, even from an academic viewpoint, was unrealistic and confused. Fortunately it never actually faced the test of practice. Turgot, during his brief term of office as minister of finance just prior to the French Revolution of 1789, was overwhelmed by the immediate problems which faced him; consequently experiments with Physiocratic doctrines were impossible. Yet however critical one may be of their practicability, the ideas propounded by the Physiocrats were important, primarily because they directed the attention of later economists to the circulation of wealth as an important factor in economic activity.

ADAM SMITH AND THE CLASSICAL ECONOMISTS

It is quite apparent that Adam Smith (1725–1790) became aware of the problems of distribution through his acquaintance with the Physiocrats. However, there is reason to believe that Smith conceived of economics as concerned largely with production; distribution seems to be a hastily added appendage to his work. But it is true that his inclusion of distribution set the pattern for later economists. Smith concerned himself with distribution in the functional sense. Like the Physiocrats, he understood society as consisting of three economic groups: the landlords, the capitalists, and the laborers. These three groups, deriving their income from rent, profit, and wages respectively, were not personalized in any sense. They were functional groups playing a necessary part in production. The return which each group received for its services was not a matter of equity or justice but of natural law. To be sure, some unfortunate situations occurred. Capitalists and landlords alike at times oppressed the wage earner. But aside from minor variations the laws of the marketplace regulated the distribution of wealth and income.

How are the shares of the landlords, the capitalists, and the laborers determined? It is the supply and demand for the various factors in production which set their price, and it is the contribution of each factor to the value of the article produced which determines the relative return obtained by land, labor, and capital. A greater supply of labor than is demanded, for example, lowers the price of labor and consequently reduces the income of labor. Such a situation was assumed to lead to a withdrawal of labor from the market until the price again rose to the natural or normal price existing when supply and demand were equal. Furthermore, if the article produced requires great labor but little or no capital, then the income derived by labor will be relatively large. Although it might be inferred from some passages in *The Wealth of Nations* that Adam Smith looked upon rent and profit as unjustifiable charges upon the value produced solely by labor, closer examination will show that he believed firmly that both land and capital were productive and hence entitled to a return commensurate with their relative contribution to the total value produced.

J. B. Say (1767–1832), the great French exponent of Adam Smith's ideas, improved Smith's doctrine of distribution. The principal change came in the concept of the *entrepreneur*, the person who brought together the necessary amount and type of land, labor, and capital to engage in production. Smith had assumed that the owner of capital and the organizer of a business enterprise were one and the same individual. Say understood that one individual might provide the capital as well as initiate the business activity, but he believed the process of distribution could be understood better by separating these two functions. Indeed, it was only through the services of the entrepreneur that distribution took place at all. Land, labor, and capital might be readily available and the demand for goods might be great, but until the entrepreneur initiated an enterprise there was no demand for the factors of production or supply of goods. Thus, the entrepreneur served as the intermediary through whom income was produced and distributed. It was, in Say's opinion, ultimately the productivity of each element in production as regulated by the law of supply and demand that determined the return each unit of land, labor, and capital received. But it was, in reality, the entrepreneur who first estimated these factors and paid the sums necessary to bring these factors into productive relationship. Say emphasized the need of separating the return on capital from the earnings of the entrepreneur. His insistence on this point was largely responsible for the extensive use of the word entrepreneur in contemporary economic literature.

It was David Ricardo (1772–1823) who took the confused ideas of distribution propounded by his predecessors and worked them into a well-rounded theory. He made the first real attempt to describe the process by which the various shares of income arise and how their quantity is determined. Although later writers have made it clear that Ricardo failed to clarify the problem of distribution, his ideas on that subject were accepted as authoritative for nearly a century.

First of all, Ricardo accepted the traditional division of income into rent, wages, and profit, corresponding to the three factors of production: land, labor, and capital. Thus no distinction was made between profit and interest. But that was secondary. The process of distribution, he believed, hinged upon the character of social development. As population increased, the increasing demand for food raised the price of food and brought into cultivation less fertile lands. Ricardo argued that in reality the rise in price of food was caused by the greater amount of labor necessary to produce food from the less fertile land. Be that as it may, each time additional land was brought under cultivation, rent—which is the differential between the costs of production on one piece of land as compared with the costs of production on the least fertile piece of land necessary to maintain an adequate supply—was increased. Thus rents continued to rise as civilization advanced.

Wages, on the other hand, were governed by the inflexible law of subsistence. Ricardo said, "The natural price of labor is the price which is necessary to enable the laborers, one with another, to subsist and to perpetuate their race, without either increase or diminution." The wages paid did not always correspond to the "natural price of labor." He maintained that when civilization is advancing, capital (including food, clothes, tools) increases and pushes upward the demand for labor. This is so because in such a state of civilization, the land under cultivation is the most fertile and consequently the productivity of labor is high, making the accumulation of capital more rapid than the growth of population. In time this trend is reversed and population advances faster than the accumulation of capital because now the less fertile lands have to be used to supply the necessities of life. With less capital there follows naturally a decrease in the demand for labor, the surplus of which is ultimately absorbed in the greater application of labor required by less fertile lands. The net result is a decline in real wages. Subsistence represents the minimum point to which wages can fall. What subsistence actually is depends upon the habitual living standards developed by the community. So Ricardo arrived at the essentially pessimistic belief that as population increased more labor had to be applied to soil of decreasing fertility, which inevitably decreased wages. Where this vicious circle stopped or how it is stopped, Ricardo did not say. It is a safe guess that he shared Malthus's views that population would be curtailed to the limit of the food supply by the increasing severity of natural forces cutting down the population, for example, vice, wars, famine, and disease.

He went on to explain, however, that with rents taking an ever larger share of income, and wages commanding a relatively fixed minimum, profits alone must suffer the loss equivalent to the gain in rents. He put the case even more strongly. Profit is essentially what is left over after labor is paid for its work on land which yields no rent. To illustrate, on a piece of marginal land—that is, land which yields no rent at present prices—the sum realized from the sale of produce is divided between wages and profits. The share going to wages can never be lower than the subsistence of the laborers; the amount going to capital must be sufficient to encourage accumulation. It must be noted that when the economist speaks of rent he usually means economic rent; that is, the natural or theoretical return which a piece of land should receive for its share in production. If the selling price of produce just equals wages and interest, there is no economic rent. Money rent, or the sum paid by a leaseholder to a landlord, may be above or below the economic rent. If above, money rent is paid by taking a share of the return rightfully belonging to labor or capital.

The net result of Ricardo's teaching was to emphasize the competitive nature of distribution; and this led logically to the idea of the class struggle. Marx, in later years, saw the implication of Ricardo's ideas, and built upon them his own system of the exploitive "squeeze" put upon labor by the landlord on the one hand and by the capitalist on the other. In spite of his insistence that distribution was the fundamental problem in political economy, later authorities claim that Ricardo did not succeed in giving an accurate description of how the relative proportions of income were determined. His unwarranted assumptions and circular reasoning eventually diminished the great respect his work initially received.

The basic assumption which preceded the ideas of the classical economists examined thus far was that distribution was controlled by natural forces which were interfered with by man to his own undoing. Even the pessimistic trend described by Ricardo might be made worse by attempts at human control. The more optimistic note struck by Smith assured all concerned that in spite of the obvious inequalities in distribution, the operation of self-interest and natural law would result in greater abundance for all. Even Ricardo agreed that in the long run land, labor, and capital received a return equivalent to their respective productivity. Hence, the mode of distribution was not only outside of human control but it also was essentially equitable.

THE EARLY SOCIALISTS AND RELATED THINKERS

J. C. L. Simonde de Sismondi (1773–1842) was one of the first to attack the abstract and unreal thinking of the classical economists. Although he began his career as an ardent advocate of classical doctrines, he became keenly aware of the terrible human costs of industrialism, and he protested strongly against the complacent trust his contemporaries put in the operation of natural economic laws. Nowhere is this better portrayed than in Sismondi's explanation of the process of distribution.

Both in his travels and in his studies of history Sismondi saw repeated over and over again the same economic process. Everywhere, as a result of the competitive nature of economic activity, society was separating into antagonistic classes: those who owned land and capital and those who worked; the rich and the poor. The middle classes were gradually disappearing, leaving only the propertyless masses and the great capitalists. The wage earner without property was utterly and completely dependent upon the sale of his labor for a livelihood. Since the numbers of workmen were far in excess of the demand for their services, they were forced to accept the first wage offered them. It was Sismondi's contention that the independent artisan could estimate the need for his produce and his probable income and hence limit his expenses and his family accordingly. But under the existing system the workers labored in a world controlled by others. Their incentive to foresight was lost. The size of families and the workers' expenses fluctuated with the capitalists' demand for labor. Uncertainty, poverty, and misery became the inevitable lot of the working class. The capitalist and the landlord focused their attention on what Sismondi called the net product rather than the gross product. For example, while a plot of land might be fertile enough to produce abundantly, the financial interest of the landowner might be better served by limiting production, thus reducing not only the amount of produce available but also the opportunities for employment of workers.

The actual process of distribution, in Sismondi's view, began with the existence of an annual national revenue which consisted of rents and profits on the one hand and wages on the other. The claims of capital and land to a return were past claims based upon labor expended upon them in the previous year. The claim of workers to wages was a future claim, realized only as a result of opportunity for employment. Although these forms of income were in opposition to each other in the present, they were derived from the same source—labor. Sismondi believed that the revenues of one year were exchanged for the production of the next. In other words, the purchasing power of one year consisted of the wages, rents, interest, and profits paid in the previous year. When equilibrium was maintained, that is, when revenue and production exactly balanced, stability and prosperity were enjoyed by all. If, however, the owners of land and capital spent their income for consumption goods rather than for more capital, or if they consumed too little so as to provide a disproportionately large amount for capital, the balance is upset. If the amount of revenue allocated to the purchase of capital equipment could be increased slightly each year, the circular process of revenue, production, revenue, production could be raised to successively higher planes, increasing the standard of living year by year. However, one of Sismondi's emphases was that the failure of revenue to be distributed proportionately among rent, profits, and wages caused general overproduction of necessities for which there was inadequate income, while the unlimited desire for luxuries by the rich absorbed more and more of the consumers' power to purchase.

Thus according to Sismondi the real cause of the inequalities in distribution of income was, first, the ownership of land and capital by relatively few persons and the lack of any property at all by the working class, and, second, the ruthlessness of economic competition under a regime of *laissez-faire*. To correct these ills, Sismondi advocated a vague and indecisive plan for the return of ownership to artisans and small capitalists with rejection of the doctrine of *laissez-faire* and a return to state paternalism. His intermediate objectives were the right of unions to organize, limitations on hours of labor and the work of women and children, and the "professional guarantee," which made the employer responsible for providing maintenance for the worker during illness, old age, and lock-out.

The importance of Sismondi's ideas in the history of economic thought lies first in the fact that he called attention to the human aspects of business activity in a time when the classical economists were concerned only with economic matters and trusted implicitly the natural benevolence of economic laws to safeguard the welfare of man. Of even greater significance was the influence which Sismondi's ideas exerted upon the important nineteenth-century economic movements, most of which can trace either their intellectual content or their inspiration to the views expressed by this earliest critic of classical doctrine. Such developments as the humanitarian reaction against the impersonal and coldly economic doctrines of Smith and Ricardo, the closer adherence to historical facts, the attack upon wealthy property owners for their complacency in the midst of human suffering and poverty, and the increasing demand for state intervention in economic matters were all foreshadowed by Sismondi. Apart from the Socialists, very few of his contemporaries openly espoused his ideas, but as the years passed a much greater number came to acknowledge him as the source of their inspiration.

While the ideas of John Stuart Mill (1806–1873) on distribution follow the general pattern of classical doctrine, he was influenced by the critical and humanitarian views of Sismondi and the Socialists. For example, he held to the classical doctrine that production was governed by economic laws which were in a real sense natural laws. Yet he believed distribution was different, as the factors governing that process were man-made and subject to human control. He said, "The laws and conditions of the production of wealth partake of the character of physical truths. There is nothing optional or arbitrary in them. . . . It is not so with the distribution of wealth. This is a matter of human institution solely. The things once there, mankind, individually or collectively, can do with them as they like." Mill stood between the full-grown power of classical dogma and the vigor and strength of newly born socialist thought. His writings show the preponderant character of the former, but the latter is responsible for a host of modifications which Mill felt it necessary to make in order to give his ideas a more humanitarian and social outlook.

The classical element in Mill's ideas of distribution represents a synthesis of ideas expounded by Ricardo and Senior. His division of income was traditional, consisting of rent, interest and profits, and wages. Rent he analyzed as the differential payment arising because of the higher costs of production on less fertile land. Mill was the first to use the term "unearned advantage" as a synonym for rent, meaning of course the same thing as the later term "unearned increment." Assuming that an increase in rent and the value of land would arise from natural causes, he advocated a periodic revaluation of land leading to the levying of a tax which would absorb the increase. Profits and interest, however, which Mill treats together, are derived from three sources: abstinence, stored-up labor, and the productivity of labor. Mill never really distinguished these three sources, his only clear contention being that profits depended on wages. When wages rose profits fell, and vice versa. Capital, Mill believed, consisted principally of advances to laborers, hence the productivity of labor would determine whether the surplus over and above the advances would be large or small. This return was presumably a payment for abstinence.

As to wages, Mill accepted with modifications the fixed wages-fund theory described in Chapter 3. Hence the way to raise wages was to limit the population. He said, "Only when in addition to just institutions, the increase in mankind shall be under deliberate guidance of judicious foresight, can the conquests made from the powers of nature . . . become the common property of the species."

The relative proportions of income which were distributed as rent, profits and interest, and wages, Mill believed, were affected by historical processes. Increases in population inevitably create a greater demand for living space and agricultural produce, hence rents tend to rise; but there is a corresponding tendency for the productivity of labor to increase, causing a fall in the price of manu-factured goods which reduces profits to a minimum.

Mill was not merely an economist. He was also a philosopher

and a student of politics. As he saw it, the goal of mankind is to increase the sum total of human happiness. This could be done through the exercise of man's mental powers: "Poverty," he said, "like most social evils, exists because men follow their brute instincts, without due consideration. But society is possible precisely because man is not necessarily a brute."

Since Mill had already indicated his belief that distribution was subject to man-made laws rather than natural laws, he urged certain reforms in order to bring about more equitable distribution. Among them were the relaxation of the laws against worker combinations, the encouragement of the cooperative movement, more control over the increase in population, the fostering of education among the working class, and the enactment by government of a land policy that would encourage more laborers to become landowners. In addition, he advocated protective legislation which would prevent the exploitation of workers and a system of inheritance taxes which would prevent the continuation of the inequalities of wealth and income through succeeding generations.

The accumulated store of socialistic ideas which caused Mill to criticize and modify classical ideas at so many points completely captivated Johann Karl Rodbertus (1805–1875), a wealthy German landowner. Rodbertus's economic ideas, expressed most completely in *Toward Knowledge of Our Economic Condition* and *Letters*, can be traced largely to Adam Smith and Saint-Simon. From Smith was taken the concept of division of labor, which Rodbertus saw as the most important socializing force in history. It brought the most divergent interests into harmony and created larger and larger units of mankind into a community of labor. A society which had been brought together by specialization had three functions according to Rodbertus: (1) the adjustment of production to need; (2) the maintenance of production at a point which would utilize all available resources; and (3) the equitable distribution of income among those who produce it.

Rodbertus rebelled against the classical idea that these functions would be carried out in the best conceivable fashion if individuals were free to pursue separately their own economic interest. The kind of society men would have was the result of their own decisions, he said; certainly it was illogical to assume that the society which permitted its institutions to grow haphazardly without plan or design would be better suited to human needs than one which was consciously directed. The goal of any system of distribution, said Rodbertus, was to assure to everyone the product of his labor. In this he differed not at all from the classical school. In the way this goal was to be achieved he differed from them altogether.

Classical doctrine said that the process of exchange, controlled as it was by the market forces of supply and demand, assured to each factor in production the market value of its contribution to production. Rodbertus maintained that while the theory was excellent, it did not agree with the process of distribution in practice. Since the value of all commodities was created solely by labor, the charges levied upon the product by the landlord and the capitalist were unjust. Raw materials and land were the gifts of nature; intellectual effort was inexhaustible and required no expenditure of time; thus only manual labor which required time and energy could be considered as productive. Like Adam Smith, Rodbertus believed that labor was the only true source of economic goods. He never contended that labor was the only source of value, but he did believe that the ideal toward which the community should strive was an equality between the exchange value of an article and the amount of labor necessary to produce it. In the process existing at the time, Rodbertus claimed that the owners of land and capital were able to control exchange so as to reap a benefit for themselves although they contributed nothing toward production. This control was made possible through socially supported rights of private property to exact payment when used in production. Hence society was really to blame for poor distribution, since as long as goods were produced and made available for use no thought was given to the justice of the rewards paid to such widely diverse elements as the continuous labor of the unskilled worker and the lazy indifference of the landlord and capitalist. The unearned return taken by the latter two, Rodbertus called rent.

Were this condition of maldistribution a temporary affair which would work itself out naturally, as some of the classical economists claimed, Rodbertus would have been less concerned; but he believed the contrary. Wages were paid only in such quantity as to enable the workers to subsist and reproduce themselves. This, as Ricardo had pointed out, was the natural or normal price of labor to which all wages tended to gravitate. The amount of the product which went to labor remained constant, but the productivity of labor was always increasing; thus the share of labor was a constantly diminishing proportion of the whole product of labor. As a result, it was perfectly true that the economic position of the worker became more degraded relative to that of other social classes.

The logical conclusion to Rodbertus's analysis was a program for the suppression of private property and unearned income: Instead of private ownership the state should own the land and capital, and labor should be rewarded according to its productivity. Labor time expended in production should be accepted as the real estimate of the exchange value of an article. This new program of distribution was to be accomplished by the gradual establishment of state socialism which would compromise the issue to the extent of allowing private enterprise and private property to exist. Rodbertus was possessed, first, by a sense of historical inevitability which would bring in the higher economic society based upon socialistic principles, and, second, by a fear of the wild and uncontrolled action of the selfish masses in the face of the complex problem of differentiating between the legitimate returns and rightful ownership resulting from labor and the exploitive charges made upon production by owners of land and capital used in production. The confidence which he expressed in the benevolence of the state was really an expression of the lack of confidence he felt in mass action. His immediate proposal for a period of transition was similar to schemes of Owen and Proudhon. The state would supply to each employer a quantity of coupons equal to the labor value of the things produced and offered for sale. The employer and his employees together would be able to keep the equivalent of the article they produced. Periodic revision of the scale of payment would be made to take account of any increases in production or changes in proportion of the total product created by the workers as contrasted to the employer. This compromise between the forces of private property and those of labor was intended to be only temporary, and it could be accomplished only through the instrumentality of the state. Hence, in the classification of economic doctrine, Rodbertus, frequently called the founder of scientific socialism, must be counted among the state socialists.

Emphasis upon the injustice of payments made to the owners of land and capital is characteristic of all socialistic writings. Saint-Simon, Proudhon, Lassalle all follow much the same analysis. It was Proudhon who coined the famous phrase, "Property is theft." He considered labor alone as productive. Since land and capital were useless without labor, the demand by the owner of land or capital for payment was based on the false assumption that land and capital were productive in themselves. Hence any payment to landlord or capitalist was theft from the rightful earnings of labor.

KARL MARX

Although his ideas are basically in accordance with those of other socialists, special mention must be made of Karl Marx (1818–1883). In terms of popularity, as well as in their profound effect upon socialist thinking of the nineteenth and twentieth centuries, the doctrines of Marx stand supreme. It is doubtful whether any other nonreligious works have been responsible for so much blind devotion, so much critical discussion, and so much emotional condemnation as the writings of Marx. Born of a moderately wealthy German Jewish family that followed the Protestant faith, he married into the lesser nobility. Educated to be a college professor, he forsook his career to become a leader of the revolutionary movement in Germany. He was forced on two occasions to flee the country because of his activities. Following his last departure he settled in London to devote the rest of his life to research and writing.

The initial chapter of Marx's great work *Das Kapital* indicates his adherence to the classical tradition especially as presented by Ricardo. Indeed, Marx, instead of disproving classical economic ideas, simply carried them to their logical conclusion. Annual income is divided into three classes: ground rent, profits, and wages; these are the return on land, capital, and labor, respectively. As a result, there exist in society three primary social classes: the landlords, the capitalists, and the laboring class.

What is the process of distribution of income to each of these classes, and what determines the share each shall receive? Marx said that there were really only two sources of income: value and surplus value, both created by labor. Out of the former, wages were paid; out of the latter, rent and profits were paid. We have already noted that surplus value arose, according to Marx, because the capitalist paid only the wages of subsistence, while he was able to sell the product of labor in the market at a price determined by the laws of supply and demand. The difference was surplus value, claimed by the capitalist by his right to the product of labor as owner of the fixed capital such as machinery, and of variable capital out of which he paid wages. The capitalist's desire to augment surplus value was achieved in two ways. (1) through the exercise of superior bargaining power which enabled him to prolong the working day beyond the time necessary for the worker to produce the equivalent value of his subsistence, or (2) by reducing the labor time necessary for the worker to produce his sustenance. The latter was accomplished through the increased use of machinery or the perfection of industrial organization.

In calculating cost of production the capitalist figured the payment of rent as a cost. This did not change the fact in Marx's mind that rent was an unearned charge upon the value produced by labor, as was profit. Essentially, Marx followed the Ricardian explanation of rent. Rent was for the most part a differential between the cost of production and the selling price of farm produce appearing on land which was more fertile than the average land under cultivation. He rejected the theory held by earlier economists that rent was interest on capital invested in the land. Instead, he placed major emphasis upon the idea that rent was a monopoly price exacted by the private owner of the land because of the limited amount of land available for use. Under certain circumstances the landowner, by his monopolistic power, was able to extract from the capitalist the total amount of the surplus value as rent, leaving him only enough to pay other necessary costs of production.

Marx believed that this process in history resulted in the increasing poverty and misery of the wage earner. Moreover, the power of competition tended to reduce the number but increase the power of capitalists and landowners, the losers dropping down into the laboring class. The remaining landowners and capitalists, having nearly identical interests, merged into a single capitalist class. Thus the process which Adam Smith believed would result in greater economic well-being for all men, Marx said would result in degradation of most men, the tremendous wealth and power of a few, and intense class conflict. It is important to note that as far as Marx was concerned the process was beyond human control. Legislation might slow the process and relieve the distress of increasing poverty, but the course of events was inherent within the process itself. The outgrowth of this economic process, which took the value produced by labor and distributed it as rent and profits to the nonproductive landlord and capitalist, was a continuous class struggle. As a result of the class struggle the numerically important but impoverished working class, organized by the economic system itself, would eventually abolish private ownership of land and capital, the source of their impoverishment, and set up a socialistic community in which the means of production were owned by all the people.

Criticism of the Marxian ideas of distribution has come from within the circle of Marx's own followers as well as from his opponents. The surplus value source of profit has been discarded along with the labor theory of value. If land and capital are useless without labor, it is just as true that labor is useless without land and capital. The question is merely whether the present arrangement which makes it necessary to pay the owner of land and capital for the right to use these factors in production is socially efficient and just, or whether profit and rent when paid the owners who perform no essential social service represents what later authors have called unearned increment. The source of the criticism of Marxian ideas lies in the pattern of distribution in modern industrial society. The lot of the wage earners has not steadily grown worse, as Marx said it would. Marx's followers have sought to interpret him to mean that in spite of an absolute rise in the standard of living of the working class the lot of the worker is relatively worse as compared to the rapid increases in wealth of the capitalist. Finally, the evolution of capitalism has not caused the separation of society into capitalists and wage earners by the annihilation of the middle class. Instead, the character of the middle class has changed. During Marx's lifetime, this class was composed of the independent owners of small tracts of land and small business enterprises. This group is declining in importance both numerically and in the amount of business activity it carries on, but a new middle class has grown up consisting of highly skilled technicians, professional people, office personnel, and salespeople. More dependent upon the continued operation of capitalist business enterprise than their predecessors, the members of the new middle class—like the members of the old—act as a stabilizing force in society, resisting radical change but ultimately assenting to progressive changes in government and economics.

THE FABIAN SOCIALISTS

With the rejection of Marxian ideas of distribution, later Socialists have cast about for other economic explanation and justification for their social theories. Their principal ideas have been elaborations of the unearned character of rent, interest, and profit. The Fabian socialists—consisting of such well-known personages in literature and economics as George Bernard Shaw, Sidney and Beatrice Webb, and H. G. Wells—proposed an alternative explanation of distribution. They contended that wealth is social. Modern industry makes it impossible to distinguish the contribution of each individual or each factor in production to the final product. Hence any attempt to distribute wealth and income according to the labor expended is likewise impossible. The only alternative is to declare wealth the property of all.

The Fabian explanation of distribution hinges on the idea of rent as a differential payment made for the productivity of good land over bad. If the same amount of labor were applied and rewarded exactly the same, the greater production of one piece of land over another would not be the result of labor or of ownership but of the nature of land itself; yet by the fact of private ownership this surplus accrues to the owner. This same process, however, applies to all kinds of capital—machinery, building sites, soils, and forms of skill. Labor that works with the least productive tools produces barely enough to pay its wages, while those working with superior tools provide a surplus which is taken by the owner of the tools. Even ability is rewarded as a differential rent. Marginal knowledge and skill produce only subsistence, while superior talents produce a surplus which is claimed by the owner of the superior talents. In their pamphlet *English Progress Toward Democracy*, the Fabian Society stated its position on distribution:

> The individuals or classes who possess social power have at all times, consciously or unconsciously, made use of that power in such a way as to leave to the great majority of their fellows practically nothing beyond the means of subsistence according to the current local standard. The additional product, determined by the relative differences in productive efficiency of the different sites, soils, capitals, and forms of skill above the margin of cultivation, has gone to those exercising control over these valuable but scarce productive factors. This struggle to secure the surplus or "economic rent" is the key to the confused history of European progress, and an underlying unconscious motive of all revolutions.

The Fabian program for more equitable distribution, unlike the Marxist doctrine, does not require that the economic surpluses be returned to the wage earner. It does call for the confiscation of these surpluses for society as a whole. Thus everyone will become a wage earner, receiving the means of subsistence as wages in return for labor. The standard of living of all will rise, however, as a consequence of equitable distribution of additional goods and services by the state. Revolutionary measures are quite unnecessary, for natural evolutionary processes will bring about the decline of the capitalist and landowner. The growing intervention of the state is the means by which the change will be brought about. Already, say the Fabians, profit and rent are drastically reduced through taxation; the use to which property may be put is restricted by legislation; the state has developed industrial enterprise which it owns and operates for the public service; and relationship of employer and employee are closely supervised by the state. "On every side the individual capitalist is being registered, inspected, controlled, and eventually superseded by the community."

ROBERT OWEN AND THE COOPERATIVE MOVEMENT

Robert Owen (1771–1858) believed that the existence of profit was an unjust addition to the cost of goods. The just price of an article was its cost of production; consequently the process of exchange which allowed producers to charge more than the cost of production, and to lay claim to the excess because of their ownership of property, created a system which was not only unjust but unworkable. He pointed out that the wages paid represented the income with which the articles produced had to be purchased. If the price was increased above the cost of production to allow for profit an economic crisis would ensue when laborers could no longer buy back the articles they produced. Thus the combination of private property, profit, and rent made for an inequitable system of distribution. A different system of exchange was necessary in order to assure to the worker his right to consume what he produced. To achieve this end it was necessary to eliminate profit and suppress the desire to buy cheaply and sell dearly. Owen's Labour Exchange plan implemented in 1832 has been described in Chapter 7. It is sufficient to note here that like other experiments of Owen's, it failed in short order.

In 1844, in the village of Rochdale in Lancashire, England, the poverty and insecurity among a group of textile workers led to the formation of a cooperative society as a means of improving their lot. The Rochdale Society of Equitable Pioneers began as a small retail store. Its original capital of £28 was secured through small subscriptions from those planning to participate in the store's activities. The intention of the founders of the store was to provide goods of high quality at the lowest possible price by eliminating profit. Ultimately, they planned to establish a self-supporting community.

The success of the Rochdale Equitable Pioneers as compared to previous societies has been attributed to the new principles which they followed. Briefly stated, capital investment would receive a return of no more than 5 percent; prices at the store would be the prevailing prices in the area; the surplus over and above the amount necessary to pay interest on capital would be returned to those who purchased at the store in proportion to their purchases; membership would be open to all who would pay a small entrance fee (1 shilling, or 25 cents) and agree to purchase a £1 share ($5), which could be paid out of purchase savings. Control of the society was democratic, each shareholder being entitled to one vote regardless of the number of shares he possessed. Although the cooperative movement has grown tremendously since these early beginnings, little change has taken place in cooperative principles. A minor variation has occurred with the development of producer cooperatives. Emphasis in these ventures is upon the rights of employees. Consumer cooperatives have also allowed employees to participate in the earnings of the cooperative. In the last century the kinds and types of cooperative societies has increased notably. Housing, credit, shipping, food service, clothing, books, are now produced and distributed through various types of cooperative enterprises. Failures have been frequent. In general, the causes of failures can be traced to inexperienced management and the power of competitive practices of private enterprises which sought to destroy the cooperative.

The ultimate goals of the cooperative movement are far-reaching. James Warbasse, the outstanding advocate of cooperatives in America, stated: "In the Co-operative Movement the ultimate tendency is toward the creation of a social structure capable of supplanting both profit-making industry and the compulsory political state." These goals were implicit in the first articles written by the Rochdale Equitable Pioneers setting forth their aims. They were to start a store, build houses, commence manufacturing giving employment to those without work, purchase farms, establish a hotel ("for the promotion of sobriety"), and "as soon as practicable the Society shall proceed to arrange the powers of production, distribution, education, and government; or, in other words, to establish a self-supporting home-colony of united interests, or to assist other Societies in establishing such Colonies."

THE OPTIMISTS: CAREY AND BASTIAT

In spite of these conflicting and critical ideas offered by advocates of socialism and cooperation, classical ideas of distribution continued to be generally accepted by the majority of economists. Following the work of John Stuart Mill, who accepted the basic formulas of Smith and Ricardo while compromising at various points with Socialism, there appeared further elaborations and modifications of classical ideas. Bastiat and Carey, respectively French and American economists of the middle nineteenth century, gave an optimistic turn to the analysis of distribution made by earlier economists. In their opinion, annual income is divided into three portions—rent, interest and profit, and wages—corresponding to the three factors in production—land, capital, and labor. Whereas Ricardo had stated that as population increased, less fertile lands were brought under cultivation, and rent (the differential payment received by the good land) increased accordingly, the Optimists (especially Carey) held that the less fertile lands were the first to be cultivated and more fertile lands, which usually required clearing and draining, came into production later. While the total rent might increase, rent tended to decrease in proportion to wages, because as richer land came into cultivation labor's productivity increased and the price of farm produce tended to fall.

Very much the same view was taken of capital. Indeed, Carey claimed that no distinction existed between land and capital. Thus as capital accumulated, the interest rate (and rate of profit) fell; so that while the total amount paid as a return on capital increased, the rate of return decreased and the proportion of total income taken by capital got smaller in relation to wages. Interests of owners of capital and workers were therefore not antagonistic; in fact the evolution of economic society would ultimately bring about equality between labor and the capitalist since the wages earned would in time equal the amount received by the owner of capital. Proof of these ideas was offered in the form of tables and historical summaries. For the most part, however, the tables were merely hypothetical situations reduced to quantitative terms, and the historical data was sketchy and obviously selective. For example, in spite of Bastiat's contention that the interest rate tended to fall, during the nineteenth century it appeared to rise, and profits increased proportionately much faster than wages.

THE AUSTRIAN SCHOOL

The attempt to explain distribution in terms of the utility of the three factors in production (land, labor, and capital) was pursued most ardently by the members of the Austrian school of economic thought. The names of Menger, von Wieser, and von Böhm-Bawerk are associated with the most elaborate development of the explanation of economic processes in terms of utility, that is, the want-satisfying power of economic goods. The process of distribution is based upon the power of each factor in production to impute value to the final product. It is the value contributed by the last unit added (marginal unit) which determines the return of all the units used. Thus the difference in the return obtained by labor in a productive process as compared to the return of capital and land is judged by a comparison of the value contributed to the final product by the last or marginal unit of labor as compared to the last or marginal units of land and capital. This is essentially von Wieser's explanation. Von Böhm-Bawerk confused the issue terribly by ignoring the idea of a factor of production imputing value to an article, and emphasizing the reverse and unreal process of the value of the final product as judged by its utility, back-tracking to the factors of production. How this could be done was never clarified. Von Wieser seems to be on fairly firm ground when he says that payment is determined by the value produced by the marginal unit of land, labor, and capital.

NEOCLASSICAL VIEWS

The idea of marginal production as applied to distribution was worked out more intelligently and more concretely by Alfred Marshall (1842–1924). In the final section of his *Principles of Economics*, entitled "The Distribution of the National Income," Marshall directs his efforts to clarifying the baffling problem of how income is distributed. First of all, there appears an annual dividend which consists of the material and immaterial goods produced in a given year. This "National Dividend" is divided up into wages, the interest on capital, the rent of land, and profits on organizing ability. The problem of distribution is essentially one of describing the forces which determine the relative quantity of income received by each of the factors responsible for producing it. In such fashion does Marshall state the problem. His answers are not so easy to grasp. In simplest language his explanation is this: The price of any commodity is determined by the operation of supply and demand. In the case of the factors in production, the *demand* is determined by the entrepreneur's estimate of the value of the land, labor, and capital, in production. The *supply* is determined by the costs (sometimes discussed as subjective costs, sometimes as real costs) of producing land, labor, capital. Land, of course being irreplaceable, has only a money cost figured in much the same fashion as Ricardo's differential payment for more productive land, labor's cost is essentially the cost of maintaining a family at a customary standard of living, capital's cost is the cost of abstaining from consumption, or the estimate of the superiority of present value over future value.

In determining the actual return which each factor is to receive, Marshall uses the concept of marginal productivity. Land, labor, and capital receive a return equivalent to the productivity of the last unit of the factor used, as judged in relation to its supply. Marshall then analyzes the way returns on land, labor, and capital are determined under different economic conditions. In each case the analysis rests upon the general idea that the return of each of the factors of production depends upon the price it can command.

This price in turn is fixed by all the factors affecting demand on one side, that is, the marginal value to the entrepreneur; and all the factors affecting supply on the other. If a homely illustration may be permitted, the price paid for any of the factors in production (and hence its share of income) is like a large rubber ball held in the air by an indefinite number of streams of water playing upon it from every angle. Roughly speaking these streams appear to line themselves off into two groups (corresponding to supply and demand), each group exerting a counteracting pressure to the other in order to hold the ball in suspended equilibrium. Marshall's explanation of distribution is still generally accepted among economists primarily for its realistic and penetrating examination of all the separate factors representing distribution rather than for the clarity of the theory itself.

Ideas similar to those of Marshall were being expressed in America at about the same time by John Bates Clark (1847–1938), a professor of economics at Columbia University and the chief exponent of neoclassical economics in America. His reputation rests principally on his *Distribution of Wealth*, published in 1899. Briefly stated, he believed that functional distribution—that is, distribution of shares of income to the factors of production—was in proportion to the marginal productivity of each of the shares. Thus labor would receive what labor had created, capital would receive what capital had created, and so on.

To demonstrate his idea Clark assumed the existence of a static society in which the amounts of capital and labor were fixed and considered as a fund, that is, a fund of social capital and social labor. To the entrepreneur who organized production by assembling land, labor, and capital, the value of each of these factors would be equivalent to the value of the last unit of each of these he engaged to produce. In order to make this situation clear Clark assumed that the entrepreneur would hire units of land, labor, and capital until it was a matter of complete indifference in production whether additional units were hired or not. Clark followed a bit of circular reasoning here when he said the entrepreneur would continue to engage additional units of production until the value contributed by the last unit hired equalled the expense incurred for that unit. Such a statement apparently means that the return for each of the factors of production is already determined by forces other than the productivity of the factor. This confusing thought is overcome by the Ricardian explanation that the long-run and not the short-run process must be considered. In the light of Clark's direct statement on the subject, marginal productivity is the key factor. The idea is better stated by saying that the wages of labor or the interest on capital is equivalent to the value or income lost when the last worker hired is again withdrawn from service.

By the law of diminishing returns this unit does not and cannot produce as much as the next above it. Whether or not it is profitable to keep the marginal unit working is determined by the price at which the final product is sold in relation to the value of the marginal unit in production. There are innumerable assumptions made by Clark in order to set forth this explanation. He assumes, for example, that all units of labor are completely interchangeable, that capital is entirely fluid and can be adjusted to any number of workers, that no distinction exists between the rent on land and the interest on capital. In addition to criticism leveled at the abstract nature of Clark's explanation of distribution, Clark himself has been criticized for seeking two mutually exclusive things: the unchanging natural laws which govern distribution, and a method of eliminating the injustice existing in present distribution. It has been asked why, if natural laws govern distribution, should one seek a more ethical plan of distribution? Like all classical economists, Clark believed in the existence of the natural laws and in the essential justice of their control; the injustice arises not from the laws but from the obstructions which stand in the way of their full operation.

ECONOMIC CONSEQUENCES OF UNEQUAL DISTRIBUTION

The economic consequences of the inequalities in wealth and income are extremely important. (Many of these are connected with the business cycle and will be discussed in the following chapter.) In the early part of the eighteenth century, the close connection between income and economic progress was discussed by Bernard Mandeville in a poem called *The Fable of the Bees*. He pointed out that while saving and being frugal were calculated to increase the estate of the family, such was not the case with the nation, since a balance of spending and saving needed to be maintained if stagnation was to be avoided. Malthus, in 1821, was even more explicit. He said, "We see in almost every part of the world vast powers of production which are not put into action, and I explain this phenomenon by saying that, from the want of proper distribution of the actual produce, adequate motives are not furnished to continued production." The wide variations in income he thought led to the over-saving of some and the under-consumption of others, a condition that was bad for a country since it impaired the usual motives of production.

Adam Smith and his followers reasoned from the analogy that what was good for a family must be good for the nation. As Smith expressed it, "What is prudence in the conduct of the private family can scarce be folly in that of a great kingdom." They believed that economy and frugality throughout the nation were desirable. It is clear, however, that if everyone saves and consumes at a minimum, the incentive to increase production disappears.

John Maynard Keynes did much to clarify the relationship between income, consumption, saving and investment opportunities. He pointed out that as income increases there arises an increasing gap between income and consumption which remains as savings. With the rise in incomes the amount of savings increases, or, as he put it, "the propensity to consume" decreases. Under such circumstances the lack of consumption decreases the need for new instruments of production. Consequently, investment opportunities decline as savings increase.

Thorstein Veblen viewed society as a pyramid-structure of people on various economic levels, each level aping the mode of life of the group just above and imitating directly or at second hand the characteristics of the leisure class at the top. Since the differences between the economic levels were expressed in money terms, and since the distinction of the leisure class was its ability to engage in wasteful and conspicuous consumption without work, a tremendous societal stress upon income was inevitable. The ruthless competition for an increasing share of the world's goods was the dynamic force of modern civilization. Where a society so motivated would end, Veblen did not say.

Karl Marx, as we have already noted, contended that the economic struggle of class against class was the chief characteristic of history, and that in fact history could only be understood in terms of the class struggle. Contrary to Veblen, however, Marx believed that a pattern of evolution was inherent in the class struggle. In every stage of civilization the struggle resulted in a new synthesis of the elements of society in a more productive economic order. The transition from capitalism to communism was the expression of the class struggle, since under communism economic inequalities would be dissolved. From "each according to his ability," to "each according to his needs," has been the economic ideal of the communist state. This aim stands in striking contrast to the most widely accepted statement of capitalist distribution, that each factor and each person tends to receive, in the long run, the equivalent of what he has produced.

The inequalities of income distribution both within our own affluent society and among less-developed nations have given rise to new emphases in economic thought and investigation. Within the United States, the persistence of poverty in the midst of plenty gave rise to the "War on Poverty" of the 1960s. Since the classical theories of income distribution—in which labor, capital, land, and entrepreneurship receive their share in accordance with their contribution to the final product—left large segments of the population below the subsistence level, more positive initiatives were taken to provide a more even distribution of income. Of course, one approach is to deal with such causes of poverty as poor education and training, lack of opportunity, old age, disability, and dependent children.

Beyond remedial programs to assist in these situations, economists have sought an incomes policy which would reduce the disparities in income and adjust consumer purchasing power to other economic conditions in order to prevent wide swings in the business cycle.

The idea of a "negative income tax" or "guaranteed family income" has received some popular support. The original formulation of a negative income tax was based upon the idea that many low-income families were treated unfairly because the income-tax exemption presupposed an income large enough to benefit from the exemption. Therefore, the government would replace for the poor family that amount of tax offset enjoyed by the wealthy because of dependents. Refinements of this idea, and a more appropriate name, have emerged as "guaranteed family income" at subsistence levels administered as part of the federal tax structure. Conservative economists such as Milton Friedman have conceded that economic support for the poor would be more efficiently administered as part of the tax procedure than as welfare grants.

Two-thirds of the world's population live in what are called underdeveloped countries, and one-half of all men, women, and children in the world live continuously on less than a subsistence diet. Because of both humanitarian considerations and the recognition that such vast inequalities in wealth and income distribution are among the foremost causes of war, economists have been giving serious thought to a new branch of economics called *development economics*. While it cannot be claimed that new economic ideas have emerged from these studies, the concentration on economic growth has led to a new emphasis upon such fields as capital formation, new and improved technology, population control, and land reform. Perhaps the most critical factor in relation to the improvement in less-developed countries is the need to balance the introduction of capital and technology to obtain more efficient use of natural resources with the need to maintain high employment levels in a labor-intensive situation. It does little good to increase the production of life-supporting elements within a nation if, in the process, masses of people become unemployed. Out of this concern to manage economic change has come a renewed interest in economic planning, a subject dealt with in Chapter 11.

9. BUSINESS CYCLES

HALES · MISSELDEN · LAW · SAY · MALTHUS · SISMONDI ·
OWEN · RODBERTUS · MARX · VON HAYEK · WICKSELL ·
CASSEL · CLARK · CARVER · PIGOU · MITCHELL · JEVONS ·
MOORE · FISHER · KEYNES · HANSEN

*What are business cycles? Are depressions caused by events
outside the economic order, or by the nature of economic
life itself? What is the government's responsibility in preventing
depressions? Are depressions inevitable or can they be
prevented by government control of further spending and
control of the money supply? Do wars cause depressions?*

THE REGULARITY with which recession has followed prosperity—
bad times followed good times—has led economists to think of
fluctuations in business in terms of *cycles.* Furthermore, the recur-
rence of these fluctuations has made many writers think of them
as inherent characteristics of our present economic order. The pattern of events which marks the course of the business cycle is now
so well known that it can be described with precision. Although
names may differ, economists seem to agree that the business cycle
passes through certain well-defined phases. Professor Wesley C.
Mitchell (1874–1948) identified four phases: prosperity, recession,
depression, and revival. Additional phases have been noted. Certainly
as information on business cycles becomes more extensive refinements will become desirable. As matters stand, however, the four
phases seem to be sufficient. The words crisis, panic, and boom

which have been so frequently associated with business cycles are reserved to indicate degrees of recession and revival.

CLASSICAL DESCRIPTIONS

Now what are the peculiar characteristics in classic terms of each of these phases? It makes little difference at what point in the cycle we begin, the fluctuations constitute an endless chain of events; but the sequence is perhaps clearer if we start with revival. During the phase of revival, production increases; unemployment begins to diminish as new jobs are opened; prices start to rise and profits enter the range of possibility; new opportunities for investment appear; stocks are traded at higher prices and fewer bond issues are defaulted; and commercial bank loans increase. The prosperity phase is merely an extension of revival: prices continue to rise; consumers' demand reaches the heavy industries; unemployment is reduced to a minimum; security prices continue to increase, encouraging speculation; the demand for bank credit rises to a point where interest rates also rise; profits are high and wages increase, but signs are already apparent of a slowing down in the movement of goods as inventories appear complete and opportunities for new investment seem fewer.

Recession sets in as rising costs of production cannot be met by any further increases in the demand for goods. Inventories are so complete that wholesalers resort to a lower price policy in order to move their supplies. New building ceases. It becomes more difficult for debtors to meet their obligations. Speculators and investors in the security markets strive to sell, causing rapid decline in the prices of stocks. Banks recall their loans, and their reserves mount steadily. Unemployment levels are abnormal. Depression is the bottom point of the downward turn of business activity. It may affect only banks and commercial enterprises, or it may shake the economic world completely and bring business activity to a standstill. The marks of this phase are rapidly falling prices, slowly moving goods, stock market collapse, an increase in bankruptcies, some bank failures, and almost a complete absence of operation in heavy industry and in the building trades. Bank loans and new investment opportunities are negligible. Then, however, economies in methods of production are introduced, a new product or two comes into large-scale production, stocks begin to move at the low prices, interest rates are set at a low figure, and bank credit is made easier. These characteristics indicate that the road is being cleared for an acceleration in business activity.

Business cycles as we have described them have been known for the past two centuries. (Reliable information is not available for earlier periods.) A chart designed by Leonard P. Ayers of the Cleveland Trust Company presents graphically the rhythmic rise and fall of business activity between 1790 and 1950. The chart indicates 23 major depressions, the one occurring during the 1930s being by far the most severe. The significant facts indicated by the chart are the almost complete absence of what one would term normal years, and the almost equal division between depression years and prosperity years. The close association of war periods first with prosperity and then with depression is clearly demonstrated by the chart. Aside from the early days of war, prosperous periods have been associated with the opening of new opportunities, for example, railroads, gold mining, maritime commerce, public lands, new energy sources, and industrial enterprise.

As we shall see later in this chapter, the model of business cycles has been greatly modified by government programs of economic direction and regulation.

THE MERCANTILISTS' KNOWLEDGE OF CYCLES

Events of such major importance as prosperity and depression, booms and panics, could not fail to receive the attention of economists. John Hales's *A Discourse of the Common Weal of This Realm of England* was written during the unsettled conditions accompanying the enclosure movement (of heretofore common land) in the seventeenth century. Turning of peasants from the land resulted in widespread poverty and the rise of food prices in England. Journeymen demanded higher wages to meet higher prices; masters could not afford to support apprentices; laborers could not find employment. Hales pictured the conditions: houses, streets, highways, and bridges were left without repair; prices rose but markets decreased, for no one had money with which to buy; charities were not maintained, and the universities were empty of young men. The cause of such conditions appeared to be two-fold. First, the enclosures reduced production of foodstuffs, raised the price of remaining food, and threw large numbers of persons out of employment. Second, debasement of English currency caused the prices of foreign goods to rise. As a remedy for depressed conditions Hales offered a mercantilist policy: Manufacture necessities at home, buy abroad as little as possible, and sell more than you buy. In addition he condemned debasement, advocating a return to a currency of established weight.

Edward Misselden (1608–1654) lived in a period when the efforts of strongly organized wool merchants succeeded in enlisting the power of the king in order to break the hold of a rival group of traders called the Merchant Adventurers. The latter group had developed strong trade relations with Dutch merchants to whom they sold undyed and undressed cloth. The Dutch traders completed the processing and sold the cloth to northern European cities. The new rival company attempted to dress and dye cloth in England and sell directly to the Continent. This move brought on a trade war with the Dutch in which English merchants not only failed in the new effort but lost the original Dutch market as well. And ultimately this brought on a depression throughout England.

Misselden noted four basic causes of the downward swing of the trade cycle: too large an importation of luxuries from abroad; the export of gold (especially as it applied to the policies of the East India Company); too much competition among English merchants; and the failure of the government to inspect carefully the quality of exports. In the remedies which he offered in his essay *Free Trade, or the Means to Make Trade Flourish*, Misselden proposed strict mercantilist principles. He suggested a means of preventing the exportation of English coins, and, by a process of overvaluation, would be attracting foreign coins to England. The coin export privileges enjoyed by the East India Company, he felt, should be curtailed. The low value of English money as compared to foreign money should be remedied by agreements with foreign nations concerning the stabilization of currencies. Some of the shallowness of Misselden's thinking on these subjects is evidenced by the fact that he reversed many of his former ideas after becoming a member of the East India Company.

Daniel Defoe in *A Plan of the English Commerce* (1728) was able to analyze the phases of the business cycle in very modern terms, indicating clearly the frenzied activity of the merchant proprietors when excess demand skyrocketed prices and the poverty and distress which accompanied business collapse. He ascribed the causes of booms and depressions to "Accidents in Trade" which first bring about an unforeseen demand. Merchant proprietors, careless of the future, expand their production, hiring new workers, setting up more looms, increasing wages. Instead of confining his production to the orders in hand, he produces to excess, and when the "Accident in Trade" is over, the proprietor finds the market glutted with his goods. The distress of declining business falls hardest upon the new workers recruited from the farm to operate the spinners and looms, who, after a short period of work, are dismissed and find it impossible to return to their original employment.

SAY'S THEORY OF MARKETS

The economic upheavals following the Napoleonic Wars excited economists' interest in business cycles. Jean Baptiste Say (1767–1832) was the first of the professional economists to treat business cycles systematically. However, his contribution is mostly negative, for he adopts the ostrich stance of hiding his head in classical theory and maintaining that crises do not exist because in theory they could not exist. To prove that this was so he developed his idea of markets. Since goods were exchanged for goods, all goods produced represented a demand for other goods; therefore increased production merely increased demand and overproduction generally could not exist. In order to be free from the inconvenience of an oversupply of some goods in relation to others it was merely necessary to free the market from unnecessary restrictions in exchange.

UNDERCONSUMPTION THEORIES OF ECONOMIC CRISES

The search for additional explanation of the business cycle leads away from classical economic theory and into the domain of its critics.

MALTHUS   Robert Malthus (1766–1834), whose niche among the world's great thinkers is due to his ideas on population, was also a truly great economist. Malthus was the first to admit that crises might arise from conditions inherent in the capitalistic system. His ideas on the causes of crisis can be stated briefly. Production he believed depended upon the continuation of effective demand. This effective demand was one which established a price high enough to allow a producer to pay all expenses of production and still provide a profit. But he pointed out that the value of products was always more than the sum paid for the labor necessary to produce them. Hence the body of laborers themselves could never represent a demand big enough to enable the producer to obtain a profit. The additional demand for goods must of necessity come from another source. The capitalists themselves could not be depended upon to provide the necessary demand since they were more interested in saving than in spending. Consequently, the demand must come from what Malthus called *unproductive consumption.* As unproductive consumers Malthus listed landlords, menial servants, statesmen, soldiers, judges, lawyers, physicians, and clergymen. If, however, the rate of capital accumulation in a very progressive country was rapid, and if the nonproductive classes were encouraged to save rather than consume, effective demand would fall and industry would come to a standstill.

Malthus was the forerunner of many who believed that crises and depressions were the result of underconsumption. In the light of later economic thought, Malthus might at first glance be classed among the revolutionary economists. He was no doubt one of the first to note the inconsistencies and contradictions in capitalism, but he noted its flaws with regret, for the ability of capitalism to produce was fully known to him. The salvation of capitalism, as Malthus saw it, was the encouragement of unproductive consumption.

SISMONDI   The implications of Malthus's exposition were taken up and elaborated by a highly competent continental writer, J. C. L. Simonde de Sismondi (1773–1842).

The ideas of Sismondi on business cycles illustrate how a slight change in perspective can identify a thinker with the future rather than with the past. Sismondi, whom we have referred to several times before, was an Italian Swiss who began as a close follower of Adam Smith's economic ideas. These ideas he reviewed for European readers in his first work, entitled *De la Richesse commerciale* (1803). Sismondi then spent several years in historical research dealing especially with medieval Italian cities. After nearly fifteen years of separation from active work on economic subjects he was asked to write an article on political economy for the *Edinburgh Encyclopaedia*. The period intervening between his first work on economics and the encyclopedia article had been one of great economic upheaval caused by the Napoleonic Wars. When Sismondi began to write his article he found that the generally accepted principles no longer stood the test of reality. In rearranging his ideas to fit conditions as they existed, he found that he had arrived at conclusions which diverged from the accepted thought. These ideas he set down in his *Nouveaux Principes d'Economie politique* published in 1819.

Sismondi's new ideas of political economy arose from his efforts to explain why it was that in a nation with relatively complete freedom of economic enterprise there continued to exist individuals who did not have enough money to buy what they needed to consume. In brief the explanation of crises was overproduction and underconsumption. The analysis which Sismondi made of this situation involved four distinct conditions.

1. Knowledge of the market is imperfect. The nature of the mar-

ket is really an unknown quantity to the producer. He has no exact information as to the taste, purchasing power, and quantities demanded. He depends upon price in relation to cost of production to dictate whether he should produce more or less. A high price in relation to production costs encourages greater production because of the desire to increase profits. But one producer has no means of knowing how much other entrepreneurs are increasing production. Consequently, overproduction of certain commodities is always in evidence.

2. The unequal distribution of income, Sismondi suggests, in the second place is a contributing factor. While wage earners' incomes are constantly depressed to the level of subsistence the surplus purchasing power gravitates into the hands of the wealthy. The reason for this maldistribution is that the ownership of private property includes the power to demand a part of the value produced by labor; and the severe competition among workers for jobs results in subsistence wages. The wealthy, having sufficient income for necessities, can use their surplus only for luxuries, but for psychological reasons foreign luxuries are more attractive than those produced at home. Thus domestic production is forced to find foreign markets. This is difficult. New luxury industries are slow in starting because of foreign competition, hence workers are dismissed, surplus stocks accumulate, and a crisis results.

3. Since the purchasing power available to purchase consumer goods is equal to last year's income, any increase in production will result in a surplus of commodities. This is true because the income of last year is less than the value of the goods produced in the present year. Hence increases in machinery are frequently responsible for gluts upon the market.

4. Production under a capitalist economy is determined by the amount of capital available for investment rather than consumers' needs. In a prosperous period the accumulation of surplus funds in the hands of the wealthy is frequently turned to the production of goods for which there is no existing market. The result is the building up of inventories which ultimately cause a curtailment of production, unemployment, and crisis.

Sismondi described clearly weaknesses of the economic system which classical economists were likely to overlook. He failed, however, to give an explanation for these weaknesses which could find a place in the system of economic ideas prevalent at the time. His unorthodox conclusions and explanations formed an important point of departure for later socialist thought, and the realism of his observations had an important bearing upon the thinking of later classical economists even though they rejected his ideas.

Sismondi's humanitarian principles led naturally to proposals which would eliminate the evils of business crisis and poverty. He suggested state intervention to regulate production and restrict the use of inventions in the interest of a more stable economy in which production and purchasing power would be kept approximately equal. Since inequalities in income were due principally to the separation of wage earners from property, Sismondi suggested a restoration of paternalism in industry and the return of the independent artisan. Until such a reunion of the worker and property could be achieved Sismondi believed that poverty and human suffering should be modified by laws permitting workers to organize, protecting women and children in industry, limiting hours, and guaranteeing workers against the hazards of unemployment, illness, and old age.

OWEN About the same time in England, Robert Owen (1771–1858) was writing on the trade cycle, expressing ideas similar to those of Sismondi. His interest in business cycles was also aroused by the depressions following the Napoleonic Wars. In his *Report to the Committee of the Association for the Relief of the Manufacturing Poor* (1817), he stated that the introduction of machinery caused production to exceed the revenues available to purchase these productions. He was quick to see that while some persons became wealthy as a result of machine production, wealth was so poorly distributed that the increases in production could not find a market. As he maintained in his *Report to the County of Lanark*, "The markets of the world are created solely by the remuneration allowed for the industry of the working classes, and those markets are more or less extended and profitable in proportion as these classes are well or ill remunerated for their labor." "But," he continued, "the existing arrangements of society will not permit the laborer to be remunerated for his industry, and in consequence all markets fail."

RODBERTUS   The effort to describe and explain economic crisis was ignored by the classical economists, but Johann Karl Rodbertus, a German economist of the middle nineteenth century, elaborated and clarified the ideas of the trade cycle advanced by Sismondi and Owen. Rodbertus's explanation of crisis begins with his conception of distribution. Although in theory land, labor, and capital receive a return corresponding to their respective services as estimated by the market, actually capitalists and landlords are able to manipulate exchange so as to take from labor part of its legitimate share. Moreover, the present economic system recognizes the right of owners to a share of income although they have contributed nothing toward production. The loss of income by the wage earners to landlords and capitalists is a permanent factor in the economic system, and the loss increases rather than decreases as time goes on, ultimately returning to labor only enough income to provide subsistence. In spite of the declining income of the workers, capitalists continue to expand production to meet the total demand represented by the income distributed. But since much of the income goes to those who either save or spend only for luxuries, overproduction follows sooner or later. During a period of depression the surpluses are disposed of and equilibrium between supply and demand is established.

Like Sismondi, Rodbertus felt an obligation not only to describe the business cycle and identify its causes, but also to suggest remedies. As one might imagine from his theories of distribution, he proposed that means of production should be owned socially. Unearned income should be eliminated. Income should be distributed in proportion to the labor of each worker. These objectives were to be achieved gradually by the establishment of a socialistic state under a benevolent monarchy.

MARX   In his explanation of the evolution of capitalism into socialism Karl Marx (1818–1883) ascribed a major role to economic crises, devoting several hundred pages to this topic in *Das Kapital.* He was one of the first authorities to point out that crises recurred periodically in capitalistic society, and perhaps without adequate proof he contended that crises were becoming more severe.

The Marxian analysis begins with the assumption made by classical economists that the normal state of the market is an equilibrium in which the supply of goods just equals the consumer demand for them. Anything which disrupts either supply or demand, therefore, disturbs the equilibrium of the market. In a crisis, immense quantities of unsold articles accumulate, while thousands of people go without basic necessities. An economic crisis, which is essentially a disturbance in equilibrium where supply outruns the demand for commodities in general, is peculiar to a capitalistic economy. It could not exist in a society where each man produced for his own needs. When division of labor and specialization are introduced, the balance between supply and demand becomes delicate and a rupture of the equilibrium is possible. However, in the Middle Ages when each community was self-sufficient and the market for goods steady and well defined, no crises occurred save those which could be traced to external causes. Under capitalism crises are the result of the nature of capitalism itself.

What then are the significant aspects of capitalism which cause crises? According to Marx there are two. First, production ceases to be governed by the needs of the consumer; it is now controlled by the needs of production. Because of the interdependence of specialized labor in a factory, an employer sees to it that his entire work force is utilized, but this may result in a productive capacity above the market needs. Nevertheless, because of the interdependence of all workers and the necessity of maintaining the maximum efficiency, no workers can be discharged. Instead, the producer endeavors to create a market for his surplus. Although originally designed to satisfy more fully consumers' needs, size and the intricate nature of production now determine how much will be produced. Thus overproduction is not only possible, it is usually present, for adaptation to the size of consumer demand is well-nigh impossible.

In addition to the impossibility of balancing production and consumption in such a complex system, as production now determines its own ends, the inequalities of income distribution add to the difficulties of maintaining equilibrium. Since the employer is able to exact surplus value from his workers in the form of extra production which he places on the market for sale, it is obvious that the wage earners alone cannot buy back the commodities they produced. The capitalist, instead of spending the surplus money which he receives on added consumption of the product, uses some of it upon luxury commodities and uses most of it to purchase additional machinery (constant capital) which enables him to produce more goods and to exact a still greater amount of surplus value. And since regardless of the laborer's power of production, he is paid only a subsistence wage, a market surplus appears which cannot be sold at a profit or even at cost.

The simultaneous existence of idle manpower and idle capital is the great paradox of capitalist crisis, and it is only by resolving the paradox that crisis turns to economic revival. This is accomplished by two movements. The first is the elimination of the surplus capital. Some disappears through business failures and the physical destruction of plant and equipment; the rest disappears through shrinkage in value. The second is the reduction of wages to a point where it is again profitable to produce. The number of the unemployed competing for jobs sooner or later reduces wages to the required level.

The inevitable consequences of this process are crises of increasing severity. On the one hand, unemployment increases, and the wage earners, growing in number, are impoverished. On the other hand, the mounting surpluses of unsold goods lead to bankruptcy of the smaller business; large corporations increase in size; ownership becomes merely 'a claim on surplus value without direct control or responsibility; and concentration of power in the hands of a few owners finally results. It is at this point that the wage earners become conscious of the inability of capitalism, in spite of its huge accumulation of the means of production, to provide and distribute the needed commodities, and the transition from capitalism takes place.

SOME MODERN THEORIES

The explanations of crises given by Malthus, Sismondi, Rodbertus, and Marx laid the general pattern of all underconsumption explanations. Until the latter part of the nineteenth century these were the only systematic treatments of the subject. Since then theories of the business cycle have come from the pens of economists in ever-increasing numbers.

VIEWS ON UNDERCONSUMPTION   In addition to the standard socialist interpretation, there are several other interpretations of underconsumption as a cause of business cycles. Underconsumption may mean that purchasing power is lost. With the disappearance of money from the economic system the value of money rises. This deflationary process causes a fall in the price level and sets in motion the recession phase of the business cycle. Underconsumption may also mean oversaving. This is the most generally accepted meaning of the term and is implicit in all the previous descriptions. The essence of the argument is that savings lead to a decrease in demand for consumer goods and an increase in production. The natural result is a fall in prices and a decline in business activity.

Another view of underconsumption is that prosperity turns to recession when the full power of production made possible by the increased saving in the early part of the revival is finally brought into operation. Thus not oversaving or underconsumption but rather an oversupply of consumer goods causes the recession. The last explanation that merits consideration here claims that wages fail to rise swiftly enough during the boom period, causing excessive profits. A dangerous credit inflation follows which ultimately collapses when wages finally reach their normal relation to profits, and raise costs of production.

TOO MUCH MONEY AND TOO LITTLE MONEY   One of the most prevalent and widely discussed explanations of business cycles involves the flow of money and credit. An outstanding exponent of this general idea was Irving Fisher (1867–1947) of Yale University, though this school of thought includes many other well-known economists. Moreover, its effect upon the monetary policies of both England and the United States during the depression of the 1930s was profound. It was Fisher's belief that depressions are caused by fluctuating price levels. Since production in modern society is constantly increasing, if the volume of money remains fixed prices will fall and a crisis will ensue. One must bear in mind that money as discussed here means not only cash but credit as well, and the rapidity with which money and credit circulate must also be considered. In the midst of the 1930s depression Fisher advocated an increase in the volume of money in circulation in order to reestablish 1926 price levels. This practical suggestion was indeed followed by the Democratic administration then in office.

OVERINVESTMENT   The essence of the overinvestment theory is that industries producing machinery and other equipment (producer- or capital-goods industries) expand faster than consumer-goods industries. The former are not as sensitive as the latter and react more strongly to fluctuations. That is, an increase in demand for capital goods reflecting an increase in demand for consumer goods sets in motion a production process that is not closely adjusted to demand and may easily oversupply the market. Great variations exist in the way the details of this theory have been worked out by various economists.

Gottfried von Haberler, in his extensive treatment of the theories of business cycles, *Prosperity and Depression* (fourth edition, 1969), classifies three types of overinvestment: overinvestment which appears as a result of monetary and credit changes; overinvestment which arises from non-monetary influences such as inventions, discoveries, and the opening of new markets; and overinvestment which is caused by changes in the demand for consumer goods—which reacts more slowly but more violently upon capital-goods industries. We shall review the general explanation and each of these modifications briefly. (Since all three represent the particular viewpoints of several noted economists we can do no more than mention their names in connection with the discussion.)

The monetary explanation of overinvestment differs only slightly from the monetary theory of business cycles as discussed above. The representatives of this body of ideas include Friedrich A. von Hayek of the University of London, Austrian economist Ludwig von Mises, and Swedish economist Knut Wicksell, all outstanding thinkers of the early twentieth century. The interest rate is here believed to be the key to credit expansion and contraction, a process which in turn controls prices and the demand for goods. When low interest rates set in motion the sequence of events leading to greater demand and still higher prices, the tendency is for investments in capital equipment to increase, since by the use of machinery expenses are reduced and profit is made larger. The increasing emphasis upon the building of capital goods reduces the consumer goods available and naturally increases their price. But by the introduction of machinery, production is made more interrelated and less flexible. Consequently, when banks can no longer advance more credit to meet the rising costs of consumer goods, the interest rate rises. The result is a complete stoppage in the production of new capital equipment, for the high margin of profit necessary to encourage production of capital equipment is no longer present. Frequently, it is impossible for manufacturers to maintain the long and expensive mass-production methods that capital equipment makes inevitable. Booms subside and ultimately lead into recessions.

The difference between the monetary and non-monetary overinvestment theories of the business cycle lies mainly in the fact that money and credit are paramount in the former and merely passive agents in the latter. Gustav Cassel (1866–1945), the great Swedish economist, was an advocate of the latter explanation of the business cycle (though his explanation of the depression of the 1930s emphasized the monetary causes). In the early period of the upswing the increase in production is caused or encouraged by an increase in saving which goes to increase capital equipment. But near the end of the boom, wages tend to rise, reducing the amount of ready capital which can be used to purchase equipment. By this time, however, the huge productive mechanism necessary to turn out such equipment, made possible by investments and credit advanced in the early period of the upswing, is just hitting its full stride. Thus the demand for capital goods—i.e., equipment—falls, while the production of such equipment rises. It is this shift in the flow of money, from saving to payment of wages, which eventually brings about the crisis and the subsequent depression. The real cause of the depression is an overestimate of the supply of ready capital, or the amount of savings available to purchase the capital equipment produced.

Now the revival begins, not as a result of the more rapid movement of consumer goods, as many economists contend, but because of increased investment. The principal stimulus to investment is the decrease in production costs such as wages, price of raw materials, and lower interest rates. Professor Cassel regarded the fall of interest rates as the most powerful influence. Other authorities, following this general analysis, have considered the appearance of new inventions, the opening up of new territories, and the introduction of new business techniques as necessary to encourage new investment.

A further modification of the overinvestment theory is that changes in consumer demand are the real cause of overinvestment. J. M. Clark of Columbia University, Thomas N. Carver of Harvard, and A. C. Pigou of Cambridge expounded what has been called the acceleration principle, which implies that the effect of variation in consumer demand for finished goods increases as it moves backward to the heavier industries which produce unfinished, durable goods. In other words, minor variations in consumer demand for finished goods may produce violent fluctuations in the demand for capital goods and equipment used in their production. This happens because a small acceleration in demand, if it is to be met, requires an increase in equipment which is expensive and long-lived. Haberler, in analyzing this proposition, shows that a 10 percent increase in demand may lead to a 100 percent increase in the production of durable equipment. As John M. Clark pointed out, this condition stimulates the business cycle when the new productive equipment is fed by an expansion of credit. From this point on the description of the business cycle follows the pattern described by those adhering to a monetary explanation of the cycle. Credit advanced for new capital equipment feeds consumer demand which continues to expand. The principle of acceleration causes a new demand for capital equipment. But the necessity of restricting credit and the rising interest rate, or the failure of investment, sooner or later react upon both consumer demand and production of capital equipment. Then the principle of acceleration acts in reverse. The decline in consumer demand causes a complete and immediate cessation of production in the capital equipment industries. Since the payments of these industries for raw material and labor contributed largely to consumer demand, their closing further reduces consumer demand. The depression is then inevitable.

Too Much Debt   The idea of overinvestment may be viewed in reverse as overindebtedness. Irving Fisher took this view of the business cycle. Though there is no real distinction between overinvestment and overindebtedness, Fisher's viewpoint has been helpful, as undoubtedly debts do intensify the fluctuation. Investments in capital equipment in the boom period are made with borrowed money. If business becomes unprofitable the debt structure remains but earnings are not sufficient to support it. Consequently, the downward trend is encouraged. As prices fall the burden of debt becomes heavier; but to meet debts producers continue to sell, thus depressing prices further. No industry has illustrated this condition so well as agriculture. During World War I, when the prices of farm produce reached fabulous heights, farmers mortgaged farms to secure new lands for cultivation. With the collapse of foreign markets following the war, farm prices dropped, but the farmers still had to meet debts contracted when wheat was selling at $2.20 per bushel. At 50 cents or 75 cents per bushel they had to sell two or three times as much wheat to meet their debts. This of course further depressed the price of grain. The depression in agriculture was much deeper and longer lasting than it was in other industries.

DECREASED EFFICIENCY   Another explanation of the business cycle was suggested by W. C. Mitchell, Professor of Economics at the University of California and Director of Research in the National Bureau of Economic Research. The decline in costs which accompanies the depression encourages renewed efforts to produce. This brings on the period of revival. The tendency to increase production, however, will eventually bring about increased costs. As production surpasses the efficient capacity of present equipment, less efficient plants are brought into service. The increase in demand for labor brings in the less efficient members of the labor force. In spite of this decline in efficiency, wages, rent, interest, and prices of raw materials all increase, many of them at a faster rate than the prices of finished goods. When, therefore, the inevitable point is reached where the margin of profit is insufficient to warrant continued production and the credit structure will not support higher prices, the downswing sets in.

CLIMATIC CHANGES   William Stanley Jevons (1835–1882) is responsible for the first statement introducing the importance of climate. In two works, *The Periodicity of Commercial Crises and Its Physical Explanation* (1878), and *Commercial Crises and Sun-Spots* (1879), he investigated the history of trade fluctuations and the appearance of sun spots in England from 1721 to 1878. The close coincidence of the sun spots and the depressions convinced him that there was a causal relationship between the two. Thus the sun spot cycle of 10.45 years was almost identical with the 10.466-year period of the commercial cycle. The sun spots were held responsible for causing stronger sun rays and more plentiful rainfall, thus producing abundant crops. This surplus of agricultural products upset the distribution of income, setting in motion the business cycle. Later authorities while rejecting the relationship to sun spots have emphasized the effect of fluctuations in agriculture in causing business cycles, recognizing the importance of good harvests and bad harvests upon demand for capital, the interest rate, and the mental outlook of the population.

KEYNES   One of the most thought-provoking and influential theories of the business cycle is the work of John Maynard Keynes (1883–1946). In his book *The General Theory of Employment, Interest, and Money* (1936), Keynes goes far beyond the bounds of the classical ideas of the business cycle, frequently offers unorthodox explanations and proposals. He challenges the generally accepted view that the way to end depressions is to cut expenses, especially wages, and by so doing encourage full employment and revival. In individual plants a reduction of wages may make it possible to expand production and increase employment. A general wage cut, however, would simply reduce consumption and accentuate the depression. In Keynes's opinion, satisfactory business conditions depend upon maintaining full employment. His argument, therefore, attempts to show why full employment is not achieved, and why declining business activity appears as a consequence. The goal of the businessman is profit. He operates his business at a level which will yield in his opinion the maximum return. In making his decision on this point he considers three variable factors: (1) the "propensity" of the population to consume; (2) the prospective return of new capital investment; and (3) the rate of interest.

In discussing the "propensity to consume," Keynes shows that as income increases expenditures also increase, but not as fast as income. Hence there is always a surplus available as savings. But income and employment cannot rise except as a result of investment. Here arises the paradox. Investment cannot rise unless there is an increase in consumption; otherwise there is no demand for increased production. Nor is it possible to consume all that is produced if saving is to be accomplished.

However, entrepreneurs will be inclined to invest in new productive enterprise if the returns to be expected are larger than the current rate of interest. A rise in the interest rate, he says, reduces productive investment and curtails employment. A reduction in the interest rate tends to have the reverse effect. Contrary to other economists, therefore, Keynes did not believe that a raising of the interest rate encourages saving and promotes investment. If the interest rate is to be helpful in controlling business activity, it must be controlled by public authority in the opposite direction to the suggestion of older economic theory. Rather than raising the interest rate to prevent overinvestment, it is necessary to keep the interest rate low in order to encourage investment as a means of maintaining full employment. A high interest rate, Keynes believed, would postpone investment and encourage hoarding. To cut wages would be to produce the most disastrous results, for income would be redistributed in favor of property owners who save more than they consume.

HANSEN Alvin H. Hansen (1887–), noted Harvard economist and author of *Fiscal Policy and Business Cycles* (1941), gave rise to the theory that secular stagnation lay at the base of business cycles. In Hansen's viewpoint there were three reasons for new investment: population growth, unoccupied land, and technological change. In the late 1920s and the 1930s each of these factors showed evidence of decline. His comments on technology are of particular interest. While technology continued to expand the financing of new economic ventures, it made older industries, which were more capital-intensive, obsolete. In developing industries, technological improvements did not open up new employment opportunities fast enough to absorb the unemployment in existing industries. This pessimistic view was quite widespread until after World War II, when the forward thrust of the economy was such that Hansen dropped the idea from his writings and became an enthusiastic exponent of Keynes's theories. Later, Hansen gave more weight to a monetary explanation of depressions, arguing that the over-extension of credit initially expands purchasing power more rapidly than additional goods can be produced, resulting in higher prices. Further credit expansión encourages more production, but credit is not inexhaustible, and soon purchasing power begins to lag behind goods available, leading to reduced business activity and unemployment.

CURRENT TRENDS Runaway inflation of the late 1970s and early 1980s poses questions about the functioning of the economy for which the current store of economic ideas provides few answers.

Rapidly rising prices, instead of curtailing consumption, have apparently increased the demand for goods and services. By means of readily accessible and seemingly inexhaustible supplies of money and credit, consumer expenditures continue to rise along with producers' demand for funds. The American dollar, long the cornerstone of international exchange and the reserve for other national currencies, is out of favor, and foreign creditors now demand payment in deutsche marks or Swiss francs. Rather than seeking to prevent a depression, as governmental authorities have for decades, a downturn in business activity is eagerly sought. Heretofore, economic thought and the principles evolved have been concerned with national economies. The international character of the forces influencing economic conditions is now apparent, and, as far as business cycles are concerned, existing tools of economic thought are simply inadequate to cope with international factors, such as the price of oil, which are beyond the power of national governments.

10. Taxation and Fiscal Policy

PETTY · THE PHYSIOCRATS · SMITH · PAINE · RICARDO · MILL ·
WALRAS · SAINT-SIMON · MARX · HENRY GEORGE · HELLER

*What is a fair or a just tax? Should taxes be levied according
to ability to pay or the benefit received? Should one class in
society be taxed for the benefit of another class? From what
taxes does the government derive the most income? Is it better
policy to tax through direct or through indirect and hidden
taxes? Is a single tax on land just? Is such a tax possible? Should
the power to tax be used for regulatory purposes as well as
for revenue? For what purposes should a nation expend its
money? Are balanced budgets essential to sound fiscal policy?*

THE HISTORY OF economic thought might well be described as the
record of the ebb and flow of government influence in economic
life. Indeed, the close parallel between economic and political
thought and institutions throughout the course of history has led
more than one great student of society to contend that the character
of economic life at any given time determines the form of its political
institutions. Lincoln Steffens, the eminent American journalist of
the early twentieth century, after his extensive investigations of existing political organization, said that politics and economics were
merely the opposite sides of the same coin. One might draw far-
reaching conclusions on this subject from the course of economic
thought. Economics had its origins in a period when the state was

all-powerful and economic activity was conducted ultimately in the interests of the state. Gradually, from 1750 onward, it achieved the full stature of an independent social science with laws of its own. In recent years, when economic controls have begun to shift from the forces of the marketplace back to the power of the state, the circle seems to be drawing to a close. Moreover, the very idea of economic activity carried on in isolation without regard for the government on the one hand and only incidentally related to other social institutions on the other, seems absurd, or at least unrealistic. Many aspects of the modern relationship of government to economics will be clarified if we begin at the origin of ideas on this subject.

THEORIES ON TAXATION

The earliest and most prevalent form of government interference with the economic life of individuals and business enterprises is *taxation*. The right of the chief authority to collect taxes, and the general policy which determines who is to be taxed, how much the tax shall be, and for what purposes it shall be levied has always been a controversial issue. In the twelfth and thirteenth centuries the revenues of rulers came from their own estates; there was no system of general taxation for the support of a public office. But the extension of the power of the monarch and the creation of the great states was expensive. One might say that the financial difficulties of governments was one of the chief causes of Mercantilism. The extravagance and waste of luxurious courts and the increased needs of government could not be met by the revenues from the monarchs' estates. The development of general taxation was inevitable.

PETTY Generally speaking, the Mercantilists believed that taxes should be paid according to the benefits the taxpayer received from the state. Sir William Petty (1623–1687) wrote the first systematic treatise on this subject. He believed in the sovereignty of the government and its obligation not only to carry on the necessary traditional functions, such as defense, maintenance of rulers, and administration of justice, but also to care for the well-being of individuals. Three functions were added: support of schools and colleges, so that the ablest students might attend rather than those who had money enough but little ability; support of orphanages and care for the dependents; and finally the maintenance of highways, navigable streams, bridges, and harbors.

As the basic formula for taxation, Petty stated that men should contribute to the state according to the share and interest they have in the "public peace," that is, "according to their Estates or Riches." In spite of the justice of the formula, Petty found that people were reluctant to pay their taxes. He attempted to give an economic justification of taxation by saying that taxes did not change the economic position of the nation in the slightest. Money taken in taxation is returned directly to the people. However, taxes ought not to be levied in such a way as to reduce the funds necessary to support the trade of the nation. Therefore, taxes are not harmful as long as they are spent for domestic products.

Petty had decided views upon two methods of taxation current in his day. These were debasement of currency and excise taxes. He claimed that debasement was really a very inequitable system of taxation, falling most heavily upon the creditors of the state and the holders of fixed incomes. The normal uses of debasement, such as the attraction of foreign money and lowering of wages, Petty found unsuccessful. He warned that debasement was "a sign that the state sinketh." He was more charitable to taxes upon domestic consumption, or excises. That each person should be taxed in proportion to his enjoyment or expenditure seemed to him essentially just. Moreover, by encouraging thrift the wealth of the nation would be increased. Duties upon imports and exports were approved if they were levied within reason and somewhat selectively. An import duty should be levied on foreign goods similar to those manufactured in England. It should be just high enough to keep the foreign product from domestic consumption. For raw materials necessary for England's industry, no duty at all or only a very light one should be levied. With luxury goods from abroad the interests of the nation would be well served if the duty were excessive. The nation would by such measures be made frugal. Export duties should never exceed a point where they would raise the cost of the product beyond the price asked by competitors in other nations.

HUME   The next English economist to deal at length with the problem of taxation was David Hume (1711–1776). He contended that both a monetary economy and a relative equality in the distribution of wealth contributed to a strong state, since the sources of revenue were more numerous and the ease with which revenue could be secured from the people was greater. Hume like Petty stood in opposition to all arbitrary taxes because they were unequal and they were costly to collect. On the other hand, he held that the laying of a tax might have good results, especially among laborers who because of the tax might be encouraged to work more efficiently. However, if industry was too heavily taxed, the result would be the death of industry rather than its growth in earning power. Hume believed levies upon luxury to be wise taxation. It taxed those who were wealthy enough to pay for luxuries; the tax was paid in small amounts entering into final price almost as a cost of production; and a person had an element of choice—he could either pay the tax or do without the unnecessary luxury.

In regard to the other relationships of the state to economics, Hume represented a compromise. He believed that commerce thrived in a state where freedom was allowed, and perished where restrictions were too numerous. It was the state's function to insure liberty and at the same time to protect business interests. Yet Hume never indicated that he considered individual welfare superior to that of the state. For the greatness of the nation it was necessary for the state to foster those conditions which cause foreign trade to prosper; at the same time, he denied the basic mercantilist thesis that a nation prospered only through a favorable balance of foreign trade.

THE PHYSIOCRATS   Much of the eighteenth-century Physiocratic system is concerned with theories of taxation. In a sense this aspect of their work remains their most significant contribution to economic thought. In spite of the large-scale reduction in the functions of the state which they advocated, the remaining duties of the state—secondary legislation, defense of rights, education, and public works—required revenues. The method of securing them was woven closely into the general pattern of Physiocratic economic theory. They held that agriculture was the only source of wealth. When all expenses are paid for agricultural enterprise, and funds are available for the next season, and capital equipment is reconditioned, the surplus or *produit net* represents the only and the true increase in wealth. This is the source of state revenue and since the entire surplus is taken over by the proprietor he must bear the entire tax. As calculated from the figures given in Quesnay's *Tableau économique*, the amount of the tax should be approximately 30 percent of the total income from agriculture.

Objections by the landed proprietors to such a system of taxation were naturally expected, especially since under the old conditions landlords paid but a small proportion of the tax burden. The Physiocrats contended that the landlord did not really pay the tax; therefore, he should not feel the burden of the tax. Land would now be sold at 30 percent less than its former value, so no one would lose. To the objection that it was unreasonable to ask one class in the population to bear the total burden of taxation, the Physiocrats replied that in taxing the *produit net* they were really taxing the annual surplus. It was true that the landlord received this surplus as income, but if the tax were to be shifted to any other class it would reduce the working capital of farm or industry which would reduce the income of the nation. Wages were irreducible at the subsistence level anyway and consequently could not support the tax. Therefore, the income of the landlords was the only source of revenue which did not affect future production or natural law.

A further advantage of a single tax on the surplus income from agriculture was that it set a natural value upon the tax and prevented arbitrary levies—a barrier against the autocracy of the sovereign. Taxes were definite as to incidence (the landlord) and amount (the *produit net*). The writings of Dupont de Nemours, Baudeau, Turgot, and Quesnay are filled with statements of their distrust of indirect taxes and their implicit faith that the *impôt unique*, that is, the single tax upon the surplus earned by land, provided an ample source of direct taxation that would injure no one.

The idea of a single tax upon land had extensive popularity among the French public until Voltaire held the idea up to scorn and ridicule in his famous literary caricature called *L'homme à quarante écus* (The Man of Forty Crowns). The chief character in the story is a peasant who by dint of strenuous toil forces from his land produce equivalent to forty crowns. The tax gatherer appears, and finding that existence is possible for the peasant on twenty crowns, taxes him the remaining twenty. An old acquaintance of the peasant, originally poor, who received an inheritance worth 400,000 crowns a year in money and securities drives by in a handsome coach with six coachmen each receiving double the peasant's income. "You pay, of course, half your income, 200,000 crowns, to the state?" asks the peasant. "You are joking, my friend," answers the rich acquaintance, "I am no landed proprietor like you. The tax gatherer would be an imbecile to assess me; for everything I have comes ultimately from the land, and somebody has paid the tax already. To make me pay would be intolerable double taxation. Ta-ta, my friend; you just pay your single tax, enjoy in peace your clear income of twenty crowns, serve your country well, and come once in a while to take dinner with my coachman. Yes, yes, the single tax it is a glorious thing." The story illustrates well the practical difficulties which so beset the followers of Henry George, the modern exponent of the single tax.

ADAM SMITH It was Adam Smith's contention that revenue to support the functions of the state could be secured from two sources: revenues from property or other interests owned by the state, or from taxation. He advocated and ardently supported the second. The canons of taxation which he proposed are often quoted in discussions of taxes, and even in the light of changed conditions they appear practical and reasonable. The canons are as follows:

"1. The subjects of every state ought to contribute towards the support of the government, as nearly as possible, in proportion to their respective abilities; that is in proportion to the revenue which they respectively enjoy under the protection of the state.

"2. The tax which the individual is bound to pay ought to be certain and not arbitrary. The time of payment, the manner of payment, the quantity to be paid, ought all to be clear and plain to the contributor and to every other person.

"3. Every tax ought to be levied at the time, or in the manner, in which it is most likely to be convenient for the contributor to pay it.

"4. Every tax ought to be so contrived as to take out of the pockets as little as possible, over and above that which it brings into the public treasury of the state."

Briefly stated, any tax should conform to the standards of justice, certainty, convenience, and economy. However, Smith did not follow through consistently. In discussing the sources of the taxation he acknowledged the fact that all taxes must be derived from income, that is, from rent, profits, or wages; but he pointed out that collections from profits were difficult, or could be shifted to the consumer, or adversely affected industry and trade, the source of wealth. Consequently, he adopted the physiocratic idea that taxes upon rent satisfied his criteria of a good tax better than taxes upon other sources. Even in the land tax, Smith modified his principles, for he contended that taxes on lands cultivated by their owners should be lower than taxes on land owned by absentee landlords.

THOMAS PAINE A far more powerful attack upon systems of taxation in England during the eighteenth century was delivered by Thomas Paine (1737–1809), best known for his pamphlets on the American and French revolutions. His basic contention was that the enormous increase in taxation suffered by the people of England in the past few centuries was due to "extravagance, corruption, and intrigue." Maintaining that of the total annual tax bill of 17 million pounds, only 1½ million was necessary, he proceeded to show how the remaining taxes should be disposed of. His plan provided subsidies for children so they might be sent to school, provision for aged persons, payment to families for childbirths and marriages, funeral payments, and accident benefits.

Instead of the small indirect taxes which lay so heavily on the poor, such as taxes on houses and windows, Paine thought the principle of the luxury tax should be applied to incomes. He said, "Admitting that any annual sum, say, for instance, a thousand pounds, is necessary to support a family, consequently the second thousand is in the nature of a luxury, the third still more so, and by proceeding on we shall arrive at a sum that may not improperly be called a prohibitable luxury. It would be impolitic to set bounds to property acquired by industry, and therefore it is right to place the prohibition beyond the probable acquisition to which industry can extend; but there ought to be a limit to property or the accumulation of it by bequest." He then proposed a system of graduated taxes upon incomes. The object of such a tax was twofold: First, it would eliminate those arduous duties imposed on the poor by the rich; and second, it would break up the large estates and return their substance to all the heirs and heiresses which "hitherto the Aristocracy have quartered . . . upon the public in useless posts, places and offices."

RICARDO The question of taxation continued to occupy a prominent place in the writings of the classical economists. Their contribution, however, was not in a modification or challenge to the basic principles, as was Thomas Paine's, for example, but rather a more elaborate attempt to answer the important question of who ultimately pays the taxes which are levied upon the various sources of income. "Taxes," says Ricardo, "are a portion of the produce of the land and labour of a country, placed at the disposal of the government; and are always ultimately paid, either from the capital, or from the revenue of the country." He then proceeded to show that taxes paid from revenue were satisfactory in the main, but that taxes paid by capital destroyed the productive efficiency of the nation and led, if continued, to economic ruin. But he added that taxes were not necessarily paid by the person nor the source of income on which they were levied. It was important, therefore, to determine in which cases taxes were and in which they were not shifted to other persons or other revenues. Adam Smith dealt at length with this topic, and Ricardo in most instances does little more than restate Smith's viewpoint, with a critical comment from time to time.

Briefly summarized, Ricardo's conclusions as to the incidence of taxation were as follows: a tax on raw materials falls on the consumer but will also diminish profits; a rent or land tax falls on the landlord; taxes on houses are paid in part by the occupier and part by the landlord; taxes on profits will be paid by the consumer, and those on wages by the capitalists. Ricardo added little that was new either as to the general theory of taxation or to the understanding of the relationship of the state to economic life. His opposition to the Corn Laws was a dramatic intervention into public affairs but it followed naturally from his general ideas on trade and wages. One must admit, however, that his explanation of rent became in later years the basis for a revival of the single tax and for proposals to nationalize land. His whole theory was based upon an assumption of freedom of economic activity from state intervention.

JOHN STUART MILL   Of the great economists in the English tradition John Stuart Mill (1806–1873) was perhaps the first to advocate a distinct change in the system of taxation with the intention of bringing about social reform. Mill considered rent an economic charge which was detrimental both to individualism and to the economic process of distribution, because it secured to individuals a return for which they had performed no labor. The main contention of individualism was that each man should enjoy the benefits of his own production. Rent nullified this aim. Mill held that this extra payment for the use of land was the result of the increasing density of population and should be returned to the state, through a tax upon rent, which would increase as the increase in population further raised the level of rent. Furthermore, Mill took exception to inheritance because it allowed persons to possess wealth which they had not produced. Mill defended the right of an owner to dispose of his property as he wished. This was merely the right of free people under a rule of individualism. Nevertheless, he held that this right no longer existed at death. He therefore suggested a limitation upon the amount which anyone might inherit. Instead of the state's curtailing the right of a person to dispose of his property as he saw fit, the state merely restricted the right of one to receive as a free gift more than a certain sum.

Although the original idea was suggested by his father (James Mill), John Stuart Mill actively supported a program of land reform based upon confiscation by the state of the unearned increases in land values. In his *Principles of Political Economy*, Mill expounded the theory which subsequently became the stated purpose of the Land Tenure Reform Association founded in 1870. The proposal called for the gradual nationalization of land through a tax upon increases in valuation. A practical beginning was to be made by evaluating the whole of the land on a given date. Subsequent evaluations would be made periodically, and the assessors would estimate how much of the increase in value was due to individual improvements and how much due to community activity such as increases in population and general improvements. A general tax would then be levied transferring this gain to the state.

WALRAS   Like Mill, Auguste Walras (1801–1866) recognized the peculiar social nature of land and the inevitable rise in the value of land. He, therefore, advocated the purchase of land by government and its lease back at rents based upon actual value. In his opinion, the income from such an arrangement would make property taxes as well as other forms of taxation unnecessary.

THE SOCIALISTS   The program of social reform advocated by the followers of Comte de Saint-Simon (1760–1825) attempted to use inheritance as a means of transferring ownership from individuals to the state. Their argument was clear. They believed that through individual ownership of capital only the needs of the individual and his immediate dependents were taken into account, resulting in a chaotic variety of uses of the capital. Crises, poverty, and economic anarchy could be traced to this condition in which there was no plan for the uses of capital. The only means of escape was through collectivism: that is, community ownership of capital. To accomplish this end, they believed the state should become the inheritor of all forms of wealth; private inheritance would no longer exist. Said Saint-Simon, "The law of progress as we have outlined it would tend to establish an order of things in which the state, and not the family, would inherit all accumulated wealth and every other form of what economists call the funds of production." Once in possession of all capital, the government could then distribute it in the way best suited to community needs. In other words, the government would become the source of capital, lending it, as it were, to those best able to use it. Each man would be assigned work for which he was best fitted, and each would be paid according to his labor. The formula is stated briefly, "Each one ought to be endowed [with capital or land] according to his merits, and rewarded according to his work."

The contribution of Karl Marx (1818–1883) to the general thought on taxation is not at all original. The ultimate goal of history is to Marx the establishment of the communistic state where private property has completely disappeared. In the process of advancing toward that goal, however, certain practical measures are necessary. Therefore in the political program for immediate action which he and Engels incorporated in the *Communist Manifesto* several types of taxation are suggested. First, there should be the abolition of all private property in land and the application of rents to public purposes. Second, a heavy progressive or graduated income tax should be introduced. Third, all inheritance should be abolished. Under the influence of Marx, every socialist program from that time forward has incorporated similar tax provisions, in some cases less confiscatory, but certainly aiming at state ownership of the means of production and the levelling of incomes within certain limits.

HENRY GEORGE   In America the idea of a single tax upon land was revived by Henry George (1839–1897). The Physiocrats, as we have seen, were the first to suggest and explain such a tax, though the economic basis upon which they justified the single tax differed greatly from that of Henry George. The motives which prompted its use were likewise different. With the Physiocrats a single tax was the logical consequence of a belief that the earnings of land were the only true source of wealth and that this *produit net* was secured by the landlords. Such a tax, therefore, levied upon a surplus interfered neither with capital expenditure nor wages. Private property in land they regarded as the cornerstone of national economic life. Henry George, however, was impressed first of all with the unearned character of the return on land; a return made possible by social processes rather than individual labor, and by the harmful economic effects of private ownership of land. The single tax therefore was a means of taxing a return for which no one had worked, and eventually, George believed, it would transfer all land from private to public ownership.

George, as a result of his own experience, became aware of the great extremes of wealth and poverty which seemed to him to increase as civilization advanced. He refused to accept the ideas of Malthus and Ricardo that this was the natural consequence of population outrunning the means of subsistence. Neither did he hold much respect for the Marxian explanation that the increasing poverty of the working classes was due to the exploitation of the wage earner by the capitalist, for both the worker and the capitalist seemed to George to be the victims of the landlord. He believed that labor and capital were merely different forms of the same thing—human effort. Wages and the return on capital, therefore, tend to be equal, rising and falling together. Furthermore the advance of civilization is marked by the increase in society's ability to produce the substance of human welfare, but the wage earner does not share in this increase proportionally, for the increased production is taken by the landlord in the form of rent. Without work landowners reap the benefits of the contributions of civilization and the labor of man. Therefore, it is imperative, said George, that private property in land should be taxed out of existence. The *single tax* would not only accomplish this end but it would also help defray the expenses of the state and other forms of taxation would become unnecessary. How is this to be done? The government needs only to levy a tax upon land sufficiently high to confiscate all rent. Ownership might continue undisturbed, but the owner would secure no benefit and land might just as well belong to the state.

Critics of Henry George's plan of reform are numerous, and many of the criticisms are hard to answer satisfactorily in spite of the plausibility of his plan. Land today is acquired mainly through purchase, and ownership of land is really no different from the ownership of capital. To confiscate the one and not the other would be quite unjust. Then what of decreases in land value? Will the owner be reimbursed for any loss he suffers? Rent is no doubt due to the increase in population and other social processes, but the value of other things—labor and capital for example—is increased by similar social activity. If justice were applied, these increases would likewise be taxed. With land, however, the increases in value and the action of society in producing those increases, and the obvious absence of labor, single out rent and increases in land value as special and particularly dangerous instances of "unearned increment." They provide a most prominent and vulnerable point for anyone bent upon attacking the present economic system.

THE AMERICAN SYSTEM OF TAXATION

Although no outstanding economist has constructed a general theory of taxation which has found its way into general practice, the problems of taxation and incidentally of government finance continue to mount. The most modern extensive work in analyzing the principles and practices of taxation is that done by E. R. A. Seligman of Columbia University (1861–1939). His significant suggestions for reform of the tax structure have not, however, been widely followed in actual taxation practice.

Under the staggering burden of billions of dollars in debt, and the necessity of spending added billions, the search for new sources of taxation goes on apace. But why should it be so difficult to establish sufficient taxes to pay the expenses of government? Explanations are not far to seek. During the past fifty years the use of taxation to redistribute wealth in addition to providing revenue for government expenditure has increased taxes far beyond the amount necessary merely to run the government. Payroll taxes, processing taxes, surplus-profits taxes, undivided-profits taxes, and a host of others are quite obviously means of taking money from one group of society in order to give added benefits to another. Underlying this system of taxation as well as increases in public debt is the economic belief that business can be improved and prosperity restored by providing people in the low income groups with purchasing power to buy the products which industry is able to produce. Consequently, surpluses which might have been available to pay added government expense have already been eliminated by previous taxation. The old doctrine that only those best able to pay should be taxed served to free the lower income group from substantive income taxes. But this group has been excessively burdened by a host of "hidden" taxes such as sales taxes and tariff duties. With old sources of taxation resentful and impoverished and new sources either already claimed by hidden taxes or protected by social philosophy, it is difficult to raise necessary revenue. Finally, it must be acknowledged that taxation in a democratic nation is always difficult. Public approval is earned by appropriations, not by taxation; therefore legislators refuse to vote taxes on the interests they represent, but are always willing to spend money in their behalf.

FISCAL POLICY

As Chapter 11 will bring out more clearly, modern forms of taxation are used as instruments of social and economic policy as well as to obtain revenue to support normal government operations. This is not new, however. Alfred Marshall in his *Principles of Economics* (1890) proposed a theory that a tax levied on industries operating under a condition of diminishing returns (or increasing costs) and distributed to industries experiencing production under increasing returns (decreasing costs) would maximize the satisfaction of society. He supported his idea by an intricate analysis of marginal costs and marginal utility. He admitted that from a practical viewpoint the difficulty and cost of levying the tax and distributing the proceeds might make the scheme unworkable. Arthur Pigou attempted to elaborate this thesis in his *Economics of Welfare* (1920), but actually called attention to many of the inconsistencies in both his own and Marshall's expositions. The objective of Marshall's proposals, nevertheless, foreshadowed a dominant interest of post-World War II economists in using taxation to control business in the interest of economic growth and general welfare.

Walter Heller, Regents Professor of Economics at the University of Minnesota, and perhaps the best exponent of the neo-Keynesian reliance upon government fiscal policies to stabilize the economy, says of the development of this modern use of fiscal policy in his Introduction to *Fiscal Policy for a Balanced Economy* (1968):

> The modern emphasis on the stabilizing effects of fiscal policy represents a fundamental shift away from traditional views of its role. Only thirty years ago, few countries would have considered that the impact on demand was a relevant criterion by which fiscal action should be judged. The traditional concerns of fiscal policy were to provide certain services believed to be desirable, raise taxes to pay for them (it was generally believed that sound economic policy required budgetary balance), and to influence the distribution of income. Higher government spending at home significantly raises overall demand, while higher taxation reduces it. . . . Under contemporary conditions fiscal policy has become the most important instrument for managing the level and composition of demand. This is a major new dimension which has transformed the day to day activity of modern governments.

11. PLANNING AND GOVERNMENT CONTROLS

MORE · BACON · UTOPIAN SOCIALISTS · TECHNOCRACY ·
CONSUMER COOPERATIVES · COUNCIL OF ECONOMIC
ADVISERS · SAMUELSON · GALBRAITH

*Can competition and private initiative be depended upon to
regulate economic activity in the public interest? In what areas
of economic activity has government regulation and control
been most evident in the United States? What planning
measures have been proposed, tried, found successful? What
has been the progress of consumer cooperatives in the United
States? What is the present outlook for economic planning?*

THE ECONOMIC SOCIETY of the nineteenth century rested upon assumptions which were accepted without question by most economists. One of these assumptions was that the wealth of the community was equal to the sum total of individual material possessions; and therefore, as each individual sought to improve his own economic position he would automatically contribute to the wealth of the community. Another assumption was that economic activity was self-regulating; that is, through the beneficial power of competition the pursuit of self-interest by one individual would be automatically checked by the self-interest of others. Consequently, there appeared no need for external control. Indeed, as Adam Smith contended, the dabbling of legislators in the problems of business did more harm than good. Events of recent years have called these assumptions into question. The exhausted soil, the decay of central cities, the problems of oil supplies and the disposal of atomic waste are dramatic testimony that the search for private profit does not inevitably lead to greater social wealth. Recurring depressions and the continuing paradox of poverty in the midst of plenty are further evidence that economic activity cannot regulate itself, that there is no automatic force organizing and directing business interests for the common good. Yet, while individual business enterprises spend ever-larger sums on research, planning, and administrative organization, the economic aspects of community life as a whole have been permitted to drift, with little evidence of purpose or plan.

Reaction to these conditions was inevitable. Of necessity, U.S. and Western European governments have begun increasingly to intervene in the economic life of their people.

EARLY PLANNING AND THE UTOPIAS

The centuries from Plato to the present have not lacked proposals for utopian communities planned and regulated so as to increase human well-being. There was Sir Thomas More, who in 1516 wrote *Utopia*. More was Lord Chancellor of England, but he was extremely critical of the inequalities in wealth and the political autocracy which was characteristic of the England of his time. Consequently his Utopia portrays a society in which property was held in common, everyone had a voice in the government, work was assigned according to ability, education was free to all, and the most able were freed from other work in order to pursue specialized study.

A century later Francis Bacon set forth his ideas of a planned society in *The New Atlantis*. He laid down certain very definite plans for his community: "First I will set forth unto you the end of our foundation. Secondly, the preparations and instruments we have for our works. Thirdly, the several employments and functions whereto our fellows are assigned. And fourthly, the ordinances and rites which we observe." No clearer statement of the characteristics of economic planning could be given even today. But in addition, Bacon's catalogue of resources, his disposition of skills, and finally the emphasis upon invention further emphasize the planned nature of his ideal community.

One and all, these writers and the later ones who wrote about ideal societies expressed the belief that economic and social well-being cannot be achieved without conscious plan or purpose. Many of the authors were protesting against the poverty and oppression that accompanied the industrial revolution; consequently it was natural for them to advocate principles of economics which they discovered to be absent or neglected in current economic doctrine. They subordinated private property to social use, emphasized the need for state control and direction, lifted the scientist and scholar to superior positions in the social hierarchy, made education free to all, and promised to each man employment in line with his capacity. The policy of drift and the superficial optimism that some beneficent principle was guiding society toward more desirable goals found no place in their writing.

In addition to sponsoring ideas for utopian societies, a considerable number of these writers tried to turn their dreams into reality by founding communities organized on the utopian principles they formulated. We have already discussed the efforts of Robert Owen (at New Harmony) in this respect, but there were others; Etienne Cabet in France and America (at Icaria); John Humphrey Noyes in America (at Oneida); Fourier and Brisbane (at Brook Farm), to mention a few. That most of these experiments ended in failure after a very short life is not so much evidence of the impossibility of planning as it is testimony to the difficulty of creating an island of collectivism amidst the sea of individualism. As the negative results of too much individualism have become apparent on a large scale, societies have more or less grudgingly accepted the principle of a planned economy as the only possible adjustment to modern economic difficulties.

PLANNING IN THE UNITED STATES

Planning, in the form of government regulation, has appeared in many forms in the United States. Protective tariff has fostered

growth of industry. Regulation of public utilities on the one hand
and of monopolies on the other has sought to advance the interest
of the consumer through fair rates or by preserving competition.
Labor legislation and food and drug regulations are designed to
protect worker and consumer against harmful industrial practices.
Conservation and environmental protection measures have been enacted to prevent a short-sighted or dangerous destruction of natural
resources. Zoning and the rehabilitation of central cities are programs
aimed at preserving healthy and prosperous urban communities.
Despite these efforts, however, and except for programs in time
of war, economic planning in the United States is minuscule compared to the comprehensive planning of communist countries.

TECHNOCRACY The most forceful and dramatic proposal for economic planning ever to arise in the United States came in the
depression years of 1932 and 1933 as a result of the work of a
research organization known as *Technocracy*.

Under the direction of Howard Scott, numerous economists, archi-
tects, and industrial engineers were organized as a group, for the
purpose of investigating the physical resources of the United States
made available through the development of modern machine methods or technology. The survey was known publicly as the *Energy
Survey of North America*. No plan of economic reorganization was
specifically recommended by the Technocrats, as members of the
organization were called, but they believed that the facts presented
made certain conclusions inevitable: for example, that the price
system alone stood in the way of utilizing for everyone's benefit
the tremendous productive power which modern invention and discovery had made available.

One basic fact brought out by Technocracy's investigations was
that by the use of machines and nonhuman sources of power we
were increasing production at a rapid rate but at the same time
utilizing the services of fewer and fewer workers. The Technocrats
also showed that the volume of debt had been increasing faster
than either the rate of production or the rate of population increase,
and that this fact was due entirely to the constant process of borrow-

ing and reinvestment necessary to sustain and improve the mechanical equipment of the nation's business enterprises. They argued that the pressure to increase the efficiency of plants and equipment accelerated artificially the rate of obsolescence and led to the scrapping of machines long before their period of usefulness was ended. Through current methods of financing, new loans were secured to purchase new machinery long before the old loans had been met. Thus business enterprise, although far more efficient than ever before, could never make savings available to consumers because all additional earnings were gobbled up by creditors and investors. Sooner or later, the Technocrats believed, the gravitation of business incomes into the hands of owners and lenders would result in the accumulation of unsaleable surpluses of goods, for neither the worker nor the consumer were benefiting by the increased efficiency of business. The fundamental conclusion of Technocracy was that bankers, merchants, and industrialists in pursuit of profit were no longer capable of managing the economic system. This function, the Technocrats believed, should be delegated to those whose technical knowledge and professional attitude would qualify them to direct economic activity in the interest of society—namely, the industrial engineers.

Technocracy appeared during a period of extreme pessimism in the economic outlook of the American people. The time was ripe for a simple formula to guide the people back to the prosperous years of the late 1920s, and for a brief time Technocracy seemed to fill this need. But closer examination of the facts showed that the Technocrats had been a bit careless with figures and too sweeping in their generalizations. Many economists deprecated their efforts, and the radical implications of their conclusions did much to destroy their popularity.

THE TENNESSEE VALLEY AUTHORITY   The major U.S. effort in control of land and water resources, a program which has inspired the admiration of the communist world and free world alike, is the Tennessee Valley Authority. Becoming owner of over 2,000 acres on the Tennessee River at Muscle Shoals used primarily as a site for nitrate manufacture during World War I, the U.S. government was at a loss to know how to use the property once the war was over. No solution to the controversy which raged over this issue was found until 1933, when Congress passed the Tennessee Valley Authority Act. The purpose of this legislation was three-fold: (1) to improve the navigability and control floods on the Tennessee River; (2) to provide for reforestation, reclamation, and profitable use of the land in the Valley; and (3) to operate the nitrate plants in the interest of national defense. The program was financed by a $50,000,000 appropriation from Congress and the sale of bonds up to a similar amount to the general public. The generation of electric power as incidental to building the dams for flood control proved to be one of the most significant phases of the program. Power thus developed is sold to public and private organizations at rates which presumably act as a yardstick for the production and sale of electric power by privately owned public utilities. Taken all together, the TVA program represents the most spectacular U.S. effort to plan the economic and social relationships of 3,000,000 people and more than 40,000 square miles of land.

ECONOMIC POLICY   Only in the last thirty-five years or so has the U.S. government attempted to maintain a careful accounting of the state of the economy and to set forth guidelines and targets for government economic policy and, indirectly, for private business. Worried by the prospect of a deep depression following World War II, Congress enacted the Employment Act of 1946. This statute states as clearly as any government document the scope and the limitations on government planning:

It is the continuing policy and responsibility of the federal government to use all practical means consistent with its needs and obligations and other essential considerations of national policy, with the assistance and cooperation of industry, agriculture, labor, and state and local governments, to coordinate and utilize all its plans, functions, and resources, for the purpose of creating and maintaining, in a manner calculated to foster and promote free competitive enterprise and the general welfare, conditions under which there will be afforded useful employment opportunities including self-employment, for those able, willing, and seeking to work, and promote maximum employment, production, and purchasing power.

The Act itself failed to provide specific authority to achieve this goal, but it did create a Council of Economic Advisers to assist the President of the United States in formulating a program to achieve the goals set up in the Act. Since that time, the President has each year forwarded to Congress his Economic Report, the body of which consists of the Annual Report of the Council of Economic Advisers. This report is the closest approximation in the United States of an economic plan. It deals with almost every conceivable economic issue of current importance, with the main subjects of each report being employment, wages and price levels, the Gross National Product, economic security, welfare programs, specific industry needs such as housing, energy production and distribution, transportation and international trade, industrial safety, and the financing and mechanics of health care. In other words, the Council presents facts and figures on a broad spectrum of the nation's economic problems, and offers constructive recommendations which the President and Congress may convert into legislation.

Needless to say, the specific proposals of the Council have not met with universal endorsement. Economists, businesspeople, labor leaders, politicians, lawyers, doctors, and other professionals have frequently taken strong exception to the objectives, methods of implementation, and the reasoning found in the Council's annual reports. Nevertheless, the Council has been able to identify goals and problems and offer specific suggestions for ways of coping with them.

For the most part the Council has been dominated by economists of neo-Keynesian persuasion, since, as Paul Samuelson said, this is the mainstream of economic thought today. Occasionally, more conservative economists, favoring the policies emanating from the Libertarian School at the University of Chicago, are appointed to the Council, and Milton Friedman, spokesman for that School, has been recognized as a chief economic adviser to Presidents.

What are the economic policies set forth by the neo-Keynesians?

As explained by Samuelson in his *Economics* (first edition, 1948), when unemployment and inflation vary beyond the normal range, government fiscal and monetary policy must aim to stabilize them. This means that taxation, expenditure policies, and budget balances must be adjusted. Corporate and personal income-tax programs already provide a stabilizing effect because tax receipts change as incomes change. Other stabilizers exist, however, in the form of unemployment and retirement benefits and transfer payments of many kinds. But it may be necessary to use other discretionary programs to reduce unemployment, such as public works and/or re-training programs. In addition, through mechanisms of the Federal Reserve System, fiscal policies can be supported or their negative effects repelled by control of money and interest rates.

Thus the post-Keynesian economist, while admitting that there are many questions about economic management still unanswered, feels that skillful adjustment of fiscal and monetary arrangements, supported by an adequate incomes policy, can keep a mixed economy such as that of the United States or the countries of Western Europe in balance, eliminating the wide swings of the business cycle, preserving high employment, price stability, and growth.

GALBRAITH'S THEORY   John Kenneth Galbraith approaches planning from a vastly different angle. In his *Economics and the Public Purpose* (1973) he contrasts two economic systems operating side by side. There is the vestige of the neoclassical model which emphasizes the efficiency of the market system in directing the production and distribution of goods. In addition, however, there is the much more important economic apparatus labelled by Galbraith the Planning System. It is his contention that the size and power of business enterprise enable business to supersede the market and, by administrative action based upon a vast array of "collective intelligence," to determine what is produced, how it is produced, and what price is charged. Planning is characteristic of big bureaucracies, whether in government or business; but unfortunately their planning is directed to the aggrandizement, through size, power, and profit, of their own enterprises. Without a market to serve as a restraint on the exercise of economic and financial power by huge business enterprises and government agencies, another force is needed to coordinate the planning of individual units and direct their planning to the public good. Galbraith says:

> The state, in short, will take steps to effect the coordination of which the planning system itself is incapable. It will impose overall planning on the planning system. This is the next and wholly certain step in economic development—one that is solidly supported by the logic of the planning system.

PLANNING FOR THE PROTECTION OF THE CONSUMER

Special interest in the consumer as a factor in economic activity is of relatively recent origin. Adam Smith and his followers assumed that the consumer would be the final arbiter of economic activity, for by his power to buy or withhold his patronage he could determine what was produced, how much was offered for sale, and the price at which goods were sold. Few people really believed this; and virtual control over economic life gravitated into the hands of the producers. Through advertising and monopoly, producers controlled consumers' desires, and prices. The consumer soon became the "forgotten man" of economics. *Caveat emptor* was the rule. Resentment against this condition has found an outlet in two directions: through legislation and through consumer organizations. Through the former the consumer has secured protection against the most dangerous and fraudulent practices of producers; through the latter consumers have used their organized power to bargain and demand fair treatment.

GOVERNMENT ACTION   In the United States, government activity on behalf of consumers has been extensive. Beginning in the early 1900s regulation of meat preparation, analysis of the content of food products (with severe proscription of certain ingredients considered harmful to health), correct labeling, and strict regulation of drugs have become important functions of government performed for the most part by the Food and Drug Administration of the U.S. Department of Agriculture. The Federal Trade Commission gives some protection to the consumer through its control both of monopolistic business practices and false advertising. Consumer protection has also been advanced by the appointment in federal, state, and municipal governments of consumer affairs officers, generally without power other than that of putting pressure on marketers and producers to treat the consumer fairly. More recent efforts to protect the consumer have emerged in the critical areas of energy, credit, and the environment. Briefly, by law or administrative regulation the government endeavors to balance limited energy supplies and consumer needs, and to protect the consumer against dangerous methods of energy production. Truth-in-lending laws are designed to make the consumer aware of the terms of his loan and the borrower's obligations. Environmental protection seeks to preserve the beauties and resources of the natural environment for the enjoyment of present and future generations.

CONSUMER COOPERATIVES   Protection is after all a negative process. The government does not assist the consumer in getting the best values for his money. Although government agencies do in fact make tests of food and drug products, they are not at liberty to publicize their findings as comparisons of various products, and much of their information is available only on specific request. If the consumer wants positive assistance, he must secure it through organizations initiated and supported by himself.

The most extensive of all consumer organizations consists of the thousands of societies in the Consumer Cooperative Movement. As we noted in Chapter 8, consumer cooperation was a product of the pioneering genius of Robert Owen, but it got its official start in England in 1844 with the organization of the Rochdale weavers. Since then consumer cooperatives have grown rapidly in the Scandinavian countries, less spectacularly in England, and somewhat slowly in the United States. In Germany, Italy, and Russia the rather extensive cooperative movements were subordinated to the totalitarian and socialistic regimes.

In the United States the strongest part of the cooperative movement was originally the farm population. Pressed on the one side by strongly organized buyers of farm products and on the other side by monopolistic sellers of essential farm materials, the farmer found his only salvation in organized buying groups, formed frequently in connection with the local grange. The movement spread, however, among all consumers, especially throughout the Middle West—where one finds gas and oil cooperatives with their own distribution service and refinery, credit unions, insurance, creameries, bakeries, and grocery stores. Although not nearly as strong as in Great Britain, cooperatives in the United States continue to play an important role in our economic system.

Only the most fanatical supporters of cooperation, however, look upon it as an eventual substitute for the present economic system. More conservative persons recognize that the great value of the cooperative movement lies in offering competition and a "yardstick" for private business enterprise.

THE IMPORTANCE OF PLANNING

As we review the various evidences of planning in the United States we realize that we are dealing with a matter of constantly growing importance. There is no more forceful summary of the necessity of planning in the modern industrial world than John Kenneth Galbraith's cogent statement in *Economics and the Public Purpose:*

> The solution is to recognize the logic of planning with its resulting imperative of coordination. And government machinery must be established to anticipate disparity and to ensure that growth in different parts of the economy is compatible. The latter on frequent occasion will require conservation measures to reduce or eliminate the socially less urgent use. On other occasions it will require public steps to expand output. The sooner the need for such action is recognized, the less the inconvenience and suffering from the crises that are now predictable and for which there is no other remedy.

CONCLUSION

The widespread use of mathematics and computer technology has pushed present-day economic thought beyond the grasp of the layperson. Yet the frequent failure of economic forecasting, with its emphasis upon mathematical models and numerical expression, to foretell the direction of economic change gives new importance to economic ideas. Without being exhaustive or analytical, this book has sought to trace the growth and development of those economic ideas which have influenced both our understanding of economic behavior and our ability to control and manage economic developments. It is at best an introduction to a world of thought which is both important to our age and exciting for its potential.

INDEX